Accepting

Saint Germain's

Golden Age

Spiritualizing the World, vol 9

Accepting Saint Germain's Golden Age

KIM MICHAELS

MORE TO LIFE PUBLISHING

www.morepublish.com

For foreign and translation rights,

contact info@ morepublish.com

ISBN: 978-87-93297-66-1

The information and insights in this book should not be considered as a form of therapy, advice, direction, diagnosis, and/or treatment of any kind. This information is not a substitute for medical, psychological, or other professional advice, counseling and care. All matters pertaining to your individual health should be supervised by a physician or appropriate health-care practitioner. No guarantee is made by the author or the publisher that the practices described in this book will yield successful results for anyone at any time. They are presented for informational purposes only, as the practice and proof rests with the individual.

For more information: *www.ascendedmasterlight.com and www.transcendencetoolbox.com*

CONTENTS

INTRODUCTION

This book belongs to the series *Spiritualizing the World*. The books in this series are given by the ascended masters as workbooks that provide the knowledge and practical tools we need in order to make a contribution to solving concrete world problems. This book contains the knowledge and the tools we need in order start manifesting the Golden Age planned by Saint Germain. These books do not contain foundational knowledge about ascended masters and their teachings. In order to make the most efficient use of this book, you need to have a general knowledge of the following topics:

- You need to know who the ascended masters are, how they give their teachings and how you can make the best use of them on a personal and planetary level. You can find extensive teachings on this in the books: *How You Can Help Change the World* and *The Power of Self.*

• You need to know how the earth functions as a cosmic schoolroom. You need to know your own role and the authority you have as a spiritual being in embodiment. You need to know the role of the ascended masters and how only we who are in embodiment can give them the authority to use their unlimited power to affect change on earth. You can find more on these topics in the first book in this series: *How You Can Help Change the World*.

• You need to know how to use the practical tools given by the ascended masters. You can find more on this topic in: *How You Can Help Change the World* and on the website: *www.transcendencetoolbox.com*.

• You need to know about the existence and methods of the dark forces who are ultimately responsible for creating war on earth. You can find foundational teachings on this in: *Cosmology of Evil*.

How to use this book

There is no one way of using the teachings and tools in this book. However, if you want to make a significant contribution to bringing society forward, it is suggested that you start by following this program:

• You read one of the chapters in the book completely in order to increase your understanding of the topic.

- You give the invocation associated with that chapter once a day for nine days while studying the same chapter again.

The reasoning behind this program is that the chapters in the book form a progression. As you give an invocation for one chapter, you are also clearing your own consciousness from certain energies and illusions. This makes it easier for you to absorb and apply the teachings from the next chapter.

You can, of course, also read the book all the way through and then select one or more invocation(s) that you give several times. It is always more powerful to give an invocation once a day for nine or 33 days.

Please note that even though the dictations in this book were given at conferences in specific nations, the teachings apply to many parts of the world. You can therefore use this book to help people anywhere move towards the Golden Age.

If you feel burdened

The purpose of this book is not to merely give you intellectual knowledge. The real purpose is that you give the invocations, whereby you give the ascended masters the authority to remove the dark forces and energies that cause people to be stuck in repeating old patterns. These forces will not be happy that you contribute to the process of removing them from the earth. They may therefore seek to direct psychic energy at you that can make you feel burdened in various ways. Their purpose is to make you stop (or prevent you from starting) your efforts.

If you feel burdened, you can use some of the decrees and invocations for spiritual protection found on *www.transcendencetoolbox.com*. Most people can quickly come to a point where they are no longer vulnerable to the attacks from dark forces.

The dark forces will always seek to inflate any condition in our personal lives that makes us vulnerable. If you have particular issues, it may be helpful to use other tools that address those issues in a more direct manner. The ascended masters have given many invocations and decrees that can help you deal with specific topics, and you can find most of them on *www.transcendencetoolbox.com*. Some tools are found in the other books by Kim Michaels, and you can find them on *www.morepublish.com*.

1 | THE DIRECT WAY TO DIRECT DEMOCRACY

I AM the Ascended Master Saint Germain. I wish to give you a discourse that applies to all of the democratic nations that have reached a higher level of democracy and are experiencing somewhat of a crisis in their nations because they do not know what is the next step for democracy. They have not seen it or they have not been willing to see it. I wish to give you my thoughts on this topic, which is a somewhat broad topic. It requires us to recognize a very simple fact that has not generally been recognized by the democratic nations, and that fact is the existence of a power elite.

I am not thereby saying that all democratic nations are ready and willing to acknowledge the teachings we have given about fallen beings on the planet. I am saying that all democratic nations need to be willing to recognize that the primary difference between a democracy and other forms of government, especially a dictatorship, is that a government that is free and democratic cannot allow the formation of a power elite.

You will see that all democratic nations had in their past a more dictatorial, centralized form of government. It needs to be understood that the central aspect of such a form of government was the formation of a small power elite that could exercise power over the majority of the population. What most democracies today call a dictatorship is a form of government where one person has near total power, and around him is a power elite that has the major function of carrying out the dictator's dictates.

The true goal of a democratic government

Nevertheless, it needs to be understood that even if you do not have a single dictator, you can still have a very small power elite that is in a privileged position where they can exercise power without accountability and where they can dictate to the people how the people should live. This, of course, is the antithesis of democracy, and it needs to be recognized that it must be the goal of a truly democratic government to make a very enlightened, aware effort to counteract the formation of power elites. It also needs to be recognized that so far, no democratic nation has done a good enough job of counteracting the formation of power elites.

It needs to be recognized also that all democratic nations had a power elite when those nations shifted to a democratic form of government. That power elite did not simply lie down and die or evaporate into thin air. They continued to exist and they have, ever since then, attempted to influence the democratic government in many different ways. These have often been hidden ways because in a democratic country they cannot exercise power as openly as in a more centralized power structure. Nevertheless, this also puts a special responsibility on democratic governments to make sure that such a power elite cannot form, even if it seems like a benign power elite.

Does anyone know better than the people?

This, of course, brings up the topic that is at the very heart of democracy. What, my beloved, is the essence of a democracy? Well, it is that the people rule. Why then is it so that all nations that call themselves democracies have what you call a representative democracy? The people are not ruling directly by voting on issues but the people vote for representatives in their parliament and then those representatives carry out what they call the will of the people but which too often becomes the will of the hidden power elite.

Why is it that so many of the older democracies know they are in a crisis because the people's confidence in the government is falling, yet they do not know what to do about it? Well, it is very simple, my beloved. It is because in those older democracies a power elite has formed and that power elite is not willing to let go of its power. Now, you may say: "Is there not a difference between the power elite in a democratic country and the power elite in a dictatorial country?"

In many cases there *is* a difference because the power elite that has formed in many of the older democracies is what you could, with a certain irony, call a "benevolent" power elite. With that I mean to some degree that it is not a power elite that is openly aggressive and openly, deliberately and maliciously seeking to suppress, manipulate and control the population. It is however an elite who is seeking to manipulate and control the population because they think they know better, they know better than the people how the country should be run. This is a topic that all democratic nations, but especially the older ones, need to consider very carefully. My beloved, if you go to just about every democratic nation, you can ask the people who are elected representatives, who are in the bureaucratic establishment, who are in the educational institutions, the financial institutions, and the press and the media. If you ask these people what they think about this topic, most of them will say that the population, the people of their nation, are not capable of running the nation, of ruling the nation, because they simply do not know enough about how to run the country. They do not understand the complicated dynamics involved with running a country.

Now my beloved, you may, if you want to be kind to this elite, say that they are right. In many nations the people, if you look at the broader population, do not know enough about how their country works or how, for example, the economy works, so that they could rule the country. Can you see that when this statement is made by a power elite, it is hollow, it is hypocritical because, my beloved, who is in charge of the educational system and the press and the media of that country? Is it not the very power elite who claim that the people do not know enough? If that power elite has not educated the people as to how the country works, whose responsibility is it?

If they have not educated the people, it is not because the people are not capable of being educated but because the power elite is not willing to educate the people because they do not want to share power. It is, my beloved, *that* simple. There is no way around it, there is no fancy argumentation you can come up with that changes the dynamic here. The power elite of the older democracies have not been willing to educate their own people as to how the country works and that is entirely their responsibility. You see my beloved, this form of democracy cannot take the world into the Golden Age. It is impossible to move into the Golden Age without educating and enlightening the people as to how a country works because in the Golden Age the people *must* rule. They must make the major decisions.

The press must serve the people, not the elite

My beloved, what needs to be done to change this dynamic? Well, it can only happen by the people beginning to stand up for themselves and demanding a different form of government where they have a more direct influence. We have talked before about this phenomenon of direct democracy where the people vote in popular referendums about major issues in the country.

There will be a considerable resistance to this idea even in many of the older democracies. Do you not see that all of these democracies are facing a situation where the population have less and less faith in their elected representatives, in those who run the economy, in those who run the educational systems and in those who run the press and the media? You may say, if you are a member of this power elite, that this is a dangerous development because the people often respond to what has lately been labeled as "fake news." But you see, my beloved, why is it that the people are so open to news that do not come from the established sources? It is because even if the people cannot articulate this, they know that they cannot trust what comes from the mainstream media because the mainstream media has as its primary objective to maintain the status quo.

They want to maintain the present power structure. So you may say that it is dangerous when people respond to these fake news (and I will not disagree that it can be dangerous) but then, what is the alternative? It is, of course, that the news media that are already there need to wake up and realize that they will only survive if they serve the interests of the people, not the elite.

It is not the job of a free press to preserve the current power structure when that power structure does not serve the people and does not serve the country in the long run. The country is moving into a new phase of its development where the old form of representative democracy is becoming obsolete, is becoming outdated. Of course, the power elite that has taken advantage of representative democracy does not want their hold on the country to be upset, to be overturned, and therefore they will do anything they can to maintain that structure.

This means that there are those among the power elite in some nations who are deliberately creating fake news in order to undermine the peoples' belief in, or faith in, alternative news media. They believe that by putting out fake news that are so outrageous that people can see through them, or that can be exposed by the mainstream media as being fake, they can scare the people to come back and only listen to mainstream media. My beloved, this is an exceptionally naive belief and it simply cannot happen. You cannot turn the clock back to a situation where most people had faith in the major media outlets. These media outlets are like the dinosaurs. It is just that those who work in them have not realized that they have become extinct.

My beloved, the major media outlets in most democratic nations are run by people who are part of this power elite. They see themselves as a benevolent power elite. They sit there in their media towers, their fortifications, and they think that they will somehow be able to survive in the Internet age and maintain their monopoly on printing newspapers, printing books, running television stations and radio stations. They think they can maintain their structure and maintain their advertising income and get people to continue to subscribe to their newspapers and magazines even though the people are losing faith in them. But it cannot be done, my beloved, and it cannot be done for one very simple reason. They are not serving the people and the people are beginning to realize this in greater and greater numbers.

Why are they not serving the people? Because they have built such an arrogance of thinking that they can know what the people should think about all topics. Therefore, they believe it is not their job to simply report the news and let the people form their own opinion. They believe it is the job of the media outlets to form the opinions of the people. They believe that they know what opinions people should have in order to maintain stability in their country. My beloved, as I have said before and as *we* have said before, we as the ascended masters do not have it as our primary goal to maintain stability but to maintain growth, to create growth, to create self-transcendence.

Representative democracy is a temporary stage

We have never considered that a representative democracy was the final stage of democracy, was the highest form of democracy, the ultimate form of democracy. This has never been our vision. We see that democracy is only a means to an end, namely the raising of the consciousness of the people. This, of course, means that we have never seen that the formation of a democratic power elite was serving that purpose in the long run. It was, as we have said before, necessary, given the state of communication that was available in the 1700s, 1800s and 1900's and the level of education and literacy among the people.

There had to be a period where the people elected representatives and those representatives made the decisions in the parliamentary assemblies. That period has become obsolete by technology that makes it possible to spread information, to communicate, that makes it easier for the people to vote on issues so that they do not have to vote only every four years by going to a ballot room and putting their crosses on a printed ballot. Now they can begin to vote over the Internet so that the process is much smoother and much quicker.

My beloved, it needs to be seen, and you who are the ascended master students need to make the calls on this, that the people wake up and realize that the age of having a democratic power elite who believes they know better than the people how to run the country is coming to an end. It has outlived its usefulness and it is time to consider what the next stage for democracy is. My beloved, let us look at a specific country and since we are here in South Korea, let us look at the nation of South Korea.

You have a typical power elite in this country that believes it knows better than the people how the country should be run. You have, which is not completely typical but still it is a phenomenon found in other countries, where you have very strong business conglomerates that have a very strong influence on the democratic power elite. You also have a media that is strongly influenced by the business conglomerates, in many cases owned by them even behind the scenes. They are not likely to write something that will rock the boat too much.

What happens here is very simple. You have what we have talked about before as a process of unnatural selection. Those who desire to become part of the political establishment and either go into the bureaucracy or run for public office by running as a representative, they all develop this attitude of arrogance of knowing better than the people. I call it unnatural selection because it is a selection process that is not the natural process in a higher way.

It should be so, my beloved, that those who consider going into the democratic government (either in the bureaucracy or as the representatives) will gradually be selected based on those who have the highest willingness and desire to serve the people. What happens instead is that you have an unnatural process of selecting those who have the tendency to feel superior to the people.

You end up with a process where those who are willing to serve the people in many cases become disillusioned with the system and decide to withdraw. Either they withdraw from the bureaucracy or they decide not to run for public office because they are not willing to "go along to get along." They are not willing to follow the culture that has developed either in the bureaucratic area or in the political area. They are not willing to follow, for example, the party discipline and to not speak out about certain issues they know about because it does not fit in with what the party wants to do based on their hidden agenda of cooperating with the business conglomerates or the media so that they do not upset the apple cart and change the power structure in society.

Many of the people who have the potential to bring forth Golden Age ideas have elected by themselves not to go into the bureaucracy, not to run for public office because they know it will be a compromise of their ideals—and their ideals are more important to them than getting a comfortable job or a position as an elected representative. They simply choose to go different ways and to seek another way to make a living or another way to have an impact on the country. You end up with a situation where the people do not feel that they have real representatives to vote for because they do not feel that either side of parliament truly represents the people. They know there is a hidden agenda. They know that the major political parties have, so to speak, sold their soul to the business conglomerates or to maintaining status quo and therefore they do not feel that anything new can be brought in.

Why the people do know best

Now, my beloved, when you look at the peaceful demonstrations that took place here in South Korea over the issue of the president and the corruption around the president, you can see this as a very, very clear sign that the people do actually know better than the elite because the people know when a change is needed. They may not know consciously everything that is involved with the situation because, again, they do not have access to the full information since the elite is withholding that information. Nevertheless my beloved, the people are quite capable of feeling in their hearts or in their gut, so to speak, when a change is needed, when something has been going on for so long, when that something is not right and when they simply cannot accept it anymore. If they had a more direct way of voting for particular issues, they would also be able to feel what would be the best for their country.

My beloved, there are many among these democratic power elites who think that if their country switched to a direct form of democracy right now, it would be a total disaster because the people would vote for things that would be dangerous to the country. My beloved, let me make a very, very clear statement as the ascended master who is the hierarch for the next 2,000 years: I do not agree with these power elites! Even if all democratic nations switched within the next year to a direct form of democracy, I, Saint Germain, would much prefer the rule of the general population to the rule of the elite.

Why is this so, my beloved? Can it not be foreseen that in some cases the people would vote for certain issues that could have some not necessarily disastrous effects but certainly would create some turmoil in the countries? Yes, it could be predicted that the people would make certain decisions that would create turmoil but again, that turmoil will lead to growth because of a very simple fact. If the people make a decision that turns out to have, not the consequences they wanted, then who can the people blame when it was a result of their direct vote?

Do you see who they are blaming now, my beloved? They are blaming the politicians. They are blaming the business conglomerates. They are blaming the media. They are pointing the finger at someone else, but if the people vote directly, they have no one else to point the finger at than themselves. This will mean that a considerable part of the people will wake up and realize that: "If we could make a decision that led to these consequences, then it was because we didn't know enough about the topic and then we need to educate ourselves so that we can make a better decision in the future."

My beloved, what happens in a democratic parliament if the parliament members make a decision that turns out to have undesirable consequences? Well, do they not go back and make another decision that has better consequences? Well, can you not have the people do the same, my beloved?

Does the fact that you have a referendum about a certain issue mean that you could never have another referendum about that issue and that the decision that was made has to stand for all time? Of course, it does not, my beloved. Do you not see here that the next stage for democracy is to put the people in a situation where they have no one else to blame, where they cannot blame the power elite?

My beloved, this is what will give maximum growth to the people of those nations, and let me tell you that the people of virtually all of the older democracies are precisely ready to have that responsibility. They may not know this consciously, they may not be ready to articulate it, but they are ready for it and you can see this by the very fact of the growing dissatisfaction with the political status quo.

You can see that the people are looking for alternatives. Now, those alternatives are not there in most democratic nations and it is because, again, we need to go back and look at the underlying attitude where you have a small elite that believes that they know how the country should be run and that the population does not know how the country should be run. This is an attitude that is the very essence of elitism that goes all the way back to when the first fallen beings started embodying on this planet.

Why elitism creates chaos

When you take our teachings about the fallen beings, you will realize that they have, from the very moment they fell into this sphere, thought they knew better than those who were created as individual lifestreams in this sphere. You could argue that at a certain level they *do* know better because they have created so much destruction in previous spheres that they have an expert knowledge of how to destroy anything, which the lifestreams that were created in this sphere simply do not have. So yes, when it comes to creating chaos and destruction, the fallen beings do know better than the people. There is no question about it. I will be the first to admit that.

You see my beloved, I do not think that creating chaos and destruction has any part in creating a Golden Age and so therefore I do not consider the knowledge of the fallen beings to be particularly useful to me. I trust that most of you and most of the people around the world would not consider it particularly useful to them either. Have you not seen enough examples in world history of the chaos and destruction that the fallen beings can create? Is it not so that in most nations the broader population is beginning to awaken and say: "We have had enough of this chaos, we don't want any more of this chaos, what's the alternative?"

The people are actually crying out; "What is the alternative to us being ruled by the fallen beings?" They would not be able to articulate it that way, but this is what they are crying out for in their hearts: "Show us an alternative to being ruled by the fallen beings, the power elite, who can only create chaos and destruction or as an alternative may be able to create a static society where the majority of the people are the virtual slaves of a small elite." This is what the people are ready for, my beloved. They are ready for freedom from the fallen beings, freedom from a small power elite who are so arrogant that they think they know better than the people.

I will therefore throw out there into the collective consciousness, radiate into the collective consciousness, the awareness that it is necessary for the older democracies to step up and give the population broader influence on the political decision making process. This begins with recognizing that the people need to know more about how the country functions. It needs to be recognized also by the people that they need to be willing to educate themselves.

The next stage beyond welfare

Now you may say, as the ruling elite will say immediately, that most of the people do not want to know better, they do not want to educate themselves. They only want to live their comfortable daily lives and not have anything that upsets their daily lives. My beloved, this no longer is the case. There was a phase for democracies where the people had grown up in such poverty that their goal was to have more material abundance. If many of you look at your grandparents' generation, they lived in poverty and therefore there was a phase for modern democracies where it was a main goal to create a somewhat more economically equal situation where no one was really poor, or there are only a few people who are poor, and where you have a broad middle class that has a reasonable standard of living.

This again was a phase. It was a legitimate phase but many of the older democracies have moved out of this phase where there now is such material affluence that the people are getting tired of materialism, they are getting tired of being consumers. They are longing for a deeper purpose with their lives and this is again why they are becoming dissatisfied with their leaders because they are not giving them an alternative to the materialistic lifestyle. Again, these leaders cannot decide what kind of beings they are and what kind of beings the population are. Are they sinners, as the Christians say, or are they evolved monkeys, as the materialists say or are they neither? Is there an alternative to the two?

Of course there is, and it is the alternative that we have given now for decades. More and more people are ready for that alternative in a universal form and therefore again, what the power elite always wants to do is to argue why status quo should not be changed. They use as their argument always that the people are not ready for changing the status quo, but who is responsible for the people not being ready other than those who are in charge of that society?

Again, I radiate into the collective consciousness the utter hypocrisy of these arguments, but can this situation be broken by the power elite? Nay, for they would already have done so if they were willing to do so, for they have had the power to do so. So who can break it? Only the people themselves.

There can come a point where there has been a rising unrest and discontent in the identity, mental and emotional bodies of the people. They feel the tension but they do not consciously know how to direct that tension in a constructive direction so that it has the best possible impact on their nation. This is where the ascended master students have a historic opportunity to step in and give your calls, give your invocations, and first of all raise your own consciousness so that you can pull up on the collective consciousness and give the population the direction they are seeking.

This again does not mean that the people will all become ascended master students but it does mean that suddenly more and more among the people will wake up and from one day to the next they will say: "Ah, but this concept of direct democracy is obvious is it not, why shouldn't we vote about the issues? Of course we are capable of knowing what to vote and what is the right direction for our nation. Why should we believe that the power elite will know better than us, isn't it obvious that we are capable of knowing?" My beloved, it *is* obvious that the people are capable of knowing and you will know this very simply when you think about it.

The limitations of intelligence

What is it that the power elite is always talking about? They are talking about intelligence, my beloved. They believe that there is an intelligent elite who know better than the people. If you look at this realistically, you will see that, among all groups of people in a society, there are people even with a high IQ (as you measure it by the standard IQ test), it is simply that those people were not given an opportunity to express that intelligence by getting an education or getting a position.

Now, on the other hand if you were willing to be completely honest, you could take those who belong to the elite, you could go in and look at the politicians and those who run the big companies and you could subject them to IQ tests and you would find that they would not score higher than the average population. It is simply a myth that the most intelligent people are the ones who have risen to the top of democratic societies. It is a myth, my beloved. Besides that, you cannot say that a country can be run only by intelligent people who score higher according to the standard IQ test because they also need to have heart, they need to have situational awareness, they need to have wisdom. And you will again find that many among the people have this.

I know you can very well go out, my beloved, and you all know people who are very focused on themselves, who are very focused on their daily lives and their own situation and what we have called petty problems. You may, from a certain objective evaluation, say that these people are simply not aware enough to make good decisions for their country.

This may be so but those people do not make up a majority of the population and those people will vote the same way the people they know vote. As long as you find that broad section of the population that are aware enough, that are knowledgeable enough, to make good decisions, then the country can indeed be run successfully by a direct democracy. I assure you, my beloved, that when you give the people an opportunity, they will step up. If you do not give the people an opportunity, you will see more and more discontent, more and more unrest in the older democracies.

Two ways towards direct democracy

There is a growing fear of what they have now named "populism" but, my beloved, it is not populism. Having the people stand up and demand change is not populism, it is the *future,* my beloved. You cannot simply label it with a fancy label. This is what the ruling elite will always do. A new movement comes up, they cannot ignore it, so they try to label it and then they try to define the label so it seems dangerous and therefore should be stopped. My beloved, why should it be stopped? If the people want to elect an untraditional candidate for president or for members of parliament, then why should not the people be allowed to do so? You can see that within the next decade or so, direct democracy will have to be created in most of the older nations. Why will it have to be created? Well, it can be created in two ways. The enlightened way is that the ruling elite realizes that their time is up and that they need to give way peacefully to direct democracy and they need to let the people vote.

The other way is that the people will continue to vote for these candidates that are outside the mainstream and that some of these candidates by their nature will be unbalanced and extreme and therefore they will create chaos. This will scare the ruling elite so much that they say it might be better to let all the people vote on an issue than to have a small minority elect such an outside candidate that it creates too much chaos and uncertainty. In other words, they will suddenly begin to see that direct democracy is the lesser of two evils and therefore they think they can still maintain some power over a direct democracy by the power they have over the media. They think that they can still trust their bureaucracy and they can still influence the country that way.

Of course, it will not happen because they do not realize that you cannot stop the development towards greater awareness among the population. As my beloved brother, Master MORE, has said: "When the people know better, they will do better." We are coming into an age where the people want to know better. They will to know better and therefore they will know better and therefore they will make better decisions, my beloved.

The potential for awakening the people

Now I wish to make just a very simple comment here on some of the elections that you see going on right now. We have in the last year seen the British people elect to exit the EU. This was not the highest decision from my perspective, but I respect that it was for the British people, at this stage, a necessary decision because they needed to see the consequences of their own attitude towards being in a union with other nations. They need to see that they have not been willing to enter the EU with the necessary attitude of desiring a higher union, a higher oneness, with other nations. They need to see the result of this and therefore, even though there can be many things said about this (and we may say more about it in Europe), it was first of all an educational decision for the British people to take this step.

You have also seen in the United States where they did not elect the president that was predicted to become president because they chose what was the more outside candidate. Again, we can debate whether this was the highest decision or not the highest decision, but it was the decision that the American people needed to make for their own education so that they could have a chance to see whether electing someone who was not from the political establishment is actually better or not. Or whether there could be another alternative so that you could transcend the entire political establishment and the two-party system.

You see also upcoming elections in France where there is a possibility of a candidate who might take France out of the

EU. Although it is unlikely that France would leave the EU, it is nevertheless a necessary phase for the French people to go through the considerations that this forces them to make.

You see here in South Korea where you have an upcoming election, and again it is not that I can sit here and say there is one particular candidate that we would like to see win. Well, there may be, but it is not necessarily realistic that you who are our students in South Korea in the few days left before the election could swing the collective consciousness so much that these candidates would be elected. Nevertheless, whichever candidate becomes elected, it is the necessary step for the people. Not necessarily that this is the highest candidate, the highest choice from an ascended master perspective, but nevertheless it is the highest choice in the sense that it is the choice that the people need to make in order to take the next step in the democratic growth of the country and the peoples' willingness to take greater responsibility for their country.

You have seen now this very significant step here in South Korea that the people realized that by coming forward, by making these demonstrations, by making them peacefully, they could force a change. This is something that many people had not believed a year ago when there first was talk about the corruption of the president. Many among the people simply shrugged their shoulders and thought: "Oh, she will never be impeached, she will never be held accountable, she will be able to get away with this as so many politicians have done before." Now you see that it is possible to hold a politician accountable. It is possible for the people to make their voice heard.

This is a very significant shift in the collective consciousness as it has been in several other democratic nations, as it will be in the coming years in all of the older democracies where the people will shift. Instead of this voter apathy where they feel: "Oh, it doesn't matter who we vote for because it will be the same old political soup," people will begin to wake up and realize: "We *can* actually influence the future of our nation, we can influence the political process. There is *something* we can do and we are willing to do it." This is where you who are the ascended master students again have the opportunity. Make the calls, change your own consciousness.

The population is not powerless

My beloved, what did Mother Mary say to you earlier? She said: "Accept that the Golden Age is a possibility, is a reality, is descending upon this planet." What will it take for you to accept it? It will take that you realize you are not powerless. What is it that democracies need to go through? The population needs to realize they are not powerless. You who are ascended master students need to be the forerunners for this realization and realize that you are not powerless. Why are you not powerless? Because you are ascended master students. You have the potential to be open doors for the light and the ideas we want to release into the collective consciousness. When you make yourselves those open doors, you are not powerless. With men this is impossible, but not with God, for with God all things are possible. With the ascended masters all things are possible.

My beloved, look at what has happened in this nation in this short time span since our first conference here. I tell you, this is not the end; it is only the beginning. We have only scratched the surface of what is possible when enough people come together and give our invocations, study our teachings, raise their consciousness and accept that we are the forerunners. I am not looking at you to form a new elite. I am not looking at you to adopt any kind of arrogance and thinking you know better than the people. I am looking for you to realize and accept that when you are willing to work with us, you can tune in to what is my vision for your nation. You can invoke that vision and you can direct the collective consciousness so that more and more people will begin to wake up and suddenly realize: "Oh yes, this is obvious, we now see that this is the next step for our country."

It is not something forced upon the people. It is a consensus that comes from within their own hearts because in their own hearts what do the people of any nation want? They want what is best for the people and what is best for their nation. So when they see what is best, they do not have to be forced to accept it. They will know better when they are presented with it and when the pathways have been cleared in the three higher octaves so there is the opening for them to have that higher vision of what is possible for their nation, what is the next step for their nation.

Thus, my beloved, I know this has been a long discourse. I know for many of you, your chakras are at their maximum capacity or even beyond the light you can receive, the light you can give out. My beloved, it is worth it for you, individually and for your growth, to come together like this and to be willing to push yourselves to receive the light, to hold the light, to give out the light, so that you can have that feeling of being in the flow from Above to below. You are in the nexus of the figure-eight flow of energy from the ascended masters that then, through your chakras, is spread out to the entire population. It gives that shift in the collective consciousness so that the discontent of the people is channeled in a positive direction and they suddenly see a positive way forward instead of just being dissatisfied and wanting to overthrow the status quo without having any direction. You have seen in past ages how the fallen beings have managed to take the discontent of the people and create a violent revolution that overthrew the old power elite, only to put in a new power elite that was even more oppressive than the old one. You have seen this so many times, even in North Korea where you saw the same thing. You saw it in China with Mao, you saw it with the Bolsheviks in Russia, and you saw it after the French revolution and so many other places. This, of course, we do not desire to see repeated and that is why again I say to the old power elite, I speak to those who are the more benevolent among the power elites in the established democracies: "It is in your own best interest to wake up and realize that you will have to bring in direct democracy either as an enlightened peaceful transition or by having the people vote for more and more extremist candidates that create more chaos in your nation than you would like to see."

It is time to awaken those who can be awakened and realize that we have entered a new phase. It is irrevocable; there is no way to turn back the clock. Status quo has been disturbed and it is a matter of bringing forth the next logical step for the democratic nations of the world—and it is Direct Democracy. Have I expressed this with sufficient directness, my beloved? I trust I have and thus I thank you for your patience and your willingness to be the open door for Saint Germain—for Saint Germain I AM.

2 | INVOKING DIRECT DEMOCRACY

In the name I AM THAT I AM, Jesus Christ, I call to all ascended masters working on manifesting the Golden Age, especially Saint Germain, to radiate into the collective consciousness a new awareness of the need for direct democracy. Help people see that we can build a new future by working with the ascended masters and letting go of the old way of looking at life, including…

[Make personal calls.]

Part 1

1. I accept that even in the democratic nations, there is a power elite that is seeking to undermine democracy.

O Saint Germain, you do inspire,
my vision raised forever higher,

with you I form a figure-eight,
your Golden Age I co-create.

**O Saint Germain, what love you bring,
it truly makes all matter sing,
your violet flame does all restore,
with you we are becoming more.**

2. I accept that the primary difference between a democracy and other forms of government, especially a dictatorship, is that a government that is free and democratic cannot allow the formation of a power elite.

O Saint Germain, what Freedom Flame,
released when we recite your name,
acceleration is your gift,
our planet it will surely lift.

**O Saint Germain, what love you bring,
it truly makes all matter sing,
your violet flame does all restore,
with you we are becoming more.**

3. I accept that the central aspect of a dictatorial, centralized form of government is the formation of a small power elite that can exercise power over the majority of the population.

O Saint Germain, in love we claim,
our right to bring your violet flame,
from you Above, to us below,
it is an all-transforming flow.

O Saint Germain, what love you bring,
it truly makes all matter sing,
your violet flame does all restore,
with you we are becoming more.

4. I accept that what most democracies today call a dictator-ship is a form of government where one person has near total power, and around him is a power elite that has the major function of carrying out the dictator's dictates.

O Saint Germain, I love you so,
my aura filled with violet glow,
my chakras filled with violet fire,
I am your cosmic amplifier.

O Saint Germain, what love you bring,
it truly makes all matter sing,
your violet flame does all restore,
with you we are becoming more.

5. I accept that even if we do not have a single dictator, we can still have a very small power elite that is in a privileged position where they can exercise power without accountability and this is the antithesis of democracy.

O Saint Germain, I am now free,
your violet flame is therapy,
transform all hang-ups in my mind,
as inner peace I surely find.

O Saint Germain, what love you bring,
it truly makes all matter sing,

your violet flame does all restore,
with you we are becoming more.

6. I accept that it must be the goal of a truly democratic government to make an enlightened, aware effort to counteract the formation of power elites. So far, no democratic nation has done a good enough job of this.

O Saint Germain, my body pure,
your violet flame for all is cure,
consume the cause of all disease,
and therefore I am all at ease.

O Saint Germain, what love you bring,
it truly makes all matter sing,
your violet flame does all restore,
with you we are becoming more.

7. I accept that all democratic nations had a power elite when those nations shifted to a democratic form of government. That power elite did not simply lie down and die or evaporate into thin air.

O Saint Germain, I'm karma-free,
the past no longer burdens me,
a brand new opportunity,
I am in Christic unity.

O Saint Germain, what love you bring,
it truly makes all matter sing,
your violet flame does all restore,
with you we are becoming more.

8. I accept that the power elite continued to exist and they have, ever since then, attempted to influence the democratic government in many different ways. These have often been hidden ways because in a democratic country they cannot exercise power as openly as in a more centralized power structure.

O Saint Germain, we are now one,
I am for you a violet sun,
as we transform this planet earth,
your Golden Age is given birth.

O Saint Germain, what love you bring,
it truly makes all matter sing,
your violet flame does all restore,
with you we are becoming more.

9. I accept that this places a special responsibility on democratic governments to make sure that such a power elite cannot form, even if it seems like a benign power elite.

O Saint Germain, the earth is free,
from burden of duality,
in oneness we bring what is best,
your Golden Age is manifest.

O Saint Germain, what love you bring,
it truly makes all matter sing,
your violet flame does all restore,
with you we are becoming more.

Part 2

1. I accept that the essence of a democracy is that the people rule.

> O Saint Germain, you do inspire,
> my vision raised forever higher,
> with you I form a figure-eight,
> your Golden Age I co-create.
>
> **O Saint Germain, what love you bring,**
> **it truly makes all matter sing,**
> **your violet flame does all restore,**
> **with you we are becoming more.**

2. I accept that in many of the older democracies people's confidence in the government is falling, and the reason is that a power elite has formed and that power elite is not willing to let go of its power.

> O Saint Germain, what Freedom Flame,
> released when we recite your name,
> acceleration is your gift,
> our planet it will surely lift.
>
> **O Saint Germain, what love you bring,**
> **it truly makes all matter sing,**
> **your violet flame does all restore,**
> **with you we are becoming more.**

3. I accept that the current form of democracy cannot take the world into the Golden Age. It is impossible to move into the

Golden Age without educating and enlightening the people as to how a country works because in the Golden Age the people *must* rule. They must make the major decisions.

> O Saint Germain, in love we claim,
> our right to bring your violet flame,
> from you Above, to us below,
> it is an all-transforming flow.

> **O Saint Germain, what love you bring,**
> **it truly makes all matter sing,**
> **your violet flame does all restore,**
> **with you we are becoming more.**

4. I accept that we, the people, are beginning to stand up for ourselves and demand a different form of government where we have a more direct influence.

> O Saint Germain, I love you so,
> my aura filled with violet glow,
> my chakras filled with violet fire,
> I am your cosmic amplifier.

> **O Saint Germain, what love you bring,**
> **it truly makes all matter sing,**
> **your violet flame does all restore,**
> **with you we are becoming more.**

5. I accept that the next logical step for the older democracies is direct democracy where the people vote in popular referendums about major issues in the country.

> O Saint Germain, I am now free,
> your violet flame is therapy,
> transform all hang-ups in my mind,
> as inner peace I surely find.

> **O Saint Germain, what love you bring,**
> **it truly makes all matter sing,**
> **your violet flame does all restore,**
> **with you we are becoming more.**

6. I accept that the older democracies are facing a situation where the people have less and less faith in their elected representatives, in those who run the economy, in those who run the educational systems and in those who run the press and the media.

> O Saint Germain, my body pure,
> your violet flame for all is cure,
> consume the cause of all disease,
> and therefore I am all at ease.

> **O Saint Germain, what love you bring,**
> **it truly makes all matter sing,**
> **your violet flame does all restore,**
> **with you we are becoming more.**

7. I accept that it is not the job of a free press to preserve the current power structure when that power structure does not serve the people and does not serve the country in the long run.

> O Saint Germain, I'm karma-free,
> the past no longer burdens me,

a brand new opportunity,
I am in Christic unity.

O Saint Germain, what love you bring,
it truly makes all matter sing,
your violet flame does all restore,
with you we are becoming more.

8. I accept that my country is moving into a new phase of its development where the old form of representative democracy is becoming obsolete, is becoming outdated.

O Saint Germain, we are now one,
I am for you a violet sun,
as we transform this planet earth,
your Golden Age is given birth.

O Saint Germain, what love you bring,
it truly makes all matter sing,
your violet flame does all restore,
with you we are becoming more.

9. I accept that we cannot turn the clock back to a situation where most people had faith in the major media outlets. These media outlets are like the dinosaurs, only those who work in them have not realized that they have become extinct.

O Saint Germain, the earth is free,
from burden of duality,
in oneness we bring what is best,
your Golden Age is manifest.

O Saint Germain, what love you bring,
it truly makes all matter sing,
your violet flame does all restore,
with you we are becoming more.

Part 3

1. I accept that the ascended masters do not have it as their primary goal to maintain stability but to maintain growth, to create growth, to create self-transcendence.

O Saint Germain, you do inspire,
my vision raised forever higher,
with you I form a figure-eight,
your Golden Age I co-create.

O Saint Germain, what love you bring,
it truly makes all matter sing,
your violet flame does all restore,
with you we are becoming more.

2. I accept that representative democracy is not the final or highest stage of democracy. Democracy is only a means to an end, namely the raising of the consciousness of the people.

O Saint Germain, what Freedom Flame,
released when we recite your name,
acceleration is your gift,
our planet it will surely lift.

**O Saint Germain, what love you bring,
it truly makes all matter sing,
your violet flame does all restore,
with you we are becoming more.**

3. I accept that there was a stage where the people elected representatives and those representatives made the decisions in the parliamentary assemblies. That period has become obsolete by technology that makes it possible to spread information and makes it easier for the people to vote.

O Saint Germain, in love we claim,
our right to bring your violet flame,
from you Above, to us below,
it is an all-transforming flow.

**O Saint Germain, what love you bring,
it truly makes all matter sing,
your violet flame does all restore,
with you we are becoming more.**

4. I accept that the next logical stage of democracy is that people do not have to vote only every four years by going to a ballot room and putting their crosses on a printed ballot. Now they can vote over the Internet so that the process is much smoother and quicker.

O Saint Germain, I love you so,
my aura filled with violet glow,
my chakras filled with violet fire,
I am your cosmic amplifier.

O Saint Germain, what love you bring,
it truly makes all matter sing,
your violet flame does all restore,
with you we are becoming more.

5. I call forth the judgment of Christ upon those who follow the party discipline and the hidden agenda of cooperating with the business conglomerates or the media so that they do not upset the apple cart and change the power structure in society.

O Saint Germain, I am now free,
your violet flame is therapy,
transform all hang-ups in my mind,
as inner peace I surely find.

O Saint Germain, what love you bring,
it truly makes all matter sing,
your violet flame does all restore,
with you we are becoming more.

6. I call for the cutting free of the people who have the potential to bring forth the Golden Age so they do not withdraw from the bureaucracy or from public office because they know it will be a compromise of their ideals.

O Saint Germain, my body pure,
your violet flame for all is cure,
consume the cause of all disease,
and therefore I am all at ease.

O Saint Germain, what love you bring,
it truly makes all matter sing,

**your violet flame does all restore,
with you we are becoming more.**

7. I call for the exposure of any hidden agenda where the major political parties have sold their soul to the big business or to maintaining status quo and therefore they do not feel that anything new can be brought in.

O Saint Germain, I'm karma-free,
the past no longer burdens me,
a brand new opportunity,
I am in Christic unity.

**O Saint Germain, what love you bring,
it truly makes all matter sing,
your violet flame does all restore,
with you we are becoming more.**

8. I accept that the people do actually know better than the elite because the people know when a change is needed. They may not know consciously everything that is involved with the situation because the elite is withholding that information.

O Saint Germain, we are now one,
I am for you a violet sun,
as we transform this planet earth,
your Golden Age is given birth.

**O Saint Germain, what love you bring,
it truly makes all matter sing,
your violet flame does all restore,
with you we are becoming more.**

9. I accept that the people are quite capable of feeling in their hearts or in their guts when a change is needed, when something has been going on for too long, when that something is not right and when they simply cannot accept it anymore.

O Saint Germain, the earth is free,
from burden of duality,
in oneness we bring what is best,
your Golden Age is manifest.

**O Saint Germain, what love you bring,
it truly makes all matter sing,
your violet flame does all restore,
with you we are becoming more.**

Part 4

1. I accept that if the people had a more direct way of voting for particular issues, they would also be able to feel what would be best for their country.

O Saint Germain, you do inspire,
my vision raised forever higher,
with you I form a figure-eight,
your Golden Age I co-create.

**O Saint Germain, what love you bring,
it truly makes all matter sing,
your violet flame does all restore,
with you we are becoming more.**

2. I accept that if all democratic nations switched to a direct form of democracy, I, along with Saint Germain, would much prefer the rule of the general population to the rule of the elite.

> O Saint Germain, what Freedom Flame,
> released when we recite your name,
> acceleration is your gift,
> our planet it will surely lift.

> **O Saint Germain, what love you bring,**
> **it truly makes all matter sing,**
> **your violet flame does all restore,**
> **with you we are becoming more.**

3. I accept that even though the people would make certain decisions that would create turmoil, that turmoil will lead to growth because if the people make a decision that turns out to have unwanted consequences, then who can the people blame when it was a result of their direct vote?

> O Saint Germain, in love we claim,
> our right to bring your violet flame,
> from you Above, to us below,
> it is an all-transforming flow.

> **O Saint Germain, what love you bring,**
> **it truly makes all matter sing,**
> **your violet flame does all restore,**
> **with you we are becoming more.**

4. I accept that if the people vote directly, they have no one else to point the finger at than themselves. This will mean that many will wake up and realize that: "If we could make a

decision that led to these consequences, then it was because we didn't know enough about the topic and then we need to educate ourselves so that we can make a better decision in the future."

> O Saint Germain, I love you so,
> my aura filled with violet glow,
> my chakras filled with violet fire,
> I am your cosmic amplifier.

> **O Saint Germain, what love you bring,**
> **it truly makes all matter sing,**
> **your violet flame does all restore,**
> **with you we are becoming more.**

5. I accept that the next stage for democracy is to put the people in a situation where they have no one else to blame, where they cannot blame the power elite. This will give maximum growth to the people.

> O Saint Germain, I am now free,
> your violet flame is therapy,
> transform all hang-ups in my mind,
> as inner peace I surely find.

> **O Saint Germain, what love you bring,**
> **it truly makes all matter sing,**
> **your violet flame does all restore,**
> **with you we are becoming more.**

6. I accept that the people of the older democracies are ready to have that responsibility. They are ready for it and we can see this by the growing dissatisfaction with the political status quo.

O Saint Germain, my body pure,
your violet flame for all is cure,
consume the cause of all disease,
and therefore I am all at ease.

O Saint Germain, what love you bring,
it truly makes all matter sing,
your violet flame does all restore,
with you we are becoming more.

7. I accept that we have seen enough examples in world history of the chaos and destruction that the fallen beings can create. Therefore, I say: "We have had enough of this chaos, we don't want any more of this chaos, what's the alternative to being ruled by the fallen beings?"

O Saint Germain, I'm karma-free,
the past no longer burdens me,
a brand new opportunity,
I am in Christic unity.

O Saint Germain, what love you bring,
it truly makes all matter sing,
your violet flame does all restore,
with you we are becoming more.

8. I accept that the people are ready for freedom from the fallen beings, freedom from a small power elite who are so arrogant that they think they know better than the people.

O Saint Germain, we are now one,
I am for you a violet sun,

as we transform this planet earth,
your Golden Age is given birth.

O Saint Germain, what love you bring,
it truly makes all matter sing,
your violet flame does all restore,
with you we are becoming more.

9. I accept that it is necessary for the older democracies to step up and give the population broader influence on the political decision making process. This begins with recognizing that the people need to know more about how the country functions.

O Saint Germain, the earth is free,
from burden of duality,
in oneness we bring what is best,
your Golden Age is manifest.

O Saint Germain, what love you bring,
it truly makes all matter sing,
your violet flame does all restore,
with you we are becoming more.

Part 5

1. I accept that the older democracies have moved into a phase where there is such material affluence that the people are getting tired of materialism, they are getting tired of being consumers.

O Saint Germain, you do inspire,
my vision raised forever higher,
with you I form a figure-eight,
your Golden Age I co-create.

O Saint Germain, what love you bring,
it truly makes all matter sing,
your violet flame does all restore,
with you we are becoming more.

2. I accept that people are longing for a deeper purpose with their lives and this is why they are becoming dissatisfied with their leaders because they are not giving them an alternative to the materialistic lifestyle.

O Saint Germain, what Freedom Flame,
released when we recite your name,
acceleration is your gift,
our planet it will surely lift.

O Saint Germain, what love you bring,
it truly makes all matter sing,
your violet flame does all restore,
with you we are becoming more.

3. I accept that only we, the people, can change the status quo by becoming aware of the power elite and by being willing to take responsibility for our nation.

O Saint Germain, in love we claim,
our right to bring your violet flame,
from you Above, to us below,
it is an all-transforming flow.

O Saint Germain, what love you bring,
it truly makes all matter sing,
your violet flame does all restore,
with you we are becoming more.

4. I accept that it is a myth that the most intelligent people are the ones who have risen to the top of democratic societies. I accept that a country cannot be run only by intelligent people because they also need to have heart, they need to have situational awareness, they need to have wisdom.

O Saint Germain, I love you so,
my aura filled with violet glow,
my chakras filled with violet fire,
I am your cosmic amplifier.

O Saint Germain, what love you bring,
it truly makes all matter sing,
your violet flame does all restore,
with you we are becoming more.

5. I accept that the broad section of the population are aware enough, are knowledgeable enough, to make good decisions, and therefore the country can indeed be run successfully by direct democracy.

O Saint Germain, I am now free,
your violet flame is therapy,
transform all hang-ups in my mind,
as inner peace I surely find.

O Saint Germain, what love you bring,
it truly makes all matter sing,

**your violet flame does all restore,
with you we are becoming more.**

6. I accept that when we give the people an opportunity, they will step up. If we don't give the people an opportunity, we will see more and more discontent, more and more unrest in the older democracies.

O Saint Germain, my body pure,
your violet flame for all is cure,
consume the cause of all disease,
and therefore I am all at ease.

**O Saint Germain, what love you bring,
it truly makes all matter sing,
your violet flame does all restore,
with you we are becoming more.**

7. I accept that having the people stand up and demand change is not populism, it is the *future*. The ruling elite will try to label this as dangerous, but if the people want to elect an untraditional candidate for president or for members of parliament, then the people should be allowed to do so.

O Saint Germain, I'm karma-free,
the past no longer burdens me,
a brand new opportunity,
I am in Christic unity.

**O Saint Germain, what love you bring,
it truly makes all matter sing,
your violet flame does all restore,
with you we are becoming more.**

8. I accept that direct democracy will be created by the ruling elite realizing that their time is up and that they need to give way peacefully to direct democracy and they need to let the people vote.

> O Saint Germain, we are now one,
> I am for you a violet sun,
> as we transform this planet earth,
> your Golden Age is given birth.

> **O Saint Germain, what love you bring,**
> **it truly makes all matter sing,**
> **your violet flame does all restore,**
> **with you we are becoming more.**

9. I accept that if this does not happen, people will continue to vote for candidates that are outside the mainstream, and this will lead to some chaos. This will scare the ruling elite into thinking that direct democracy is the lesser of two evils.

> O Saint Germain, the earth is free,
> from burden of duality,
> in oneness we bring what is best,
> your Golden Age is manifest.

> **O Saint Germain, what love you bring,**
> **it truly makes all matter sing,**
> **your violet flame does all restore,**
> **with you we are becoming more.**

Part 6

1. I accept that nothing can stop the development towards greater awareness among the population. We are coming into an age where the people want to know better.

> O Saint Germain, you do inspire,
> my vision raised forever higher,
> with you I form a figure-eight,
> your Golden Age I co-create.

> **O Saint Germain, what love you bring,**
> **it truly makes all matter sing,**
> **your violet flame does all restore,**
> **with you we are becoming more.**

2. I accept that people will to know better and therefore they *will* know better and therefore they will make better decisions.

> O Saint Germain, what Freedom Flame,
> released when we recite your name,
> acceleration is your gift,
> our planet it will surely lift.

> **O Saint Germain, what love you bring,**
> **it truly makes all matter sing,**
> **your violet flame does all restore,**
> **with you we are becoming more.**

3. I accept that in the coming years, the people in the older democracies will shift and realize: "We *can* actually influence

the future of our nation, we can influence the political process.
There is *something* we can do and we are willing to do it."

> O Saint Germain, in love we claim,
> our right to bring your violet flame,
> from you Above, to us below,
> it is an all-transforming flow.

> **O Saint Germain, what love you bring,**
> **it truly makes all matter sing,**
> **your violet flame does all restore,**
> **with you we are becoming more.**

4. I accept that the Golden Age is a possibility, is a reality,
is descending upon this planet because the people will realize
that we are not powerless.

> O Saint Germain, I love you so,
> my aura filled with violet glow,
> my chakras filled with violet fire,
> I am your cosmic amplifier.

> **O Saint Germain, what love you bring,**
> **it truly makes all matter sing,**
> **your violet flame does all restore,**
> **with you we are becoming more.**

5. I accept that Saint Germain's vision does not have to be
forced upon the people because the people of any nation want
what is best for themselves and what is best for their nation.
When they see what is best, they do not have to be forced to
accept it.

O Saint Germain, I am now free,
your violet flame is therapy,
transform all hang-ups in my mind,
as inner peace I surely find.

**O Saint Germain, what love you bring,
it truly makes all matter sing,
your violet flame does all restore,
with you we are becoming more.**

6. I accept that people will know better when they are presented with a higher vision and when the pathways have been cleared in the three higher octaves so there is the opening for them to have the vision of what is possible for their nation.

O Saint Germain, my body pure,
your violet flame for all is cure,
consume the cause of all disease,
and therefore I am all at ease.

**O Saint Germain, what love you bring,
it truly makes all matter sing,
your violet flame does all restore,
with you we are becoming more.**

7. I speak to those who are the more benevolent among the power elites in the established democracies: "It is in your own best interest to wake up and realize that you will have to bring in direct democracy, either as an enlightened peaceful transition or by having the people vote for more and more extremist candidates that create more chaos in your nation than you would like to see."

> O Saint Germain, I'm karma-free,
> the past no longer burdens me,
> a brand new opportunity,
> I am in Christic unity.
>
> **O Saint Germain, what love you bring,**
> **it truly makes all matter sing,**
> **your violet flame does all restore,**
> **with you we are becoming more.**

8. I accept that it is time to awaken those who can be awakened and realize that we have entered a new phase. It is irrevocable; there is no way to turn back the clock.

> O Saint Germain, we are now one,
> I am for you a violet sun,
> as we transform this planet earth,
> your Golden Age is given birth.
>
> **O Saint Germain, what love you bring,**
> **it truly makes all matter sing,**
> **your violet flame does all restore,**
> **with you we are becoming more.**

9. I accept that status quo has been disturbed and it is a matter of bringing forth the next logical step for the democratic nations of the world—and it is Direct Democracy.

> O Saint Germain, the earth is free,
> from burden of duality,
> in oneness we bring what is best,
> your Golden Age is manifest.

**O Saint Germain, what love you bring,
it truly makes all matter sing,
your violet flame does all restore,
with you we are becoming more.**

Sealing

In the name of the Divine Mother, I call to all ascended masters for the sealing of myself and all people in my circle of influence in the creative flow of the Divine Mother, the River of Life. I call for the multiplication of my calls by all ascended masters so that we form the perfect figure-eight flow of "As Above, so below." Thus, I accept that this is fully manifest, because the mouth of the Lord, the Divine Mother that I AM, has spoken it. Amen.

3 | INVOKING THE JUDGMENT OF THOSE WHO OPPOSE DIRECT DEMOCRACY

In the name I AM THAT I AM, Jesus Christ, I call to all ascended masters working on manifesting the Golden Age, especially Archangel Michael, to bind, consume and remove the dark forces that oppose direct democracy and Saint German's Golden Age. Help people see that we can build a new future by working with the ascended masters and letting go of the old way of looking at life, including…

[Make personal calls.]

Part 1

1. I call forth the judgment of Christ upon the power elite that has formed in many of the older democracies, the elite that is seeking to manipulate and control the

population because they think they know better than the people how the country should be run.

> Archangel Michael, light so blue,
> my heart has room for only you.
> My mind is one, no longer two,
> your love for me is ever true.

> **Archangel Michael, you are here,**
> **your light consumes all doubt and fear.**
> **Your Presence is forever near,**
> **you are to me so very dear.**

2. I call forth the judgment of Christ upon the elite that says the people don't know enough about how their country works, the elite that is in charge of the educational system and the media.

> Archangel Michael, I will be,
> all one with your reality.
> No fear can hold me as I see,
> this world no power has o'er me.

> **Archangel Michael, you are here,**
> **your light consumes all doubt and fear.**
> **Your Presence is forever near,**
> **you are to me so very dear.**

3. I call forth the judgment of Christ upon the power elite that claims the people don't know enough, but it is because the power elite has not educated the people as to how the country works.

Archangel Michael, hold me tight,
shatter now the darkest night.
Clear my chakras with your light,
restore to me my inner sight.

**Archangel Michael, you are here,
your light consumes all doubt and fear.
Your Presence is forever near,
you are to me so very dear.**

4. I call forth the judgment of Christ upon the power elite that is not willing to educate the people because they don't want to share power.

Archangel Michael, now I stand,
with you the light I do command.
My heart I ever will expand,
till highest truth I understand.

**Archangel Michael, you are here,
your light consumes all doubt and fear.
Your Presence is forever near,
you are to me so very dear.**

5. I call forth the judgment of Christ upon the power elite that says the spread of alternative news is a dangerous development because the people often respond to fake news.

Archangel Michael, in my heart,
from me you never will depart.
Of hierarchy I am a part,
I now accept a fresh new start.

**Archangel Michael, you are here,
your light consumes all doubt and fear.
Your Presence is forever near,
you are to me so very dear.**

6. I call forth the judgment of Christ upon the mainstream media that has as its primary objective to maintain the status quo and preserve the present power structure with the elite on top.

Archangel Michael, sword of blue,
all darkness you are cutting through.
My Christhood I do now pursue,
discernment shows me what is true.

**Archangel Michael, you are here,
your light consumes all doubt and fear.
Your Presence is forever near,
you are to me so very dear.**

7. I call forth the judgment of Christ upon the news media so they will wake up and realize that they will only survive if they serve the interests of the people, not the elite.

Archangel Michael, in your wings,
I now let go of lesser things.
God's homing call in my heart rings,
my heart with yours forever sings.

**Archangel Michael, you are here,
your light consumes all doubt and fear.
Your Presence is forever near,
you are to me so very dear.**

8. I call forth the judgment of Christ upon the power elite that has taken advantage of representative democracy and does not want their hold on the country to be overturned, and therefore they will do anything they can to maintain that structure.

Archangel Michael, take me home,
in higher spheres I want to roam.
I am reborn from cosmic foam,
my life is now a sacred poem.

**Archangel Michael, you are here,
your light consumes all doubt and fear.
Your Presence is forever near,
you are to me so very dear.**

9. I call forth the judgment of Christ upon those among the power elite who are deliberately creating fake news in order to undermine the peoples' belief in alternative news media.

Archangel Michael, light you are,
shining like the bluest star.
You are a cosmic avatar,
with you I will go very far.

**Archangel Michael, you are here,
your light consumes all doubt and fear.
Your Presence is forever near,
you are to me so very dear.**

Part 2

1. I call forth the judgment of Christ upon those among the power elite who believe that by putting out fake news, they can scare the people to come back and only listen to mainstream media.

> Archangel Michael, light so blue,
> my heart has room for only you.
> My mind is one, no longer two,
> your love for me is ever true.

> **Archangel Michael, you are here,**
> **your light consumes all doubt and fear.**
> **Your Presence is forever near,**
> **you are to me so very dear.**

2. I call forth the judgment of Christ upon the major media outlets in most democratic nations, those who are run by people who are part of the power elite and who think they will be able to maintain their monopoly on news.

> Archangel Michael, I will be,
> all one with your reality.
> No fear can hold me as I see,
> this world no power has o'er me.

> **Archangel Michael, you are here,**
> **your light consumes all doubt and fear.**
> **Your Presence is forever near,**
> **you are to me so very dear.**

3. I call forth the judgment of Christ upon those in the media who think they can maintain their structure and maintain their advertising income and get people to continue to subscribe to their newspapers.

> Archangel Michael, hold me tight,
> shatter now the darkest night.
> Clear my chakras with your light,
> restore to me my inner sight.
>
> **Archangel Michael, you are here,**
> **your light consumes all doubt and fear.**
> **Your Presence is forever near,**
> **you are to me so very dear.**

4. I call forth the judgment of Christ upon the media people who are not serving the people because they have built such an arrogance of thinking that they can know what the people should think about all topics.

> Archangel Michael, now I stand,
> with you the light I do command.
> My heart I ever will expand,
> till highest truth I understand.
>
> **Archangel Michael, you are here,**
> **your light consumes all doubt and fear.**
> **Your Presence is forever near,**
> **you are to me so very dear.**

5. I call forth the judgment of Christ upon the media people who believe it is not their job to simply report the news and let the people form their own opinion. They believe they

should form the opinions of the people and that they know what opinions people should have in order to maintain stability in their country.

> Archangel Michael, in my heart,
> from me you never will depart.
> Of hierarchy I am a part,
> I now accept a fresh new start.

> **Archangel Michael, you are here,**
> **your light consumes all doubt and fear.**
> **Your Presence is forever near,**
> **you are to me so very dear.**

6. I call for people to be cut free to realize that the age of having a democratic power elite who believes they know better than the people is coming to an end. It has outlived its usefulness and it is time to consider the next stage for democracy.

> Archangel Michael, sword of blue,
> all darkness you are cutting through.
> My Christhood I do now pursue,
> discernment shows me what is true.

> **Archangel Michael, you are here,**
> **your light consumes all doubt and fear.**
> **Your Presence is forever near,**
> **you are to me so very dear.**

7. I call forth the judgment of Christ upon people in the bureaucracy or those in public office who have developed an attitude of arrogance of knowing better than the people.

Archangel Michael, in your wings,
I now let go of lesser things.
God's homing call in my heart rings,
my heart with yours forever sings.

**Archangel Michael, you are here,
your light consumes all doubt and fear.
Your Presence is forever near,
you are to me so very dear.**

8. I call forth the judgment of Christ upon those who follow the party discipline and the hidden agenda of cooperating with the business conglomerates or the media so that they do not upset the apple cart and change the power structure in society.

Archangel Michael, take me home,
in higher spheres I want to roam.
I am reborn from cosmic foam,
my life is now a sacred poem.

**Archangel Michael, you are here,
your light consumes all doubt and fear.
Your Presence is forever near,
you are to me so very dear.**

9. I call for the cutting free of the people who have the potential to bring forth the Golden Age so they do not withdraw from the bureaucracy or from public office because they know it will be a compromise of their ideals.

Archangel Michael, light you are,
shining like the bluest star.

You are a cosmic avatar,
with you I will go very far.

Archangel Michael, you are here,
your light consumes all doubt and fear.
Your Presence is forever near,
you are to me so very dear.

Part 3

1. I call for the exposure of any hidden agenda where the major political parties have sold their soul to big business or to maintaining status quo and therefore they do not feel that anything new can be brought in.

Archangel Michael, light so blue,
my heart has room for only you.
My mind is one, no longer two,
your love for me is ever true.

Archangel Michael, you are here,
your light consumes all doubt and fear.
Your Presence is forever near,
you are to me so very dear.

2. I call forth the judgment of Christ upon the fallen beings who from the moment they fell into this sphere thought they knew better than those who were created as individual lifestreams in this sphere.

Archangel Michael, I will be,
all one with your reality.
No fear can hold me as I see,
this world no power has o'er me.

Archangel Michael, you are here,
your light consumes all doubt and fear.
Your Presence is forever near,
you are to me so very dear.

3. I call for the cutting free of the people to see that they need to be willing to educate themselves, instead of focusing on their comfortable daily lives.

Archangel Michael, hold me tight,
shatter now the darkest night.
Clear my chakras with your light,
restore to me my inner sight.

Archangel Michael, you are here,
your light consumes all doubt and fear.
Your Presence is forever near,
you are to me so very dear.

4. I call forth the judgment of Christ upon the power elite people who argue why status quo should not be changed. They use as their argument that the people are not ready for changing the status quo, but who is responsible for the people not being ready other than those who are in charge of that society?

Archangel Michael, now I stand,
with you the light I do command.

My heart I ever will expand,
till highest truth I understand.

Archangel Michael, you are here,
your light consumes all doubt and fear.
Your Presence is forever near,
you are to me so very dear.

5. I call for people to be cut free so they will wake up and say: "Ah, but this concept of direct democracy is obvious is it not, why shouldn't we vote about the issues?"

Archangel Michael, in my heart,
from me you never will depart.
Of hierarchy I am a part,
I now accept a fresh new start.

Archangel Michael, you are here,
your light consumes all doubt and fear.
Your Presence is forever near,
you are to me so very dear.

6. I call for people to be cut free so they will wake up and say: "Of course we are capable of knowing what to vote and what is the right direction for our nation. Why should we believe that the power elite will know better than us, isn't it obvious that we are capable of knowing?"

Archangel Michael, sword of blue,
all darkness you are cutting through.
My Christhood I do now pursue,
discernment shows me what is true.

Archangel Michael, you are here,
your light consumes all doubt and fear.
Your Presence is forever near,
you are to me so very dear.

7. I call forth the judgment of Christ upon the elite who think they can allow direct democracy and still maintain some power over society by the power they have over the media.

Archangel Michael, in your wings,
I now let go of lesser things.
God's homing call in my heart rings,
my heart with yours forever sings.

Archangel Michael, you are here,
your light consumes all doubt and fear.
Your Presence is forever near,
you are to me so very dear.

8. I call forth the judgment of Christ upon the elite who think that they can still trust their bureaucracy and they can still influence the country that way.

Archangel Michael, take me home,
in higher spheres I want to roam.
I am reborn from cosmic foam,
my life is now a sacred poem.

Archangel Michael, you are here,
your light consumes all doubt and fear.
Your Presence is forever near,
you are to me so very dear.

9. I call forth the judgment of Christ upon the elite who are so blinded that they will not see the need for change and therefore will resist it with all the means at their disposal instead of giving way for the inevitable.

> Archangel Michael, light you are,
> shining like the bluest star.
> You are a cosmic avatar,
> with you I will go very far.
>
> **Archangel Michael, you are here,**
> **your light consumes all doubt and fear.**
> **Your Presence is forever near,**
> **you are to me so very dear.**

Sealing

In the name of the Divine Mother, I call to all ascended masters for the sealing of myself and all people in my circle of influence in the creative flow of the Divine Mother, the River of Life. I call for the multiplication of my calls by all ascended masters so that we form the perfect figure-eight flow of "As Above, so below." Thus, I accept that this is fully manifest, because the mouth of the Lord, the Divine Mother that I AM, has spoken it. Amen.

4 | THE LEGAL SYSTEM OF THE GOLDEN AGE

I AM the Ascended Master, Nada, and I wish to give you some perspective on the remark made by Jesus so many years ago when he said: "Woe unto ye lawyers." What does this mean for the Golden Age and for the bringing in of the Golden Age? Well, it means simply that the profession that you now see as the legal profession will have to change dramatically in order to align itself with the vision of Saint Germain. This, of course, must start, not just with the lawyers who are, so to speak, interpreting the law but also with the lawmakers who make the laws.

Lawmaking for the privileged elite

What you have today is a tradition that is very, very old. The purpose of making laws and the purpose of setting up a legal system, a court system, that is interpreting these laws is affected by the mindset of the fallen beings to such an extent that in many countries the real purpose of the entire system is to give special privileges to the ruling elite of people or to give them a way to escape accountability. There is, of course, in many democratic nations a certain limit to how they can set up the laws in order to give themselves privileges because a democracy is based on the fundamental principle that all of its citizens should be equal to the law. Yet even in democratic countries there are always those who seek to create laws in such a way that they set up exceptions for certain people or certain segments of society. You have seen this especially with the business community where in many countries there are certain corporations that are so big that they are considered too important for the country so that the country cannot risk that they will either go down or move their businesses elsewhere. Therefore, there is a tendency to create laws in such a way that these businesses are, in effect, given a favorable position.

This is something that, of course, cannot exist in the Golden Age. It is necessary for you to make calls on this so that there will be a rising awareness of the need to remove all such special privileges or exemptions in the laws of democratic countries so that they do not favor particular businesses or organizations. This will require a change in the mindset, but this will be brought about by other things that we will talk about and other calls you can make. Of course, there needs to be a trust in the nations that we do not need to give special privileges to certain companies. We do not need to, in effect, give them monopolies in order for our economy to survive.

There is today a widespread belief in many countries that the economy of certain nations simply could not survive without these huge corporations. It is, of course, not correct because it is indeed very possible that many smaller businesses can make up for the loss of one big business. It is a perception created by the fallen beings in order to give them power and to give them privileges and maintain those privileges so that they, in effect, do not have to run a business that is geared toward serving its customers. Therefore, they can get away with this because there is no effective competition due to the favored position they have been given.

Unnecessarily complicated laws

Once you remove such barriers in the laws, then what remains is to look at the legal system and how the courts and the lawyers are interpreting, and in many cases manipulating, the laws. When you look at democratic countries, it is not so difficult to bring about a situation where certain organizations no longer have these special privileges. You still have the fact that you have created a culture in the legal system of most nations where those who are part of the legal system do not want to change the system in fundamental ways because they make their living off of that system.

You know very well that in most countries the lawyers are often among the wealthiest people because they can charge very high fees. They can charge high fees because the country has such a complicated set of laws and such a complicated legal system that in effect it gives a privileged position, even in some cases a kind of monopoly position, to the lawyers. They are the only ones who can interpret the system. This, of course, you need to make calls on so that countries will come to realize that this entire culture is based on a simple fact, namely that the law system, the system of the laws, is becoming increasingly complicated, increasingly large. There is simply an unnecessary burden of all of these laws that are becoming more and more complex in all countries. Now, obviously, you cannot create a very simple law in a complex country because there are many considerations that need to be put into the system of laws. Nevertheless, what you can make calls on is that people will realize the need to simplify the laws so that there is not as much room for interpretation. What often makes the law system complex is that the entire legal profession in a country has created a culture where, for example, they say that the laws must not discriminate. In order to avoid discriminating, we have to write various conditions into the laws so that no-one is discriminated against. Even this can be used, not only to create complexity but also to create a situation where the efforts to seemingly not discriminate actually become an openness for an almost endless interpretation of the laws so that there is no clarity in how to implement these laws.

Once you start creating such a complex system of laws that hardly anyone can interpret them, you end up in a situation where the people who are writing the laws often simply do not have the vision of how a new law they are creating might potentially contradict what is said in a previous law. You end up with these situations where everything is so complicated that no one can really foresee the consequences of a new law and how it might contradict a previous law. This, again, gives leeway for the lawyers to begin to interpret, and all of a sudden the laws that were meant to, for example, prevent discrimination against certain groups actually become a tool whereby those who can afford to hire the expensive lawyers can use the laws as a form of loophole. They can actually use the law that was meant to prevent discrimination to create a new form of discrimination where they themselves can manipulate the laws so that they are claiming a certain freedom that they are not entitled to because they are not actually being discriminated against. They are using it to set themselves up in an exempt position where they do not have to follow the same rules as others.

I know, my beloved, that this is abstract but I do not wish to go into giving you too many concrete examples because again this would become something that could be interpreted and interpreted and interpreted. What I wish you to make calls on is that there is a need for the democratic nations to wake up and realize that they need to step back and look at their legal system and look how it is being misused by the lawyers to give exemptions to a small elite who can afford to pay the attorneys. They can continue to pay these attorney's fees and create these court cases that seem to go on forever and ever. In the end, they end up giving them special privileges that no ordinary citizens could ever claim because they simply could not afford to pay the legal fees.

Only the elite can afford legal fees

What you have created here is a legal system that has become very complicated. Even though it is based on good intentions of preventing the discrimination against certain groups of people, the complication of the system, the level of complexity of the system, is actually reinforcing the situation where there is an upper class who can afford to play the legal game. Then, there is the broader population who simply have no recourse because they cannot afford to run a court case that costs tens of thousands, hundreds of thousands, millions of dollars in legal fees.

You end up creating this privileged position where those who can take advantage of the system do so and therefore can set themselves up to either have privileges or to generate profits. They can effectively destroy competition by running these lawsuits against their competitors that no smaller businesses can afford. Therefore, the smaller businesses cannot challenge the older established businesses. There is also a tendency in most countries, to create so many rules that, for example, businesses have to comply with that this in itself creates a privileged position for the large businesses that can afford to hire the lawyers or the experts or build the facilities that are required. In essence, you have a situation where the legal system that actually was meant to protect the people, is being used by large established businesses to destroy their competition or to prevent the competition from even arising because they cannot afford to comply with the elaborate rules.

It is necessary for you to make the calls that there is a rising awareness. Again, we do not need people to know about ascended master teachings, we do not need them to understand the dynamic of the fallen beings. But it is not beyond the capability of the people in most nations to realize that there is always a power elite that is seeking to gain special power and privileges for themselves and they will use any aspect of society, including the legal system and the bureaucratic system.

It is not beyond the capacity of most people to realize that for the ordinary citizen in a democratic country, it is in their best interest to have a relatively simple legal system and a relatively simple set of bureaucratic rules so that they themselves can figure out what their rights are. It is certainly something to make calls on so that people will realize that the tendency to complicate everything (to complicate the legal system, to complicate the bureaucracy) only serves the elite. They are the only ones who can afford to hire the attorneys to take advantage of this complex system. They are using it over and over and over again to set themselves up so that the people cannot challenge them. Thereby, this system of complexity creates a privileged position for the few and effectively shuts out the many from attaining these privileges.

Difficulties of starting new businesses

You will see in many nations how the rules that are set in place for establishing a new business in many areas are so complicated, so elaborate and so expensive to comply with, that a new business effectively cannot be started. Or at least, it cannot be started by a single person or a few people. It could only be started by someone who had enough experience and enough connections so that the person could manipulate the system and so that the person could also gain financing from the major financial institutions. This would then mean that such a business, in order to even get started, has to, so to speak, become part of the establishment.

You will see that there has been created this privileged position where only those who are part of the establishment can start a new business. In order to get that business going, they must then, as I said, become part of the establishment. This means they accept the establishment (the rules that they are based on) and they will perpetuate the system, they will not challenge the system.

When you look back at the way many nations got their economies going, it was often that a single person could take the initiative and could start with very little capital and start a new business that eventually would grow to become a bigger business. Effectively, in many nations this is no longer possible in the main areas of business. It is only possible in new areas such as you, for example, saw a few decades ago with the computer industry. Anyone who had the expertise could start a new company, such as a software company, and simply by their know-how start a new business. The reason for this was very simply that the old established businesses did not understand the computer industry in the beginning, did not see its potential and therefore it was one of those rare opportunities for the small independent entrepreneur. It is the small independent entrepreneurs that will drive the innovation that will bring about the new technology and the new business models in the Golden Age.

The elite cannot receive new technology

My beloved, have we not so many times talked about the power elite that you realize, of course, that the new inventions and the new business models that are necessary in the Golden Age are not likely to be brought by the huge established businesses? They are more concerned about protecting their position and their interests than bringing forth something new.

Now, we have talked about the fact that there are many businesses who become so large and they become so complicated that they cannot invent. You see why! It is simply because when a business becomes so big that it becomes a part of the establishment in a country, then it is inevitable that the business that is taking advantage of a complicated legal system will itself have to create a set of internal rules. These will also become more and more complicated so that the business itself eventually becomes so bogged down in these internal procedures that there is no room for invention, there is no room for creativity. Therefore, it begins to, as we have said, have this process of unnatural selection where it selects *out* the people who can invent and selects *in* the people who are willing to follow rules.

It is clear that for Saint Germain's Golden Age to be manifest, many new business methods, business visions, much new technology needs to be brought forth. This is not likely to be brought by the big established companies because they either will not see a new invention as a possibility or they will see it as a threat to their business and therefore want to suppress it. You need to make the calls for this entire conglomerate because there are some very, very powerful demons and collective entities that have been created by these huge corporations.

You can make the calls for this in every country because every country is affected by this. You especially need to make calls for the binding and the consuming of the demons behind the big multinational corporations. Here in South Korea, you need to make calls for the big business conglomerates that you have nationally so that they will be exposed and that their privileged positions will be removed.

Make calls on multinational corporations

You also need to be aware, as does every nation, that there are these huge international, multinational corporations that are simply seeking to take over the economy in any country. You will see that these corporations will move in. If you study, for example, the situation in Eastern Europe after the fall of Communism, you will see that in every country these big multinational corporations attempted to move in and dominate the business world because they had the capital, they could afford to hire the attorneys. They wanted to make sure that they would take over the market in these newly freed-up economies instead of having a situation where the local people would act as entrepreneurs and start up businesses that eventually would take over most of the market. Instead, the big multinationals wanted to dominate these markets and they were in many countries allowed to establish this form of dominance.

Well, it is time, of course, for you who are our students to make the calls for this and to increase people's awareness of the need to limit, as Saint Germain has said before, the size of corporations so that they cannot become so powerful that they can begin to influence the political process in democratic nations. You especially need to make the calls for the multinational corporations. It is one thing to have a national business that influences that nation's business because that national business may at least have some loyalty to the country in which it was established. When you look at these large multinational corporations, they have no loyalty to any nation nor to any people. They are simply looking at the people as either employees that they can use and take advantage of or as customers where they would like to establish themselves in a monopoly so that the people effectively have very little choice.

You also need to make the calls that people become aware of this as consumers so that they can make wiser choices, my beloved. To give you an obvious example, you can see that even though there are two multinational corporations that sell soft drinks, they have in many countries attempted to, so to speak, divide the territory so that they can tolerate each other. They shut out any competing companies so that even though the people have a choice, the only choice is the choice between Pepsi or Coca-Cola. That really is not the kind of choices that we would like to see in the Aquarian Age.

The problem of unjust court decisions

These are areas that it is important for you to make calls on because it is clear that in the Golden Age the legal system will be *of* the people, *by* the people, *for* the people. Not *of* the elite, *by* the elite and *for* the elite, as it is today in most nations. It is not that I in any way want to promote a negative view of lawyers and attorneys, as you see in some countries. It is obvious that there are some countries where the people are beginning to be aware that attorneys have set themselves up in a position where they are interpreting and manipulating the laws endlessly.

Therefore, they are able to command these enormous fees without in the end being able to really give people a just treatment in the legal system. It is clear that there are nations where people are becoming more and more aware that they cannot get real justice in the court system because the attorneys can come up with interpretations that, in a sense, paralyze the judges from making just judgments.

This is a situation to make calls on so that there is a simplification of the legal system where again the rules become more clear. Have you done something that is illegal? Well then, you will be held accountable for that according to the rules of the system. Today, it is so that if you are a person without much money, you may be held accountable by the law, but if you have enough money to hire the attorneys, then you will not be held accountable.

Using the legal system against other people

Of course, you also can make the calls that there will be a rising awareness where the people will refuse to, so to speak, use the legal system to gain a personal advantage over other people. You see so many times, my beloved, where there are personal disagreements between different people, it can be in business dealings, it can be in divorce cases, it can be in inheritance or many other things. You will see that the people are so eager to sue each other as a way to get back at the other side. What happens in most cases is that both sides end up paying enormous legal fees and there is really no decisive outcome of the case, precisely because of the conditions and the complexity of the legal system, which makes it impossible to make these just judgments.

You can make the calls for this also and that there is an awareness here that the people are not sucked in by these beasts, by these conglomerate entities, collective entities that have been created by the legal system. This has been created because those who are part of the system want to perpetuate their existence, they want to make more and more money.

Therefore, there has been created these entities, in the emotional realm especially, that are so good at putting hooks into people's auras, into their emotional bodies and making them angry so that they want to sue each other because they think that they will get some kind of justice. There is in many cases in these disagreements no justice. The only solution here is not even to create a better legal system because it would be impossible to create a legal system that could settle every disagreement between the people in a nation. There are simply so many disagreements that people can come up with that any system would be bogged down by the volume of disagreements when people are in this state of consciousness.

You can make the calls for the binding of these demons and entities so that the people will be cut free and they will see that the real solution to these personal disagreements is not to go to the courts but to raise your own consciousness. You can make the calls that people become aware that they need to make a very realistic assessment here of what they want out of these disagreements. The simple karmic consequence of engaging in these legal battles with other people is that you tie yourself to these people karmically.

Regardless of what the outcome of a court case may be, you are tying yourself karmically to the people you are suing. You need to therefore be realistic and say: "Do I want to tie myself to these people, so that I may have to reincarnate with them again in my next lifetime? Or do I want to be free of these people so that I can move on? In that case, I might need to look to raise my own consciousness so I can see a different way to approach this situation." You can make the calls that people will rise to this new awareness that there are better ways to settle things between them.

You can even make calls for the awareness that if you go back just a few decades, there was in most nations not the tradition for suing each other that you see today. Therefore, people can begin to ask themselves: "Well, how come we could settle things back then without going to court and now all of a sudden, we have to go to court about everything? What is it that has changed in our psychology, in our national psychology, that we have suddenly become so sue-happy that we are suing each other at every opportunity?"

It is indeed possible for you to make these calls and there can be an awakening where people will begin to realize that things have simply gone too far. It is necessary to return to some original principles or even to rise up to some new principles that make it possible for people to be able to communicate openly and freely so that they can settle differences without having to take recourse with attorneys who are not giving them recourse because they are only complicating matters.

You can make the calls that people are awakened to the fact that the primary goal of many attorneys is to complicate a case so that they can extract more legal fees. The longer it goes on, the more money they make. The attorneys in many cases do not care about the outcome for the people, they do not care about justice. You need to make the calls also for the binding of these entities and demons that are enveloping the legal profession in many countries. The attorneys, even if they started out with a certain sense of idealism, have, so to speak,

sold their souls to the devil because they have become so disillusioned with the entire legal system that they do not anymore care about their ideals and principles. They realize that in
most cases, they cannot give justice to their clients. They have
decided that since this is their profession and since they went
to school and this is the only thing they know, they are just in
it for the money.

You can make the calls for the binding of these entities
that are overshadowing the minds of these attorneys and other
people involved with the system. You will see that there can
indeed be a change towards a Golden Age system where the
laws are simple, the laws are clear, the laws do not give exemptions to those who can afford to hire attorneys. There is no
room for interpretation whereby a privileged elite can gain and
maintain privileges and where there is an attitude to the legal
system that it is only a last recourse. You create a system of
mediation among people where there are more effective ways
to settle conflicts than by going to court.

A new type of justice system

You realize my beloved, that in the present situation a court-
room procedure is such a complicated interaction of energy, of
demons, of collective entities, of the emotional bodies of the
people involved, of the mental bodies of especially the attorneys, that the entire situation is so complex that the chances of
creating any form of higher justice here is very, very remote.
When you realize this, you can see that there is a need for a
new awareness for creating an entirely different system that
actually appeals to people's discernment rather than their anger
or their emotions of wanting to get back at people. The only

way to create a completely just justice system is to create a situation where the judges have a certain measure of Christ discernment. Even the people need to have some Christ discernment to know what is in their own best long-term interest.

My beloved, these are indeed complicated matters and I realize it is easy to overwhelm you. I have no desire to make you feel burdened by this personally. I simply have a desire to make you aware of what you can make calls for and then you make the calls. Then, you allow us to step in and bring forth the changes that can be brought forth because you have cleared the energetic pathway whereby this awareness can descend all the way to the physical. Once again, people wake up and say: "Oh, this is obvious. We now see it."

Do you see, my beloved, that one of the underlying themes for radiating the Golden Age consciousness is that you who are our students become the electrodes for radiating these energies from us, these ideas from us? It clears the three higher bodies of the planet so that those people who have the potential from past lifetimes suddenly wake up and see how obvious a certain change is. This is what it really means to radiate the Golden Age consciousness.

It is not that you force anything upon people. It is simply that you set them free to see the obvious and when they *know* better, they will *do* better. They will know better as soon as they are not overwhelmed by this cloud of lower energy that clogs up the flow from the ascended realm through the identity, mental, emotional realm and into the physical level where they can consciously recognize the validity of a new idea.

With this, I give you my gratitude for being the electrodes for radiating this, not only here in Korea, but throughout the world. For this is, of course, a planetary problem. I can assure you that those of you who are here have radiated an extraordinary measure in your own nation here in Korea. When you reinforce it with your calls, you will begin to see changes happening, my beloved. Thus, I give you my gratitude for enduring this long discourse.

5 | INVOKING THE LEGAL SYSTEM OF THE GOLDEN AGE

In the name I AM THAT I AM, Jesus Christ, I call to all ascended masters working on manifesting the Golden Age, especially Nada and Astrea, to radiate into the collective consciousness a new awareness of the legal system of the Golden Age. Help people see that we can build a new future by working with the ascended masters and letting go of the old way of looking at life, including…

[Make personal calls.]

Part 1

1. I call forth the judgment of Christ upon the demons and fallen beings behind the tradition of making laws and setting up a legal system that is interpreting these laws according to the mindset of the fallen beings.

Master Nada, beauty's power,
unfolding like a sacred flower.
Master Nada, so sublime,
a will that conquers even time.

**Master Nada, peace you give,
forevermore in peace we live,
our planet has a peaceful morn,
the Golden Age is hereby born.**

2. I call forth the judgment of Christ upon the demons and
fallen beings who are responsible for the fact that in many
countries the real purpose of the legal system is to give special
privileges to the ruling elite of people or to give them a way to
escape accountability.

Master Nada, you bestow,
upon us wisdom's rushing flow.
Master Nada, mind so strong
rising on your wings of song.

**Master Nada, peace you give,
forevermore in peace we live,
our planet has a peaceful morn,
the Golden Age is hereby born.**

3. I call forth the judgment of Christ upon those in democratic
countries who seek to create laws in such a way that they set up
exceptions for certain people or certain segments of society,
especially the business community.

Master Nada, precious scent,
your love is truly heaven-sent.

Master Nada, kind and soft
on wings of love we rise aloft.

**Master Nada, peace you give,
forevermore in peace we live,
our planet has a peaceful morn,
the Golden Age is hereby born.**

4. I call forth the judgment of Christ upon the people behind the mindset that certain corporations are so big and so important for the country that there is a tendency to create laws that give these businesses a favorable position.

Master Nada, mother light,
our hearts are rising like a kite.
Master Nada, from your view,
all life is pure as morning dew.

**Master Nada, peace you give,
forevermore in peace we live,
our planet has a peaceful morn,
the Golden Age is hereby born.**

5. I call for the cutting free of people so there will be a rising awareness of the need to remove all such special privileges or exemptions in the laws of democratic countries so that they do not favor particular businesses or organizations.

Master Nada, truth you bring,
as morning birds in love do sing.
Master Nada, we now feel,
your love that all four bodies heal.

Master Nada, peace you give,
forevermore in peace we live,
our planet has a peaceful morn,
the Golden Age is hereby born.

6. I accept that we do not need to give special privileges to certain companies. We do not need to, in effect, give them monopolies in order for our economy to survive.

Master Nada, serve in peace,
as all emotions we release.
Master Nada, life is fun,
the solar plexus is a sun.

Master Nada, peace you give,
forevermore in peace we live,
our planet has a peaceful morn,
the Golden Age is hereby born.

7. I call forth the judgment of Christ upon the mindset that the economy of certain nations could not survive without these huge corporations. I accept that many smaller businesses can make up for the loss of one big business.

Master Nada, love is free,
conditions we no longer see.
Master Nada, rise above,
all human forms of lesser love.

Master Nada, peace you give,
forevermore in peace we live,
our planet has a peaceful morn,
the Golden Age is hereby born.

8. I call forth the judgment of Christ upon the demons and fallen beings who have created this mindset in order to give them power and to give them privileges and maintain those privileges so that they do not have to run a business that is serving its customers. They can get away with this because there is no effective competition due to their favored position.

Master Nada, balance all,
the seven rays upon our call.
Master Nada, rise and shine,
your radiant beauty most divine.

Master Nada, peace you give,
forevermore in peace we live,
our planet has a peaceful morn,
the Golden Age is hereby born.

9. I call forth the judgment of Christ upon the demons and fallen beings behind the mindset where those who are part of the legal system do not want to change the system in fundamental ways because they make their living from that system.

Nada Dear, your Presence here,
filling up the inner sphere.
Life is now a sacred flow,
God Peace we do on all bestow.

Master Nada, peace you give,
forevermore in peace we live,
our planet has a peaceful morn,
the Golden Age is hereby born.

Part 2

1. I call forth the judgment of Christ upon the demons and fallen beings behind the fact that many countries have such a complicated set of laws and such a complicated legal system that in effect it gives a privileged position, even in some cases a monopoly position, to the lawyers who are the only ones who can interpret the system.

> Beloved Astrea, your heart is so true,
> your Circle and Sword of white and blue,
> cut all life free from dramas unwise,
> on wings of Purity our planet will rise.
>
> **Beloved Astrea, in oneness with you,**
> **your circle and sword of electric blue,**
> **with Purity's Light cutting right through,**
> **raising the earth into all that is true.**

2. I call for the cutting free of people to see that the law system is becoming increasingly complicated, and there is an unnecessary burden of all of these laws that are becoming more and more complex in all countries.

> Beloved Astrea, in God Purity,
> accelerate all of our life energy,
> we're rising beyond every impurity,
> as Purity's Light forever we see.
>
> **Beloved Astrea, in oneness with you,**
> **your circle and sword of electric blue,**

**with Purity's Light cutting right through,
raising the earth into all that is true.**

3. I call for the cutting free of people to realize the need to simplify the laws so there is not as much room for interpretation.

Beloved Astrea, from Purity's Ray,
send forth deliverance to all life today,
acceleration to Purity, we are now free
from all that is less than love's Purity.

**Beloved Astrea, in oneness with you,
your circle and sword of electric blue,
with Purity's Light cutting right through,
raising the earth into all that is true.**

4. I call forth the judgment of Christ upon the demons and fallen beings behind the culture where any consideration is used to create complexity and an almost endless interpretation of the laws so that there is no clarity in how to implement these laws.

Beloved Astrea, accelerate us all,
as for your deliverance we fervently call,
set all life free from vision impure
beyond fear and doubt, we're rising for sure.

**Beloved Astrea, in oneness with you,
your circle and sword of electric blue,
with Purity's Light cutting right through,
raising the earth into all that is true.**

5. I call forth the judgment of Christ upon the demons and fallen beings behind the complex system of laws that hardly anyone can interpret so the people who are writing the laws often do not have the vision of how a new law might contradict what is said in a previous law.

> Beloved Astrea, we're willing to see,
> all of the lies that keep us unfree,
> we surrender all lies causing the fall,
> forever affirming the oneness of All.

> **Beloved Astrea, in oneness with you,**
> **your circle and sword of electric blue,**
> **with Purity's Light cutting right through,**
> **raising the earth into all that is true.**

6. I call forth the judgment of Christ upon the demons and fallen beings behind the situation where everything is so complicated that no one can really foresee the consequences of a new law and how it might contradict a previous law.

> Beloved Astrea, accelerate life
> beyond all duality's struggle and strife,
> consume all division between God and man,
> accelerate fulfillment of God's perfect plan.

> **Beloved Astrea, in oneness with you,**
> **your circle and sword of electric blue,**
> **with Purity's Light cutting right through,**
> **raising the earth into all that is true.**

7. I call forth the judgment of Christ upon the demons and fallen beings behind the system where laws are so complex that

they become a tool whereby those who can afford to hire the expensive lawyers can use the laws as a loophole.

> Beloved Astrea, we lovingly call,
> break down separation's invisible wall,
> raising our minds into true unity
> with the Masters of love in Infinity.

> **Beloved Astrea, in oneness with you,**
> **your circle and sword of electric blue,**
> **with Purity's Light cutting right through,**
> **raising the earth into all that is true.**

8. I call forth the judgment of Christ upon those who manipulate the laws so that they are claiming a certain freedom that they are not entitled to, using it to set themselves up in an exempt position where they do not have to follow the same rules as others.

> Beloved Astrea, help all of us find,
> the secret that we create with the mind,
> and thus what in ignorance we decreate,
> in knowledge we easily can recreate.

> **Beloved Astrea, in oneness with you,**
> **your circle and sword of electric blue,**
> **with Purity's Light cutting right through,**
> **raising the earth into all that is true.**

9. I call for people to be cut free to see that in the democratic nations we need to step back and look at the legal system and how it is being misused by the lawyers to give exemptions to a small elite who can afford to pay the attorneys. They end up

giving them special privileges that no ordinary citizens could ever claim because they simply could not afford to pay the legal fees.

Beloved Astrea, we all do aspire,
to learning to use your purity's fire,
to raise every form in infamy sown,
as Saint Germain makes this planet his own.

Beloved Astrea, in oneness with you,
your circle and sword of electric blue,
with Purity's Light cutting right through,
raising the earth into all that is true.

Part 3

1. I call forth the judgment of Christ upon the demons and fallen beings behind the legal system where the complication of the system is reinforcing the situation where there is an upper class who can afford to play the legal game. Then, there is the broader population who have no recourse because they cannot afford to run a court case.

Master Nada, beauty's power,
unfolding like a sacred flower.
Master Nada, so sublime,
a will that conquers even time.

Master Nada, peace you give,
forevermore in peace we live,

**our planet has a peaceful morn,
the Golden Age is hereby born.**

2. I call forth the judgment of Christ upon the demons and fallen beings behind the creation of this privileged position where those who can take advantage of the system do so and therefore can set themselves up to either have privileges or to generate profits.

Master Nada, you bestow,
upon us wisdom's rushing flow.
Master Nada, mind so strong
rising on your wings of song.

**Master Nada, peace you give,
forevermore in peace we live,
our planet has a peaceful morn,
the Golden Age is hereby born.**

3. I call forth the judgment of Christ upon those using the legal system to effectively destroy competition by running these lawsuits against their competitors that no smaller businesses can afford. Therefore, the smaller businesses cannot challenge the older established businesses.

Master Nada, precious scent,
your love is truly heaven-sent.
Master Nada, kind and soft
on wings of love we rise aloft.

**Master Nada, peace you give,
forevermore in peace we live,**

**our planet has a peaceful morn,
the Golden Age is hereby born.**

4. I call forth the judgment of Christ upon the demons and fallen beings behind the tendency to create so many rules that this in itself creates a privileged position for the large businesses that can afford to hire the lawyers or the experts or build the facilities that are required.

Master Nada, mother light,
our hearts are rising like a kite.
Master Nada, from your view,
all life is pure as morning dew.

**Master Nada, peace you give,
forevermore in peace we live,
our planet has a peaceful morn,
the Golden Age is hereby born.**

5. I call forth the judgment of Christ upon the demons and fallen beings behind the situation where the legal system, that was meant to protect the people, is being used by large established businesses to destroy their competition or to prevent the competition from even arising because they cannot afford to comply with the elaborate rules.

Master Nada, truth you bring,
as morning birds in love do sing.
Master Nada, we now feel,
your love that all four bodies heal.

**Master Nada, peace you give,
forevermore in peace we live,**

**our planet has a peaceful morn,
the Golden Age is hereby born.**

6. I call for the cutting free of people to realize that there is always a power elite that is seeking to gain special power and privileges for themselves and they will use any aspect of society, including the legal system and the bureaucratic system.

Master Nada, serve in peace,
as all emotions we release.
Master Nada, life is fun,
the solar plexus is a sun.

**Master Nada, peace you give,
forevermore in peace we live,
our planet has a peaceful morn,
the Golden Age is hereby born.**

7. I call for the cutting free of people to realize that for the ordinary citizen in a democratic country, it is in their best interest to have a relatively simple legal system and a relatively simple set of bureaucratic rules so that they themselves can figure out what their rights are.

Master Nada, love is free,
conditions we no longer see.
Master Nada, rise above,
all human forms of lesser love.

**Master Nada, peace you give,
forevermore in peace we live,
our planet has a peaceful morn,
the Golden Age is hereby born.**

8. I call for the cutting free of people to realize that the tendency to complicate everything only serves the elite. They are the only ones who can afford to hire the attorneys to take advantage of this complex system. They are using it to set themselves up so that the people cannot challenge them.

Master Nada, balance all,
the seven rays upon our call.
Master Nada, rise and shine,
your radiant beauty most divine.

**Master Nada, peace you give,
forevermore in peace we live,
our planet has a peaceful morn,
the Golden Age is hereby born.**

9. I call forth the judgment of Christ upon the demons and fallen beings behind the system of complexity that creates a privileged position for the few and effectively shuts out the many from attaining these privileges.

Nada Dear, your Presence here,
filling up the inner sphere.
Life is now a sacred flow,
God Peace we do on all bestow.

**Master Nada, peace you give,
forevermore in peace we live,
our planet has a peaceful morn,
the Golden Age is hereby born.**

Part 4

1. I call forth the judgment of Christ upon the demons and fallen beings behind the situation where the rules for establishing a new business are so complicated and so expensive to comply with that a new business effectively cannot be started by a single person or a few people.

> Beloved Astrea, your heart is so true,
> your Circle and Sword of white and blue,
> cut all life free from dramas unwise,
> on wings of Purity our planet will rise.

> **Beloved Astrea, in oneness with you,**
> **your circle and sword of electric blue,**
> **with Purity's Light cutting right through,**
> **raising the earth into all that is true.**

2. I call forth the judgment of Christ upon the demons and fallen beings behind the situation where a new business could only be started by people who have enough experience and enough connections so that they can manipulate the system and gain financing from the major financial institutions.

> Beloved Astrea, in God Purity,
> accelerate all of our life energy,
> we're rising beyond every impurity,
> as Purity's Light forever we see.

> **Beloved Astrea, in oneness with you,**
> **your circle and sword of electric blue,**

**with Purity's Light cutting right through,
raising the earth into all that is true.**

3. I call forth the judgment of Christ upon the demons and fallen beings behind the creation of a privileged position where only those who are part of the establishment can start a new business. In order to get that business going, they must become part of the establishment and accept the rules that perpetuate the system.

> Beloved Astrea, from Purity's Ray,
> send forth deliverance to all life today,
> acceleration to Purity, we are now free
> from all that is less than love's Purity.

> **Beloved Astrea, in oneness with you,
> your circle and sword of electric blue,
> with Purity's Light cutting right through,
> raising the earth into all that is true.**

4. I accept that it is the small independent entrepreneurs that will drive the innovation that will bring about the new technology and the new business models in the Golden Age. New inventions are not likely to be brought by the huge established businesses that are more concerned about protecting their position than bringing forth something new.

> Beloved Astrea, accelerate us all,
> as for your deliverance we fervently call,
> set all life free from vision impure
> beyond fear and doubt, we're rising for sure.

**Beloved Astrea, in oneness with you,
your circle and sword of electric blue,
with Purity's Light cutting right through,
raising the earth into all that is true.**

5. I accept that for Saint Germain's Golden Age to be manifest, many new business methods, business visions, much new technology needs to be brought forth. This is not likely to be brought by the big established companies because they either will not see a new invention as a possibility or they will see it as a threat to their business and therefore want to suppress it.

Beloved Astrea, we're willing to see,
all of the lies that keep us unfree,
we surrender all lies causing the fall,
forever affirming the oneness of All.

**Beloved Astrea, in oneness with you,
your circle and sword of electric blue,
with Purity's Light cutting right through,
raising the earth into all that is true.**

6. I call forth the judgment of Christ upon the demons and fallen beings behind the big business conglomerate and the huge corporations. I call especially for the binding and the consuming of the demons behind the big multinational corporations.

Beloved Astrea, accelerate life
beyond all duality's struggle and strife,
consume all division between God and man,
accelerate fulfillment of God's perfect plan.

> **Beloved Astrea, in oneness with you,**
> **your circle and sword of electric blue,**
> **with Purity's Light cutting right through,**
> **raising the earth into all that is true.**

7. I call forth the judgment of Christ upon the demons and fallen beings behind the huge international, multinational corporations that are seeking to take over the economy in any country.

> Beloved Astrea, we lovingly call,
> break down separation's invisible wall,
> raising our minds into true unity
> with the Masters of love in Infinity.

> **Beloved Astrea, in oneness with you,**
> **your circle and sword of electric blue,**
> **with Purity's Light cutting right through,**
> **raising the earth into all that is true.**

8. I call forth the judgment of Christ upon the demons and fallen beings behind the corporations that moved into Eastern Europe after the fall of Communism and attempted to dominate the business world because they had the capital, they could afford to hire the attorneys.

> Beloved Astrea, help all of us find,
> the secret that we create with the mind,
> and thus what in ignorance we decreate,
> in knowledge we easily can recreate.

> **Beloved Astrea, in oneness with you,**
> **your circle and sword of electric blue,**

**with Purity's Light cutting right through,
raising the earth into all that is true.**

9. I call forth the judgment of Christ upon the demons and fallen beings behind the corporations that wanted to take over the market in these newly freed-up economies instead of having the local people act as entrepreneurs and start up businesses that eventually would take over most of the market.

Beloved Astrea, we all do aspire,
to learning to use your purity's fire,
to raise every form in infamy sown,
as Saint Germain makes this planet his own.

**Beloved Astrea, in oneness with you,
your circle and sword of electric blue,
with Purity's Light cutting right through,
raising the earth into all that is true.**

Part 5

1. I call for the cutting free of people to see the need to limit the size of corporations so that they cannot become so powerful that they can begin to influence the political process in democratic nations.

Master Nada, beauty's power,
unfolding like a sacred flower.
Master Nada, so sublime,
a will that conquers even time.

Master Nada, peace you give,
forevermore in peace we live,
our planet has a peaceful morn,
the Golden Age is hereby born.

2. I call forth the judgment of Christ upon the demons and fallen beings behind the multinational corporations that have no loyalty to any nation nor to any people.

Master Nada, you bestow,
upon us wisdom's rushing flow.
Master Nada, mind so strong
rising on your wings of song.

Master Nada, peace you give,
forevermore in peace we live,
our planet has a peaceful morn,
the Golden Age is hereby born.

3. I call forth the judgment of Christ upon the demons and fallen beings behind the multinational corporations that are looking at the people as either employees that they can use and take advantage of or as customers where they would like to establish themselves in a monopoly so that the people have very little choice.

Master Nada, precious scent,
your love is truly heaven-sent.
Master Nada, kind and soft
on wings of love we rise aloft.

Master Nada, peace you give,
forevermore in peace we live,

**our planet has a peaceful morn,
the Golden Age is hereby born.**

4. I call forth the judgment of Christ upon the demons and fallen beings behind the multinational corporations that have in many countries attempted to divide the territory so that they can tolerate each other and shut out any competing companies.

Master Nada, mother light,
our hearts are rising like a kite.
Master Nada, from your view,
all life is pure as morning dew.

**Master Nada, peace you give,
forevermore in peace we live,
our planet has a peaceful morn,
the Golden Age is hereby born.**

5. I accept that in the Golden Age the legal system will be *of* the people, *by* the people, *for* the people. Not *of* the elite, *by* the elite and *for* the elite, as it is today in most nations.

Master Nada, truth you bring,
as morning birds in love do sing.
Master Nada, we now feel,
your love that all four bodies heal.

**Master Nada, peace you give,
forevermore in peace we live,
our planet has a peaceful morn,
the Golden Age is hereby born.**

6. I call for the cutting free of people to see how attorneys have set themselves up in a position where they are interpreting and manipulating the laws endlessly. They command enormous fees without in the end being able to give people a just treatment in the legal system.

> Master Nada, serve in peace,
> as all emotions we release.
> Master Nada, life is fun,
> the solar plexus is a sun.

> **Master Nada, peace you give,**
> **forevermore in peace we live,**
> **our planet has a peaceful morn,**
> **the Golden Age is hereby born.**

7. I call for the cutting free of people to see that they cannot get real justice in the court system because the attorneys can come up with interpretations that paralyze the judges from making just judgments.

> Master Nada, love is free,
> conditions we no longer see.
> Master Nada, rise above,
> all human forms of lesser love.

> **Master Nada, peace you give,**
> **forevermore in peace we live,**
> **our planet has a peaceful morn,**
> **the Golden Age is hereby born.**

8. I accept a simplification of the legal system where the rules become more clear so that those who have enough money to hire the attorneys, cannot escape accountability.

> Master Nada, balance all,
> the seven rays upon our call.
> Master Nada, rise and shine,
> your radiant beauty most divine.

> **Master Nada, peace you give,**
> **forevermore in peace we live,**
> **our planet has a peaceful morn,**
> **the Golden Age is hereby born.**

9. I call forth the judgment of Christ upon the demons and fallen beings behind the mindset that causes people to use the legal system to gain a personal advantage over other people, making people eager to sue each other as a way to get back at the other side.

> Nada Dear, your Presence here,
> filling up the inner sphere.
> Life is now a sacred flow,
> God Peace we do on all bestow.

> **Master Nada, peace you give,**
> **forevermore in peace we live,**
> **our planet has a peaceful morn,**
> **the Golden Age is hereby born.**

Part 6

1. I call forth the judgment of Christ upon the beasts, the conglomerate entities, collective entities that have been created by the legal system. This has been created because those who are part of the system want to perpetuate their existence, they want to make more and more money.

> Beloved Astrea, your heart is so true,
> your Circle and Sword of white and blue,
> cut all life free from dramas unwise,
> on wings of Purity our planet will rise.
>
> **Beloved Astrea, in oneness with you,**
> **your circle and sword of electric blue,**
> **with Purity's Light cutting right through,**
> **raising the earth into all that is true.**

2. I call forth the judgment of Christ upon the entities in the emotional realm that are putting hooks into people's auras, into their emotional bodies and making them angry so that they want to sue each other because they think they will get some kind of justice.

> Beloved Astrea, in God Purity,
> accelerate all of our life energy,
> we're rising beyond every impurity,
> as Purity's Light forever we see.
>
> **Beloved Astrea, in oneness with you,**
> **your circle and sword of electric blue,**

**with Purity's Light cutting right through,
raising the earth into all that is true.**

3. I call for the people to be cut free to see that the solution is not to create a better legal system because it would be impossible to create a legal system that could settle every disagreement between the people in a nation.

Beloved Astrea, from Purity's Ray,
send forth deliverance to all life today,
acceleration to Purity, we are now free
from all that is less than love's Purity.

**Beloved Astrea, in oneness with you,
your circle and sword of electric blue,
with Purity's Light cutting right through,
raising the earth into all that is true.**

4. I call for the binding of these demons and entities so that the people will be cut free to see that the real solution to these personal disagreements is not to go to the courts but to raise your own consciousness.

Beloved Astrea, accelerate us all,
as for your deliverance we fervently call,
set all life free from vision impure
beyond fear and doubt, we're rising for sure.

**Beloved Astrea, in oneness with you,
your circle and sword of electric blue,
with Purity's Light cutting right through,
raising the earth into all that is true.**

5. I call for people to be cut free to see that they need to make a very realistic assessment of what they want out of these disagreements. The simple karmic consequence of engaging in these legal battles with other people is that you tie yourself to these people karmically.

> Beloved Astrea, we're willing to see,
> all of the lies that keep us unfree,
> we surrender all lies causing the fall,
> forever affirming the oneness of All.

> **Beloved Astrea, in oneness with you,**
> **your circle and sword of electric blue,**
> **with Purity's Light cutting right through,**
> **raising the earth into all that is true.**

6. I call for people to be cut free to say: "Do I want to tie myself to these people, so that I may have to reincarnate with them again in my next lifetime? Or do I want to be free of these people so that I can move on? In that case, I might need to raise my own consciousness so I can see a different way to approach this situation."

> Beloved Astrea, accelerate life
> beyond all duality's struggle and strife,
> consume all division between God and man,
> accelerate fulfillment of God's perfect plan.

> **Beloved Astrea, in oneness with you,**
> **your circle and sword of electric blue,**
> **with Purity's Light cutting right through,**
> **raising the earth into all that is true.**

7. I call for people to be cut free to say: "How come we could settle things in the past without going to court and now all of a sudden, we have to go to court about everything? What is it that has changed in our psychology, in our national psychology, that we have suddenly become so sue-happy that we are suing each other at every opportunity?"

> Beloved Astrea, we lovingly call,
> break down separation's invisible wall,
> raising our minds into true unity
> with the Masters of love in Infinity.

> **Beloved Astrea, in oneness with you,**
> **your circle and sword of electric blue,**
> **with Purity's Light cutting right through,**
> **raising the earth into all that is true.**

8. I call for the cutting free of people to see that things have simply gone too far. It is necessary to return to original principles or to rise up to new principles that make it possible for people to be able to communicate openly and freely so that they can settle differences without having to take recourse with attorneys who are not giving them recourse because they are only complicating matters.

> Beloved Astrea, help all of us find,
> the secret that we create with the mind,
> and thus what in ignorance we decreate,
> in knowledge we easily can recreate.

> **Beloved Astrea, in oneness with you,**
> **your circle and sword of electric blue,**

with Purity's Light cutting right through,
raising the earth into all that is true.

9. I call for people to be cut free to see that the primary goal of many attorneys is to complicate a case so that they can extract more legal fees. The attorneys often do not care about the out-come for the people, they do not care about justice.

Beloved Astrea, we all do aspire,
to learning to use your purity's fire,
to raise every form in infamy sown,
as Saint Germain makes this planet his own.

Beloved Astrea, in oneness with you,
your circle and sword of electric blue,
with Purity's Light cutting right through,
raising the earth into all that is true.

Part 7

1. I call for the binding of the entities and demons that are enveloping the legal profession in many countries.

Master Nada, beauty's power,
unfolding like a sacred flower.
Master Nada, so sublime,
a will that conquers even time.

Master Nada, peace you give,
forevermore in peace we live,

**our planet has a peaceful morn,
the Golden Age is hereby born.**

2. I call forth the judgment of Christ upon the attorneys who
sold their souls to the devil because they have become so disillusioned with the legal system that they do not care about their
ideals and principles.

Master Nada, you bestow,
upon us wisdom's rushing flow.
Master Nada, mind so strong
rising on your wings of song.

**Master Nada, peace you give,
forevermore in peace we live,
our planet has a peaceful morn,
the Golden Age is hereby born.**

3. I call forth the judgment of Christ upon the attorneys who
realize that they cannot give justice to their clients. They have
decided that since this is their profession and since they went
to school and this is the only thing they know, they are just in
it for the money.

Master Nada, precious scent,
your love is truly heaven-sent.
Master Nada, kind and soft
on wings of love we rise aloft.

**Master Nada, peace you give,
forevermore in peace we live,
our planet has a peaceful morn,
the Golden Age is hereby born.**

4. I call for the binding of the entities that are overshadowing the minds of these attorneys and other people involved with the system.

> Master Nada, mother light,
> our hearts are rising like a kite.
> Master Nada, from your view,
> all life is pure as morning dew.

> **Master Nada, peace you give,**
> **forevermore in peace we live,**
> **our planet has a peaceful morn,**
> **the Golden Age is hereby born.**

5. I accept a change towards a Golden Age system where the laws are clear and do not give exemptions to those who can afford to hire attorneys. There is no room for interpretation whereby a privileged elite can gain and maintain privileges, and the legal system is seen only a last recourse.

> Master Nada, truth you bring,
> as morning birds in love do sing.
> Master Nada, we now feel,
> your love that all four bodies heal.

> **Master Nada, peace you give,**
> **forevermore in peace we live,**
> **our planet has a peaceful morn,**
> **the Golden Age is hereby born.**

6. I accept the creation of a system of mediation among people where there are more effective ways to settle conflicts than by going to court.

Master Nada, serve in peace,
as all emotions we release.
Master Nada, life is fun,
the solar plexus is a sun.

**Master Nada, peace you give,
forevermore in peace we live,
our planet has a peaceful morn,
the Golden Age is hereby born.**

7. I call for the cutting free of the people who can create an entirely different system that appeals to people's discernment rather than their anger or their emotions of wanting to get back at people. I accept a system where both the judges and the people have a certain measure of Christ discernment.

Master Nada, love is free,
conditions we no longer see.
Master Nada, rise above,
all human forms of lesser love.

**Master Nada, peace you give,
forevermore in peace we live,
our planet has a peaceful morn,
the Golden Age is hereby born.**

8. I accept that when I make the calls, the ascended masters will step in and bring forth the changes that can be brought forth because I have cleared the energetic pathway whereby this awareness can descend all the way to the physical. I accept that people will wake up and say: "Oh, this is obvious. We now see it."

Master Nada, balance all,
the seven rays upon our call.
Master Nada, rise and shine,
your radiant beauty most divine.

**Master Nada, peace you give,
forevermore in peace we live,
our planet has a peaceful morn,
the Golden Age is hereby born.**

9. I call for the clearing of the three higher bodies of the planet so that those people who have the potential from past lifetimes suddenly wake up and see how obvious a certain change is. I call for the consuming of the cloud of lower energy that clogs up the flow from the ascended realm through the identity, mental, emotional realm and into the physical so that people can consciously recognize the validity of a new idea.

Nada Dear, your Presence here,
filling up the inner sphere.
Life is now a sacred flow,
God Peace we do on all bestow.

**Master Nada, peace you give,
forevermore in peace we live,
our planet has a peaceful morn,
the Golden Age is hereby born.**

Sealing

In the name of the Divine Mother, I call to all ascended masters for the sealing of myself and all people in my circle of influence in the creative flow of the Divine Mother, the River of Life. I call for the multiplication of my calls by all ascended masters so that we form the perfect figure-eight flow of "As Above, so below." Thus, I accept that this is fully manifest, because the mouth of the Lord, the Divine Mother that I AM, has spoken it. Amen.

6 | A BUDDHIC PERSPECTIVE ON THE MILITARY

The Buddha I AM, Maraytaii is my name. As the path of the Buddha is open to both men and women in embodiment, naturally once you become an ascended master, you can continue to raise your consciousness until you reach the level of Buddhahood. I would, however, caution you that even though we present our-selves as male and female masters, what you transcend when you ascend is the concept of men and women that you have on earth. Thus, you should not think that you can project those earthly concepts upon us, for we are not nearly as tied into the roles that are defined on earth for men and women. We have a much greater flexibility and can take on an appearance that is suited for a particular purpose.

We generally do not switch between male and female roles in order to avoid confusing you, but in the many tasks we perform in the ascended realm, we nat-urally do take on the appearance or the concentration of our Beings that is required for the task.

The demons behind the military-industrial complex

What I wish to discourse with you on today is an aspect of society in virtually every nation on earth that is very much a hindrance to the progress and transcendence of that society. My discourse is, naturally, very relevant to the situation between North and South Korea but it is truly applicable to any nation on earth. What I wish to make you aware of is the role of the military and the businesses that are making a profit off of supplying what the military needs. This is what has sometimes been called, the military-industrial complex.

If you take a look at world history, you will see that in many cases the military has decided to stage a coup where they have taken over the government. This has even happened in a number of democratic nations, such as you have seen here in South Korea as well. In most cases where this has been done, the military has played a very conservative role, in other words being against major changes to society that would spread the power. Thus, what has in most cases happened is that the military, instead of defending the people has defended the power elite. This, of course, you can make calls on so that this will not happen in your nation. There is especially a need to make calls for this here in Korea.

Envision, my beloved, that you have a situation where the regime in North Korea has collapsed. You now face the question of how to deal with the re-unification of the two Koreas. Do you realize, my beloved, that one of the biggest difficulties in such a scenario would be that both the North and the South has a very large military? They also both have businesses or at least institutions that are producing and supplying what the military needs, such as weapons, uniforms, food, shelter and housing and any other things. What you will see is that if there was a re-unification of Korea, suddenly the North Korean military and military-industrial complex could easily be seen as obsolete. Also, in South Korea, is there really a need to have as large of a military if you do not have to deal with the threat north of the border?

As Mother Mary explained so eloquently in her book on stopping war, anything human beings do, any endeavor where they focus the attention of many people, will create a collective entity. As more and more energy is fed into it, it eventually can reach the stage that we call a demon, which is a being that very aggressively seeks to perpetuate its own existence.

How was the demon created? By people pouring their energy into a particular fear-based matrix. How will the demon sustain its existence? Only by getting people to continue to pour their energies into the fear-based matrix that created the demon in the first place. The military as an institution goes very far back into history, but I wish especially to focus on the fact that ever since you have had nation states (nations with a clear sense of identity), those nations have in most cases had a military. There are nations where the existence of a military force goes back many centuries and you can see how much energy has been poured into this by the people over this long time span. Therefore, you need to recognize that any country that has had a military for a long time has created some very powerful demons that are owing their existence to the military and to the energies that have been fed into it by the people. Now, my beloved, there are many, many people on earth who have grown up to take it for granted that you need a military, you need an army; you need to be able to defend yourself against attack.

Why war is never justified

Well, my beloved, there has, of course, been certain time periods in the history of the earth where there have been certain peoples or certain nations that have been very aggressive in expanding their power over other nations by conquering them with a military. Therefore, one can say that for a nation to survive, it has had to have a military that could deter such an attack or even turn it back if it occurred. I am not trying to say that we can take a completely idealistic view of the military and say that it has never been necessary at the practical level. However, I wish to go to a higher level and consider whether a military truly is necessary and this is where you simply cannot understand the dynamic around the military unless you understand the teachings we have been giving about fallen beings.

My beloved, as Mother Mary explains in her book, and as we have explained before, war is not a naturally occurring phenomenon on any planet. War is an invention of the fallen beings and the real purpose of war is not actually to conquer other people, to extend ones territory or extend ones system. You may think that it was the purpose of Communism to conquer the entire world and turn it into a communist world, but this was not the real cause behind the communist aggression. The real cause of war as designed by the fallen beings is one thing and one thing only: destruction. There is no positive, constructive purpose for war whatsoever, there never has been, there never will be.

This means that when you look at the situation from a spiritual perspective, you see that war is never justified—*never* justified. You may go into the human perspective, the more immediate, practical perspective and you may say that from such a perspective war is justified. I would like to make a distinction, a very clear distinction, between these temporary, situation-based justifications that human beings define based on the circumstances in this world. What I wish you who are spiritual students to be aware of, is that there is a higher perspective, the ascended-master perspective and according to this war is never justified.

You may look at a human situation, a historical situation on earth, and you may ask: "Well, was it not justified that the so-called free world defeated Nazism in the Second World War? Was it not justified that the so-called free world resisted the spread of Communism so that the entire world was not conquered by the Soviet Union or other communist states?" My beloved, the shocking truth from the Buddhic level is that it was not justified from the ascended perspective.

You might say that given the state of the collective consciousness, it was unavoidable. It was perhaps even necessary for the outplaying of the dualistic state of consciousness so that people might come to see the futility of it. Nevertheless, it cannot be construed, my beloved, (and you need to listen very carefully here) it cannot be construed that the ascended masters did in any way feel that these wars were justified from our perspective. The reason for this is that we are not dualistic beings.

I realize full well that many of our students, especially in previous decades, have projected upon us that we share the same dualistic reasoning that they have allowed to enter their minds but we have never shared it, my beloved. Regardless of what you may feel and project upon us, we know very well the dualistic dynamic created by the fallen beings.

War seeks to destroy people's spiritual potential

We know very well that the real purpose of war is destruction. Not just the destruction of the physical environment or a nation or a planet but the destruction of human beings; the destruction of their potential to raise their consciousness towards the level of Christhood and Buddhahood. My beloved, has anything had a more destructive influence on people's ability to follow the spiritual path than these huge wars you have seen over the past century?

Look at how many people were killed prematurely. Look at how many people were displaced. Look at how many people had their entire energy and attention consumed by these wars. You recognize, my beloved, that the purpose of a war is never just what it is claimed to be at the surface level. The Second World War was not a fight between good on one side and evil on the other. It was the result of a manipulation by the fallen beings that caused human beings to polarize towards two dualistic extremes whereby the fallen beings manipulated them into seeking to destroy each other. The fallen beings have done this over and over and over again on this planet.

War never has a benign purpose

What I am telling you here is that there is never a benign or constructive purpose for war. This means that there is never a higher necessity to have an army. It is not a natural condition that a nation should have to have an army in order to survive. It is an artificial condition created by the fallen beings.

What does this mean, my beloved? It means that the entire consciousness behind armed forces is based on fear. If you did not have fear, you would not have a military. There is no way to create a military that is not based on fear. You may say: "But what about those empires that have created an army not to defend themselves but to attack others?" Even there, there is fear. You cannot engage in aggression against other human beings, you cannot engage in killing other human beings, unless you are driven by fear.

You may have some excuse of extending civilization or spreading Communism or spreading freedom and democracy by engaging in war, but behind that motivation is some fear-based motive. Your minds are taken over by fear—that is why you arm yourself. Whether you arm yourself for the purpose of conquest or for the purpose of defense, it is always based on fear.

My beloved, again anything human beings do from a fear-based state of consciousness will create these entities and demons and they will then eventually become so powerful that they can overpower individuals very easily, they can over-power groups of people and they can even overpower entire nations. What was it that caused the Soviet aggression against non-communist states? It was fear. When you recognize, at least sub-consciously, that your entire ideology is based on fear (as Communism is indeed a fear-based ideology), then you nat-urally, unavoidably feel a need to extend your ideology to all nations because you are threatened by the existence of nations that do not recognize your ideology. You feel fear that maybe your ideology could be wrong and that is why these other peo-ple are resisting it. In order to overcome your fear, you want to force all others to accept your ideology.

Why did the communist forces in the North absolutely have to conquer all of Korea? Because they could not live with the fact that some people in Korea did not embrace their ide-ology. So you see there is always a fear-based dynamic. When-ever you have an armed force, my beloved, you must have an enemy to fight. Otherwise, what is the justification, and why would people then pay their taxes to support the armed forces?

Dark forces behind the military

You see, my beloved, in the vast majority of cases a nation has an army that is paid for by the taxes paid by all of the people. How do you then get the people to pay these taxes, especially in a democracy where you cannot force them? Well, you do so only by perpetuating the fear-based mindset so that the people are so afraid that they think it is necessary to maintain the armed force. Do you see that behind this are the demons who are not concerned about the people whatsoever but only about perpetuating their own existence? Even further behind it all is the fallen beings who are not concerned about the people either. They are only concerned about either controlling the population on the earth or destroying those who will not be controlled. There are even some fallen beings who are not primarily concerned about control because they are focused on destruction and nothing else. Behind every military in the world there is a conglomerate of forces. There are these collective entities, there are the stronger demons and then there are the fallen beings.

It does not necessarily mean that the people in the military are fallen beings. But their minds are so controlled by the consciousness and the doctrines, the military doctrines, created by the fallen beings that they have very little ability to think clearly, to think individually and to think in an independent manner. What I am telling you is that we have talked about the unnatural selection process where a certain system filters out those who do not agree with the basic philosophy of the system. The armed forces of any nation is precisely a closed system and therefore it filters out all of those people who have the ability to question the system.

You understand, my beloved, that when you look at some of the armed forces in the world, you can see that, for example, the armed forces in the United States are still to a large degree trapped in what has been called the cold war mindset. When the Soviet Union collapsed and when it (at least for a time) seemed like Russia would no longer be the military threat it had been during the cold war, there were many people in the United States' military, in the industrial complex and in the political arena who had a kind of withdrawal symptom, almost like a drug addict who does not have access to his drug. They simply did not know what to do with themselves now that it seemed like they did not have a clearly defined enemy to fight. You will see that many of these people drew a sigh of relief when Vladimir Putin stepped into the role of seeming like Russia could again become a threat against which the armies of the West needed to be ready to defend themselves.

Forces against reunification

You will see the same dynamic here in Korea where there are many people in the armed forces who are so trapped in the mindset that was created by the war and has been perpetuated since the war that they cannot, they *will* not, even consider the potential for a re-unification. Their mindset is geared toward one thing only and that is fighting the North Korean army.

Naturally, you see in North Korea also many people in the military who would not even consider that they could give up and surrender and allow a re-unification. Their entire mindset is geared towards fighting South Korea. You will see the same with those who represent the American armed forces in South Korea. They are also geared towards fighting North Korea. You can go to the large industrial corporations that are producing and supplying the army's needs and you can see again in their mindset they do not want to seriously consider a re-unification.

There are forces in America who, as we said last time, are making profits out of selling military equipment to South Korea and there are those armed forces who are also basing their existence on having to be ready to fight North Korea and they likewise do not want a re-unification. There are politicians in America who do not want a re-unification because they want to perpetuate the dualistic mindset where America is the one who has to guarantee freedom and democracy by always being ready to fight any enemy, real or imagined—mostly imagined, my beloved.

You see, again, in the political arena in South Korea, there are those people who will not consider re-unification. Of course in North Korea they likewise will not consider it. What you can do, what you have the opportunity to do, is make the calls for the binding and the consuming of these demons and collective entities that have taken over the minds of the people and make it impossible for people to even re-think the status quo, to ever question the status quo and say: "Do we actually need to continue this situation, to perpetuate this situation indefinitely? Is there an alternative? Is there a different way to look at this?"

The potential for dramatic changes

As I started out saying, if there was a collapse of the regime in the North, if there was a real potential for a re-unification of the two Koreas, then the biggest obstacle would be the armed

forces in both the North and the South along with the industrial complex supporting them. They would not want a re-unification for the simple reason that it would take away much of
the justification for their existence and their profits.

This of, course, is the demons that are working through
people and the fallen beings who do not want to lose the
potential they have engineered for destruction if there was a
war. When you know this, you do not need to feel discour-
aged, you do not need to feel fearful. You need to recognize
something very, very simple: It is true that there are people in
embodiment who have a great resistance to change but this
resistance to change comes primarily because the people's
minds have been taken over by the demons, or the people have
been fooled by the fallen beings.

We of the ascended masters respect the Law of Free Will.
There is a limit to what we can do in the physical octave but
there is no limit to what we can do in the emotional, mental
and identity octaves. The only limit is that we need the authorization from someone in embodiment who is aware and is
willing to make the calls. When you make the calls, we can step
in and bind and consume these demons. When we do this,
some people will respond because their minds will suddenly
be freed from this veil that has been put upon them. Suddenly,
as we have said so many times, people will wake up and it will
seem obvious to them that there is a new way to look at the
old problems. Suddenly, some people will begin to question
whether we need to continue to take the stand we have taken
so far or whether there is a more constructive approach.

We have talked about it before, how a first step could be
a greater openness towards the North Korean government, a
willingness to engage in dialogue and an interchange of energy
through businesses. Beyond this it is entirely possible that,
when people's minds are freed from the veil of the dark forces,

the people who have the potential and who are in positions in society will suddenly begin to question the status quo that has existed on the Korean peninsula now for so many decades. They will begin to question if there is a different way to deal with this, if there is a different way to look at it, and I can assure you, my beloved, that there is a potential for very swift and very dramatic changes.

I am not thereby saying this potential will come about, for free will is always free will and free will can never be predicted except in probabilities. But there is a considerable probability that the situation could shift in a fundamental way so that enough people have their minds freed from the dualistic mode of thinking. Therefore, they can be open to the new ideas that we of the ascended masters are ready to release from our level. We know that *your* minds are open but you are not in positions in society to carry out such decisions and therefore we need you to make the calls so that those people who are in position can also have their minds open to a different, non-dualistic view of the situation.

The agenda of destroying human beings

Now my beloved, even though this is a long discourse I have one more topic I wish to bring to your attention. I represent the Mother aspect of God, of the Divine. We have previously talked about a phenomenon called hatred of the mother. This is where self-aware beings, co-creators, experience such severe consequences in the physical realm that they become very resentful of the mother realm. This is because they forget that the mother realm can only reflect back to human beings what they are projecting upon the Ma-ter light. They forget that the consequences are self-created, or at least that they have been collectively created by humankind. They feel it is the mother that is unjustly forcing them to experience these very severe and long-lasting consequences.

My beloved, hatred of the mother takes many forms but the most extreme form of hatred of the mother is that you are willing to kill other human beings. Now, if you come from the Buddhic tradition, you may say is it only the killing of other human beings; is it not the killing of all sentient creatures? Well, my beloved, here we face a delicate issue. If you go to an overall level, an overall perspective, you see that, naturally, as this planet moves further into the Golden Age there will come a point where it is not necessary to kill any creature; human or animal. This, however, will require that a substantial portion of the animal species that exist today will simply vanish.

I am not here trying to say that you cannot swat a mosquito, for in the Golden Age, as we move further into it (which is a matter of a long time-span), there will be no mosquitos or other such animals on the planet. What I am pointing out to you is that in the current situation on earth, we are not primarily concerned here with the killing of animals. The topic I wish to bring to your attention is the killing of people.

You understand, my beloved, that the fallen beings have an agenda of destroying human beings. The reason for this is very simple. A human being is the only being on earth that has the potential to attain Christhood and Buddhahood. It is when you exercise your potential to attain Christhood that you become a threat to the fallen beings, their control on this planet and their survival, even their very existence. This is what they want to prevent, my beloved, and that is why they have a desire to kill anyone that manifests Christhood. In order to achieve this. they are willing to kill large numbers of people.

You have the story, even though it is a myth, that when Jesus was born, King Herod was willing to kill all male babies in order to kill the one Living Christ. This is the attitude of the fallen beings. This is one of the primary motivations behind war. They want to kill those who have a Christ potential by killing as many people as possible.

There are, of course, also those fallen beings whose only agenda is destruction and they want to kill as many people as possible, Christed beings or not, because the demons can always extract energy when people are killed violently. There is no more efficient way for these demons to extract people's energies than to get two groups of people, two nations, to wage an all-out destructive war against each other. My beloved, what I wish you to understand here is that killing a human being is the extreme outpicturing of hatred of the mother.

The military is based on hatred of the mother

Now my beloved, what is the entire purpose of a military? Is it not to kill human beings? Do you see, my beloved, that in the very mindset that generates an army, is the need, the desire, the willingness to kill human beings? You can go into the people in the military, the people in the political establishments who support the military, the people in the industrial establishment that support the military and you will see in the minds of these people a very characteristic dynamic.

If you look at these people as individuals when they act, for example, towards others or even in private settings like their families, you might say they are perfectly normal people. Some of them may be very nice people; some of them may be very well-meaning, very idealistic, very dedicated towards their task as they see it. Yet if you go deeper into the psychology, you see that they all have a mechanism in their psychology. We might call it an implant, a psychic implant, put there by the fallen beings. This mechanism means not that these people are psychopaths, not that they are indiscriminate killers. It does mean that when a situation arises that calls for their military to perform its defined task, then these people become willing to kill and to kill indiscriminately. Once they have a defined enemy, they will do whatever they can, whatever they think is necessary, to defeat that enemy. In order to achieve that objective, they are willing to kill any numbers of people among the enemy but they are also willing to sacrifice any number of their own soldiers.

Again, my beloved, be careful to listen to what I am saying. I am not saying these people are evil or bad people. I am not saying they are fallen beings in embodiment, although, of course, some people in the military, in the political establishment, in the industrial establishment are fallen beings. What I am saying is that there are many, many people who have elected to be in the military and to rise to prominent positions in the military precisely because they have this mechanism where they believe that under certain circumstances killing is fully justified.

It is justified to the point where they do not even need to think about what they are doing. They do not need to recognize that they are actually killing living human beings, individuals just like themselves and their own children. They are willing to step into a mindset where they see the enemy as non-humans and where they also see their own soldiers as non-humans. They may even see the civilians among the enemy as non-humans. They may even see their own civilians as non-humans, accepting that there will be a certain collateral damage, as they call it, to waging a war and that you cannot always avoid the killing of civilians.

You see, my beloved, this is the extreme outcome of hatred of the mother where you think it is justified to kill human beings and that collateral damage is acceptable. You actually do not think you are killing human beings because you see them as non-humans. This is a consciousness that is so deeply ingrained in the military forces of the world and the industries and the politicians who support them that there is virtually none of them that are willing to question it.

There are, of course, people in many democratic nations who have throughout the decades been willing to question the military even to demonstrate against war but what you often see is that these people go to an opposite extreme. They swing to an unbalanced extreme and they take these rather extremist pacifist positions that are simply the opposite dualistic polarity to the mindset of those in the military.

A balanced way to look at the military

What we are asking you to make the calls on is first of all the binding and the consuming of the demons behind this mindset but also the awakening of the people who are able to find a middle way. Again, as we have said before, there are young people who have been brought into embodiment because they have the potential to question this dynamic, to stand up and say there is a balanced way to look at this. They have the potential to create a debate in society that is not dominated by the extreme viewpoints of wanting to blindly defend the military, wanting to blindly attack the military.

There is a middle way where you can have a more aware discussion about the role of the military, the necessity to perpetuate the current situation. You can begin then to create an openness where you can see solutions that have simply not been seen before. Do you see, my beloved, that whenever a debate gets polarized between the extremes, it seems to people as if they either have to choose to support the military completely or they have to choose to abandon the military completely. But there is always a higher perspective where you can find a new way to look at the entire dynamic and suddenly you begin to see perspectives, solutions that were not seen by anyone before.

You see that the trick of the fallen beings in polarizing a debate is to make people group themselves into two extremes. One is focused on the one dualistic polarity, the other is focused on the other. There is nobody in between who can see anything besides these two polarities. You often have a situation where there is a debate in society and where hardly anyone can see beyond the dualistic polarities, hardly anyone can see different perspectives, different solutions. We ask you to make the calls for this so that more and more people will begin to see that there are actually alternatives.

Naturally, it is not practical, right now, for South Korea to abandon its military. Naturally, it is not practical but it would be possible for South Korea to begin to debate whether there is a different way to deal with the entire situation of the division between North and South. Could we perhaps find a way to trick the North Koreans into feeling less threatened by our military? Could we perhaps find a way to free our own society from the mindset upheld by the military and by the industry behind them that the only possible solution is confrontation?

Could we perhaps find a way to see that what the military says is that they cannot step down until North Korea steps down? Of course, the military in North Korea says that they cannot step down until the military in the South steps down. Who should blink first? Well, none of them will blink, but perhaps you could find a way to recognize that this is not the only way to look at the situation and that it may actually be possible for South Korea to take an initiative that North Korea would not be capable of taking because they are much more trapped in dualistic thinking.

You see, my beloved, we have given a concept of the wisdom of the mother. The core of the wisdom of the mother is that it does not require an idealistic solution to a problem. It is often so that the wisdom of the father looks at the overall perspective, looks at it from an ideal perspective of what is ultimately the best and what is not constructive. Then it works towards promoting that ideal solution. The wisdom of the mother recognizes that, right here and right now, we have a specific situation. It is very far from the ideal solution. Therefore, we cannot jump from the present conditions to the ideal solution. We need to look at the conditions and then find a way to break up the stalemate so that instead of being locked in a stale, stationary situation, we can begin to move. The first and primary concern of the wisdom of the mother is to take a situation that is locked and shift something so that the situation begins to move.

It is the image of a river that has been frozen in the winter and then, as the weather warms up in the spring, there comes a point where the ice begins to break. As the ice breaks, it can very slowly begin to move. As it moves faster and faster, suddenly an area of clear, open water appears, then another one, then another one. Then, they begin to blend together until suddenly, instead of a river covered with ice with a few open holes, you now have an open river with a few areas of ice. Then, eventually, all of the ice moves downstream and melts and the river is again flowing. This is a very realistic potential to achieve in the Korean situation, when you make the calls to free the minds of the people who have taken embodiment specifically to break up the stalemate and to create a new approach to the situation.

My beloved, it has been a long discourse. I thank you for being the open doors, for I have sent a very powerful impulse into the collective consciousness of South Korea as I have been speaking and as you have been listening and we have had this figure-eight flow between us that has been extended through your chakras to create a figure-eight flow between the ascended realm and the collective consciousness in your beautiful nation. Thus, my deep gratitude for you coming together at this conference and inviting the messenger here. My beloved, I bid you go in the peace of the Buddha Maraytaii.

7 | INVOKING A BUDDHIC PERSPECTIVE ON THE MILITARY

In the name I AM THAT I AM, Jesus Christ, I call to all ascended masters working on manifesting the Golden Age, especially Maraytaii and Astrea, to radiate into the collective consciousness a new awareness of the role of the military in the Golden Age. Help people see that we can build a new future by working with the ascended masters and letting go of the old way of looking at life, including…

[Make personal calls.]

Part 1

1. I call forth the judgment of Christ upon any military that, instead of defending the people, has defended the power elite.

O Cosmic Mother, sound the gong,
that calls me home where I belong.
I know you love me tenderly,
and in that knowing I am free.

**Maraytaii, I resonate
with song that opens cosmic gate.
Your melody makes me vibrate
my sense of self I recreate.**

2. I call for the cutting free of people to see that in any endeavor that focuses the attention of many people, we will create a collective entity. As more and more energy is fed into it, it can reach the stage of a demon, which is a being that aggressively seeks to perpetuate its own existence.

O Cosmic Mother, hold me tight,
I resonate with your own light.
Your music purifies my heart,
your love to all I do impart.

**Maraytaii, I resonate
with song that opens cosmic gate.
Your melody makes me vibrate
my sense of self I recreate.**

3. I call for the cutting free of people to see that a demon was created by people pouring their energy into a particular fear-based matrix. The demon will sustain its existence only by getting people to continue to pour their energies into the fear-based matrix that created the demon.

O Cosmic Mother, we are one,
your heart is like a blazing sun.
My being can but amplify,
the sacred sound you magnify.

Maraytaii, I resonate
with song that opens cosmic gate.
Your melody makes me vibrate
my sense of self I recreate.

4. I call for the cutting free of the people to see that in nations where the existence of the military force goes back many centuries, there are some very powerful demons that are owing their existence to the military and to the energies that have been fed into it by the people.

O Cosmic Mother, I now hear,
the subtle sound of Sacred Sphere.
As I attune to Cosmic Hum,
the lesser self I overcome.

Maraytaii, I resonate
with song that opens cosmic gate.
Your melody makes me vibrate
my sense of self I recreate.

5. I call forth the judgment of Christ upon the mindset that we need a military, we need an army, we need to be able to defend ourselves against attack.

O Cosmic Mother, take me home,
I am in sync with Sacred OM,

The sound of sounds will raise me up,
so only light is in my cup.

**Maraytaii, I resonate
with song that opens cosmic gate.
Your melody makes me vibrate
my sense of self I recreate.**

6. I accept that war is not a naturally occurring phenomenon on any planet. War is an invention of the fallen beings and the real purpose of war is not to conquer other people, to extend ones territory or extend ones system.

O Cosmic Mother, I will be,
a part of cosmic symphony.
All that I AM, an instrument,
for sound that is from heaven sent.

**Maraytaii, I resonate
with song that opens cosmic gate.
Your melody makes me vibrate
my sense of self I recreate.**

7. I call forth the judgment of Christ upon the fallen beings for whom the purpose of war is destruction.

O Cosmic Mother, I now call,
to enter sacred music hall.
I will be part of life's ascent,
towards the starry firmament.

**Maraytaii, I resonate
with song that opens cosmic gate.**

**Your melody makes me vibrate
my sense of self I recreate.**

8. I accept that there is no positive, constructive purpose for war whatsoever, there never has been, there never will be. According to the ascended-master perspective, war is never justified.

O Cosmic Mother, tune my strings,
my total being with you sings.
Your song I now reverberate,
as cosmic love I celebrate.

**Maraytaii, I resonate
with song that opens cosmic gate.
Your melody makes me vibrate
my sense of self I recreate.**

9. I accept that the ascended masters never felt that wars were justified because they are not dualistic beings.

O Cosmic Mother, I love you,
your love song keeps me ever true.
You fill me with your sacred tone,
and thus I never feel alone.

**Maraytaii, I resonate
with song that opens cosmic gate.
Your melody makes me vibrate
my sense of self I recreate.**

Part 2

1. I accept that the real purpose of war is destruction, not just the destruction of the physical environment or a nation but the destruction of human beings, the destruction of their potential to raise their consciousness towards the level of Christhood and Buddhahood.

> Beloved Astrea, your heart is so true,
> your Circle and Sword of white and blue,
> cut all life free from dramas unwise,
> on wings of Purity our planet will rise.
>
> **Beloved Astrea, in oneness with you,**
> **your circle and sword of electric blue,**
> **with Purity's Light cutting right through,**
> **raising the earth into all that is true.**

2. I accept that the purpose of a war is never what it is claimed to be at the surface level. The Second World War was not a fight between good and evil. It was the result of a manipulation by the fallen beings.

> Beloved Astrea, in God Purity,
> accelerate all of our life energy,
> we're rising beyond every impurity,
> as Purity's Light forever we see.
>
> **Beloved Astrea, in oneness with you,**
> **your circle and sword of electric blue,**
> **with Purity's Light cutting right through,**
> **raising the earth into all that is true.**

3. I call forth the judgment of Christ upon the fallen beings who caused human beings to polarize towards two dualistic extremes whereby the fallen beings manipulated them into seeking to destroy each other.

> Beloved Astrea, from Purity's Ray,
> send forth deliverance to all life today,
> acceleration to Purity, we are now free
> from all that is less than love's Purity.
>
> **Beloved Astrea, in oneness with you,**
> **your circle and sword of electric blue,**
> **with Purity's Light cutting right through,**
> **raising the earth into all that is true.**

4. I accept that there is never a benign or constructive purpose for war. There is never a higher necessity to having an army. It is not a natural condition that a nation should have to have an army in order to survive. It is an artificial condition created by the fallen beings.

> Beloved Astrea, accelerate us all,
> as for your deliverance we fervently call,
> set all life free from vision impure
> beyond fear and doubt, we're rising for sure.
>
> **Beloved Astrea, in oneness with you,**
> **your circle and sword of electric blue,**
> **with Purity's Light cutting right through,**
> **raising the earth into all that is true.**

5. I call for the cutting free of people to see that the entire consciousness behind armed forces is based on fear. If we did

not have fear, we would not have a military. There is no way to create a military that is not based on fear.

> Beloved Astrea, we're willing to see,
> all of the lies that keep us unfree,
> we surrender all lies causing the fall,
> forever affirming the oneness of All.
>
> **Beloved Astrea, in oneness with you,**
> **your circle and sword of electric blue,**
> **with Purity's Light cutting right through,**
> **raising the earth into all that is true.**

6. I call for the cutting free of people to see that behind the outer motivation is some fear-based motive. Our minds are taken over by fear—that is why we arm ourselves. Whether we arm ourselves for the purpose of conquest or for the purpose of defense, it is always based on fear.

> Beloved Astrea, accelerate life
> beyond all duality's struggle and strife,
> consume all division between God and man,
> accelerate fulfillment of God's perfect plan.
>
> **Beloved Astrea, in oneness with you,**
> **your circle and sword of electric blue,**
> **with Purity's Light cutting right through,**
> **raising the earth into all that is true.**

7. I call for the cutting free of people to see that anything we do from a fear-based state of consciousness will create these entities and demons and they will eventually become so powerful that they can overpower individuals very easily, they can

overpower groups of people and they can even overpower entire nations.

> Beloved Astrea, we lovingly call,
> break down separation's invisible wall,
> raising our minds into true unity
> with the Masters of love in Infinity.

> **Beloved Astrea, in oneness with you,**
> **your circle and sword of electric blue,**
> **with Purity's Light cutting right through,**
> **raising the earth into all that is true.**

8. I call forth the judgment of Christ upon the demons and fallen beings who are perpetuating the fear-based mindset so that the people are so afraid that they think it is necessary to maintain the armed forces.

> Beloved Astrea, help all of us find,
> the secret that we create with the mind,
> and thus what in ignorance we decreate,
> in knowledge we easily can recreate.

> **Beloved Astrea, in oneness with you,**
> **your circle and sword of electric blue,**
> **with Purity's Light cutting right through,**
> **raising the earth into all that is true.**

9. I call forth the judgment of Christ upon the demons who are not concerned about the people whatsoever but only about perpetuating their own existence.

Beloved Astrea, we all do aspire,
to learning to use your purity's fire,
to raise every form in infamy sown,
as Saint Germain makes this planet his own.

**Beloved Astrea, in oneness with you,
your circle and sword of electric blue,
with Purity's Light cutting right through,
raising the earth into all that is true.**

Part 3

1. I call forth the judgment of Christ upon the fallen beings who are not concerned about the people, but only about either controlling the population on the earth or destroying those who will not be controlled.

O Cosmic Mother, sound the gong,
that calls me home where I belong.
I know you love me tenderly,
and in that knowing I am free.

**Maraytaii, I resonate
with song that opens cosmic gate.
Your melody makes me vibrate
my sense of self I recreate.**

2. I call forth the judgment of Christ upon the fallen beings who are not primarily concerned about control because they are focused on destruction and nothing else.

O Cosmic Mother, hold me tight,
I resonate with your own light.
Your music purifies my heart,
your love to all I do impart.

Maraytaii, I resonate
with song that opens cosmic gate.
Your melody makes me vibrate
my sense of self I recreate.

3. I call forth the judgment of Christ upon the conglomerate of forces behind every military in the world, the collective entities, the stronger demons and the fallen beings.

O Cosmic Mother, we are one,
your heart is like a blazing sun.
My being can but amplify,
the sacred sound you magnify.

Maraytaii, I resonate
with song that opens cosmic gate.
Your melody makes me vibrate
my sense of self I recreate.

4. I call for the people in the military to be cut free from being controlled by the consciousness and the military doctrines created by the fallen beings, so they can come to think clearly, to think individually and to think in an independent manner.

O Cosmic Mother, I now hear,
the subtle sound of Sacred Sphere.
As I attune to Cosmic Hum,
the lesser self I overcome.

**Maraytaii, I resonate
with song that opens cosmic gate.
Your melody makes me vibrate
my sense of self I recreate.**

5. I call for the people to be cut free to see that the armed forces of any nation form a closed system and therefore it filters out all of those people who have the ability to question the system.

O Cosmic Mother, take me home,
I am in sync with Sacred OM,
The sound of sounds will raise me up,
so only light is in my cup.

**Maraytaii, I resonate
with song that opens cosmic gate.
Your melody makes me vibrate
my sense of self I recreate.**

6. I call forth the judgment of Christ upon the armed forces that are still trapped in the cold war mindset and actually want to have an enemy to fight so they can maintain their lifestyle.

O Cosmic Mother, I will be,
a part of cosmic symphony.
All that I AM, an instrument,
for sound that is from heaven sent.

**Maraytaii, I resonate
with song that opens cosmic gate.
Your melody makes me vibrate
my sense of self I recreate.**

7. I call forth the judgment of Christ upon the people in South Korea who are so trapped in the warring mindset that they *will* not even consider the potential for a re-unification. Their mindset is geared toward one thing only and that is fighting the North Korean army.

O Cosmic Mother, I now call,
to enter sacred music hall.
I will be part of life's ascent,
towards the starry firmament.

Maraytaii, I resonate
with song that opens cosmic gate.
Your melody makes me vibrate
my sense of self I recreate.

8. I call forth the judgment of Christ upon the people in North Korea who are so trapped in the warring mindset that they *will* not even consider the potential for a re-unification. Their mindset is geared toward one thing only and that is fighting the South Korean army.

O Cosmic Mother, tune my strings,
my total being with you sings.
Your song I now reverberate,
as cosmic love I celebrate.

Maraytaii, I resonate
with song that opens cosmic gate.
Your melody makes me vibrate
my sense of self I recreate.

9. I call forth the judgment of Christ upon the American armed forces in South Korea who are so trapped in the warring mindset that they *will* not even consider the potential for a re-unification. Their mindset is geared toward one thing only and that is fighting the North Korean army.

O Cosmic Mother, I love you,
your love song keeps me ever true.
You fill me with your sacred tone,
and thus I never feel alone.

Maraytaii, I resonate
with song that opens cosmic gate.
Your melody makes me vibrate
my sense of self I recreate.

Part 4

1. I call forth the judgment of Christ upon the people in the large industrial corporations that are producing and supplying the army's needs and who are trapped in a mindset where they do not want to seriously consider a re-unification.

Beloved Astrea, your heart is so true,
your Circle and Sword of white and blue,
cut all life free from dramas unwise,
on wings of Purity our planet will rise.

Beloved Astrea, in oneness with you,
your circle and sword of electric blue,

**with Purity's Light cutting right through,
raising the earth into all that is true.**

2. I call forth the judgment of Christ upon the forces in America who are making profits out of selling military equipment to South Korea and who likewise do not want a re-unification.

Beloved Astrea, in God Purity,
accelerate all of our life energy,
we're rising beyond every impurity,
as Purity's Light forever we see.

**Beloved Astrea, in oneness with you,
your circle and sword of electric blue,
with Purity's Light cutting right through,
raising the earth into all that is true.**

3. I call forth the judgment of Christ upon the politicians in America who do not want a re-unification because they want to perpetuate the dualistic mindset where America is the one who has to guarantee freedom and democracy by always being ready to fight any enemy, real or imagined.

Beloved Astrea, from Purity's Ray,
send forth deliverance to all life today,
acceleration to Purity, we are now free
from all that is less than love's Purity.

**Beloved Astrea, in oneness with you,
your circle and sword of electric blue,
with Purity's Light cutting right through,
raising the earth into all that is true.**

4. I call forth the judgment of Christ upon the people in North and South Korea who will not consider re-unification.

> Beloved Astrea, accelerate us all,
> as for your deliverance we fervently call,
> set all life free from vision impure
> beyond fear and doubt, we're rising for sure.

> **Beloved Astrea, in oneness with you,**
> **your circle and sword of electric blue,**
> **with Purity's Light cutting right through,**
> **raising the earth into all that is true.**

5. I call for the binding and the consuming of the demons and collective entities that have taken over the minds of the people and make it impossible for people to even re-think the status quo, to ever question the status quo.

> Beloved Astrea, we're willing to see,
> all of the lies that keep us unfree,
> we surrender all lies causing the fall,
> forever affirming the oneness of All.

> **Beloved Astrea, in oneness with you,**
> **your circle and sword of electric blue,**
> **with Purity's Light cutting right through,**
> **raising the earth into all that is true.**

6. I call for the people to be cut free to say: "Do we actually need to continue this situation, to perpetuate this situation indefinitely? Is there an alternative? Is there a different way to look at this?"

Beloved Astrea, accelerate life
beyond all duality's struggle and strife,
consume all division between God and man,
accelerate fulfillment of God's perfect plan.

**Beloved Astrea, in oneness with you,
your circle and sword of electric blue,
with Purity's Light cutting right through,
raising the earth into all that is true.**

7. I call for the binding and consuming of the demons that are working through people and the fallen beings who do not want to lose the potential they have engineered for destruction if there was a war.

Beloved Astrea, we lovingly call,
break down separation's invisible wall,
raising our minds into true unity
with the Masters of love in Infinity.

**Beloved Astrea, in oneness with you,
your circle and sword of electric blue,
with Purity's Light cutting right through,
raising the earth into all that is true.**

8. I accept that there are people in embodiment who have a great resistance to change, but this resistance to change comes primarily because the people's minds have been taken over by the demons, or the people have been fooled by the fallen beings.

Beloved Astrea, help all of us find,
the secret that we create with the mind,

and thus what in ignorance we decreate,
in knowledge we easily can recreate.

**Beloved Astrea, in oneness with you,
your circle and sword of electric blue,
with Purity's Light cutting right through,
raising the earth into all that is true.**

9. I accept that there is no limit to what the ascended masters can do in the emotional, mental and identity octaves. The only limit is that the masters need the authorization from someone in embodiment who is aware and is willing to make the calls.

Beloved Astrea, we all do aspire,
to learning to use your purity's fire,
to raise every form in infamy sown,
as Saint Germain makes this planet his own.

**Beloved Astrea, in oneness with you,
your circle and sword of electric blue,
with Purity's Light cutting right through,
raising the earth into all that is true.**

Part 5

1. I call forth the judgment of Christ upon the fallen beings who have an agenda of destroying human beings because a human being is the only being on earth that has the potential to attain Christhood and Buddhahood.

O Cosmic Mother, sound the gong,
that calls me home where I belong.
I know you love me tenderly,
and in that knowing I am free.

**Maraytaii, I resonate
with song that opens cosmic gate.
Your melody makes me vibrate
my sense of self I recreate.**

2. I call forth the judgment of Christ upon the fallen beings who have a desire to kill anyone that manifests Christhood and who are willing to kill large numbers of people.

O Cosmic Mother, hold me tight,
I resonate with your own light.
Your music purifies my heart,
your love to all I do impart.

**Maraytaii, I resonate
with song that opens cosmic gate.
Your melody makes me vibrate
my sense of self I recreate.**

3. I call forth the judgment of Christ upon the fallen beings whose primary motivation behind war is that they want to kill those who have a Christ potential by killing as many people as possible.

O Cosmic Mother, we are one,
your heart is like a blazing sun.
My being can but amplify,
the sacred sound you magnify.

Maraytaii, I resonate
with song that opens cosmic gate.
Your melody makes me vibrate
my sense of self I recreate.

4. I call forth the judgment of Christ upon the fallen beings whose only agenda is destruction and who want to kill as many people as possible, Christed beings or not, because the demons can always extract energy when people are killed violently.

O Cosmic Mother, I now hear,
the subtle sound of Sacred Sphere.
As I attune to Cosmic Hum,
the lesser self I overcome.

Maraytaii, I resonate
with song that opens cosmic gate.
Your melody makes me vibrate
my sense of self I recreate.

5. I call for people to be cut free to see that there is no more efficient way for demons to extract people's energies than to get two groups of people to wage an all-out destructive war against each other.

O Cosmic Mother, take me home,
I am in sync with Sacred OM,
The sound of sounds will raise me up,
so only light is in my cup.

Maraytaii, I resonate
with song that opens cosmic gate.

**Your melody makes me vibrate
my sense of self I recreate.**

6. I accept that killing a human being is the extreme outpicturing of hatred of the mother. Since the entire purpose of a military is to kill human beings, any military is based on hatred of the mother.

O Cosmic Mother, I will be,
a part of cosmic symphony.
All that I AM, an instrument,
for sound that is from heaven sent.

**Maraytaii, I resonate
with song that opens cosmic gate.
Your melody makes me vibrate
my sense of self I recreate.**

7. I call forth the judgment of Christ upon the people in the military, the people in the political establishments who support the military, the people in the industrial establishment that support the military, all those who have a mechanism in their psychology so that when a situation arises that calls for their military to perform its defined task, then these people become willing to kill and to kill indiscriminately.

O Cosmic Mother, I now call,
to enter sacred music hall.
I will be part of life's ascent,
towards the starry firmament.

**Maraytaii, I resonate
with song that opens cosmic gate.**

Your melody makes me vibrate
my sense of self I recreate.

8. I call forth the judgment of Christ upon the people who, once they have a defined enemy, will do whatever they can to defeat that enemy. In order to achieve that objective, they are willing to kill any numbers of people among the enemy but they are also willing to sacrifice any number of their own soldiers.

O Cosmic Mother, tune my strings,
my total being with you sings.
Your song I now reverberate,
as cosmic love I celebrate.

Maraytaii, I resonate
with song that opens cosmic gate.
Your melody makes me vibrate
my sense of self I recreate.

9. I call forth the judgment of Christ upon the people who have elected to be in the military and rise to prominent positions precisely because they have this mechanism where they believe that under certain circumstances killing is fully justified.

O Cosmic Mother, I love you,
your love song keeps me ever true.
You fill me with your sacred tone,
and thus I never feel alone.

Maraytaii, I resonate
with song that opens cosmic gate.

**Your melody makes me vibrate
my sense of self I recreate.**

Part 6

1. I call forth the judgment of Christ upon the people who do not even need to think about what they are doing. They do not need to recognize that they are killing living human beings, individuals just like themselves and their own children.

> Beloved Astrea, your heart is so true,
> your Circle and Sword of white and blue,
> cut all life free from dramas unwise,
> on wings of Purity our planet will rise.

> **Beloved Astrea, in oneness with you,
> your circle and sword of electric blue,
> with Purity's Light cutting right through,
> raising the earth into all that is true.**

2. I call forth the judgment of Christ upon the people who have stepped into a mindset where they see the enemy as non-humans and where they also see their own soldiers as non-humans. They may even see civilians, even their own, as non-humans.

> Beloved Astrea, in God Purity,
> accelerate all of our life energy,
> we're rising beyond every impurity,
> as Purity's Light forever we see.

Beloved Astrea, in oneness with you,
your circle and sword of electric blue,
with Purity's Light cutting right through,
raising the earth into all that is true.

3. I call forth the judgment of Christ upon the people who think that there will be a certain collateral damage to waging a war and that you cannot always avoid the killing of civilians.

Beloved Astrea, from Purity's Ray,
send forth deliverance to all life today,
acceleration to Purity, we are now free
from all that is less than love's Purity.

Beloved Astrea, in oneness with you,
your circle and sword of electric blue,
with Purity's Light cutting right through,
raising the earth into all that is true.

4. I call forth the judgment of Christ upon the hatred of the mother that makes people think it is justified to kill human beings and that collateral damage is acceptable, a consciousness that is so ingrained in the military forces of the world and the industries and the politicians who support them that there is virtually none of them that are willing to question it.

Beloved Astrea, accelerate us all,
as for your deliverance we fervently call,
set all life free from vision impure
beyond fear and doubt, we're rising for sure.

Beloved Astrea, in oneness with you,
your circle and sword of electric blue,

**with Purity's Light cutting right through,
raising the earth into all that is true.**

5. I call for people in democratic nations to be cut free so they can question the military without swinging to an unbalanced extreme that is simply the opposite dualistic polarity to the mindset of those in the military. I call for the binding and the consuming of the demons behind this mindset.

Beloved Astrea, we're willing to see,
all of the lies that keep us unfree,
we surrender all lies causing the fall,
forever affirming the oneness of All.

**Beloved Astrea, in oneness with you,
your circle and sword of electric blue,
with Purity's Light cutting right through,
raising the earth into all that is true.**

6. I call for the awakening of the people who are able to find a middle way and question this dynamic, and who can create a debate in society that is not dominated by the extreme viewpoints of wanting to blindly defend the military, wanting to blindly attack the military.

Beloved Astrea, accelerate life
beyond all duality's struggle and strife,
consume all division between God and man,
accelerate fulfillment of God's perfect plan.

**Beloved Astrea, in oneness with you,
your circle and sword of electric blue,**

**with Purity's Light cutting right through,
raising the earth into all that is true.**

7. I call for people to be cut free to see that there is a middle way where we can have a more aware discussion about the role of the military and the necessity to perpetuate the current situation. I call forth an openness where we can see solutions that have not been seen before.

Beloved Astrea, we lovingly call,
break down separation's invisible wall,
raising our minds into true unity
with the Masters of love in Infinity.

**Beloved Astrea, in oneness with you,
your circle and sword of electric blue,
with Purity's Light cutting right through,
raising the earth into all that is true.**

8. I call for people to be cut free to see that whenever a debate gets polarized between the extremes, it seems as if we either have to choose to support the military completely or to abandon the military completely. But there is always a higher perspective where we can find a new way to look at the entire dynamic and see perspectives, solutions that were not seen by anyone before.

Beloved Astrea, help all of us find,
the secret that we create with the mind,
and thus what in ignorance we decreate,
in knowledge we easily can recreate.

> **Beloved Astrea, in oneness with you,**
> **your circle and sword of electric blue,**
> **with Purity's Light cutting right through,**
> **raising the earth into all that is true.**

9. I call for people to be cut free to embrace the wisdom of the mother that does not require an idealistic solution to a problem but always looks for the practical solution that will bring us one step forward.

> Beloved Astrea, we all do aspire,
> to learning to use your purity's fire,
> to raise every form in infamy sown,
> as Saint Germain makes this planet his own.

> **Beloved Astrea, in oneness with you,**
> **your circle and sword of electric blue,**
> **with Purity's Light cutting right through,**
> **raising the earth into all that is true.**

Sealing

In the name of the Divine Mother, I call to all ascended masters for the sealing of myself and all people in my circle of influence in the creative flow of the Divine Mother, the River of Life. I call for the multiplication of my calls by all ascended masters so that we form the perfect figure-eight flow of "As Above, so below." Thus, I accept that this is fully manifest, because the mouth of the Lord, the Divine Mother that I AM, has spoken it. Amen.

8 | TALKING YOUR WAY INTO THE GOLDEN AGE

I AM the Ascended Master Mother Mary, and it is with great joy that I come to you today. The joy that I feel is the joy of watching you as you have come together for this gathering. Not just the fact that you are physically together, but the fact that you are so spiritually together as well. You are so openly and freely talking to each other, sharing of your hearts, talking about your personal issues and you feel free and safe to talk about things that you normally would not feel free to talk about with many other people. Strangely, if you observe yourselves, you will see that in many cases you have talked to a person that you have never met before, but still felt free to share something deeply personal about yourself without fearing that it would be used against you or misunderstood.

Free communication

Why I am bringing this to your attention is that I want to show you that what you have here at this gathering is in one sense, a glimpse of heaven on earth because, naturally, we communicate freely in the ascended realm. You also have a glimpse of the future for what the Golden Age will be like. My beloved, how can we bring a Golden Age if people cannot freely communicate; if they cannot communicate at the level of the heart rather than communicating, as is so often the case, at the level of the outer mind or the ego.

Consider your conversations and the way you interact with each other here compared to the way, in many cases, you yourselves have to interact with people out in the world. See how many games are being played around people that prevents a free and open communication at the heart level. There is always some agenda, there is always some unresolved pattern of psychology that is being outplayed, and this prevents people from connecting at the heart level.

It is obvious, is it not, that there needs to be better communication for there to be a Golden Age. This is obvious to you once you have experienced a more free level of communication that is actually a heart-based level of communication rather than being based on the ego or the outer mind. You see, my beloved, what I desire to see for you, as the one who holds the Mother Flame, is that all of you can feel free to share yourselves, to share who you are. This does not mean that you need to go out in the world and talk about deeply personal issues with every person you meet, but I wish you could be free to share more of yourself regardless of the reaction you get from other people.

You see, my beloved, here, in a community like this where you feel safe because you feel you will not be attacked for sharing of yourself, it is much easier to share. What I am seeking to point out to you is that the sharing from the heart is a flow that comes from the higher part of your being through your outer mind. Truly, it is a flow that, once you establish it, is independent of how the other person receives it. In other words, you can learn by a relatively simple switch of the mind, to disconnect the flow through the heart from the desire to have a certain reaction from the person with whom you are communicating.

Communication without expecting a certain return

You can actually learn to come to the point where your real goal is not to change the other person, or to convince the other person of anything. Your real goal is to establish the flow from your higher being through your heart and having it be expressed in this world. You can learn to find the joy in feeling that flow. You can learn to find satisfaction, fulfillment and completeness in having the flow go forth from you without having any expectations of what the other person's reaction should be, and what kind of a return you will get.

Surely, as you have experienced yourselves, when the other person responds positively, then two or more people who are freely sharing, can very quickly build an upward spiral that uplifts all of them and pulls you higher and higher. Many of you have experienced this today, even in this brief time you have been together. Yet, still, there is a joy in feeling the flow go out regardless of whether anything positive comes back to multiply the flow. You can learn to be willing and daring to share from the heart no matter what other people's reactions might be. You can come to the point where you are not expecting a particular reaction from other people. You are not wanting them to react a certain way. You are not needing them to validate or affirm you because you have come to that point where you realize that the best gift you can give on this planet is to be yourself, to share of yourself, and to have a flow from your higher being through your heart.

As was also said, it is very important for you to realize, my beloved, that you do not need to have any particular state of perfection. You do not need to reach a certain level on the spiritual path, although you generally need to be above the 48th level, which all of you are. You do not need to reach a certain level of Christhood in order to have the flow through the heart. It is truly a matter of being willing to have that flow by opening yourself to allow the flow to happen. In order to allow it to happen, most of you will have to find a way to neutralize this concern for other people's reactions.

Fallen beings limit communication

Now, my beloved, we have given many, many teachings in these last few years about dark forces seeking to limit you, about fallen beings seeking to manipulate you. My beloved, there are many ways that the fallen beings have attempted to manipulate you in order to prevent you from expressing your Christhood, but if there was one overall simple mechanism that is very easy to understand, it is simply this: They have managed to get you into thinking that when you express yourself on this planet, you should be concerned about their reactions. Therefore, you should adapt your expression to other people's reactions. You may think this is the people around you, but really when you step back, my beloved, you see that it is a mechanism created by the fallen beings where they want all people to think that they have to adapt the expression of their hearts to the expectations and standards of the fallen beings.

You do not know this consciously, of course. Most people do not know this consciously but this is what they have managed to create, my beloved, so that you do not feel free in expressing yourself. If you do not feel free in expressing yourself, well, then it is very difficult to have the flow because the flow needs an open door to flow through. It needs freedom to express because many times when you are in the flow of the spirit, you find yourself saying things that you had not planned, that you had not thought out, that you had not even thought about before. Suddenly, they come out and you realize that this is not your little concerned, frustrated, angry, afraid mind that is saying this. This is your higher being that this is coming from. Sometimes you become surprised yourself at what wisdom and insight can come from you in these situations when you allow the free flow.

Sometimes this is how you have the greatest learning experiences, not by hearing some external being speak through a dictation, or another person, or by reading a book, but actually when you have that flow from your higher being and it is your higher being speaking through you. It is speaking exactly in a way that goes right into your mind and resolves one of these enigmas you have had, resolves one of these limitations. Suddenly, it helps you see something you could never see before because nobody had expressed it in words that were exactly right for you and that clicked in your mind so that you were instantly seeing this mechanism, and instantly free from it. The greatest teacher you have, my beloved, is actually your own higher being, the teacher within yourself. The being that you already are but that you have been manipulated by the fallen beings into thinking that you are not allowed to express while you are in a physical body on a planet as limited and as dark as earth.

You can overcome the programming

My beloved, do you think it was any easier for me when I was in physical embodiment to express my higher being and share who I am? It was just as difficult for me as it is for you because I also had certain mechanisms and beliefs I had taken on from the mass consciousness and other people. Therefore, it was as difficult for any [unascended] ascended master to express themselves freely as it is for you. Therefore, I want you to understand that on the one hand I know it is difficult for you and I am not trying to give you an impossible, unreachable goal. I am not trying to make you feel guilty because you cannot always freely share from the heart.

On the other hand, I also have gone through the process myself of overcoming these limitations, learning to see through them and coming to the point where, in my last few embodiments on earth, I could express myself much more freely. I did so, in my last embodiment, many times, especially as we formed a community after Jesus had left, and we stood there alone and we had to find out what we would do now. This was a very difficult situation where there was a certain amount of power games and ego plays that came into the situation and someone had to dare to speak up and speak freely from the heart, and therefore realign all of these disciples. They had good intentions but could not necessarily see how to proceed, how to turn them into action, and how to avoid these conflicts with each other where several people thought that they had the only right way to do things. It was necessary for someone to be the kind of focal point who could speak out and bring them back into alignment with the Spirit that was ready to flow through most of them whenever they would open themselves up to it.

I was often the one who had to remind the disciples of the gift that Jesus had given us by the release of the Holy Spirit, the release of his Spirit as it happened on Pentecost, described in the scriptures, but as it happened numerous times when there was a gathering of the disciples. Someone would become the instrument for speaking something that came from the flow of the Spirit, and the others would then learn to recognize it. It was not a matter of competition; it was not a matter of someone who always had to do it, but it could be different people at different times. They all had to learn to recognize that the Spirit would choose who would be the one who would speak at that particular gathering. Then, the others had to allow this to happen, otherwise they would go into an ego reaction. In many cases, this was my role to be the one who would say: "Now let us come into unity with the Spirit because it is, after all, the Spirit that will build our community, not our outer beings."

Recognizing the flow of the Spirit

The Spirit bloweth where it listeth. It expresses itself through whomever it desires, and chooses at that moment. Therefore, none have a monopoly, none are the exclusive ones, and none are excluded from being the instrument of the Spirit if they are willing. My beloved, you will see in yourselves, in your gathering today, how you could feel that certainly someone spoke with a deeper sense of love, of heartfeltness, of sincerity than they normally did. You may think that this was not the flow of the Spirit, but it was. It was the flow of the Spirit through you from your higher being.

It does not always have to be in some dramatic fashion, like you hear a dictation spoken here. Many times in conversations you can have that flow of the Spirit. Most of you have had it, most of you have recognized it at times. Many times you do not recognize it, you do not quite acknowledge that you are able to be the open doors of the Spirit and you can be more and more conscious of allowing this flow of the Spirit, being the open door. It does not necessarily have to be some pompous thing, some long thing. It can be one sentence that is said with a greater feeling than normal, and that can be enough to shift another person's consciousness as they need to be shifted at that moment.

All of you, my beloved, have the capability of being the open door in this way. That is why, as the mother that I am, I do not want to put before you an impossible goal; but I am not putting before you an impossible goal. That is what I desire you to see because I see the potential that you all have.

There is not a single person, who has walked the path for some time, who does not have the potential to help others. If you have overcome one aspect of your ego, then you can help other people overcome that aspect. You might be the only one they will meet for a long time, and therefore you need to be more willing to be the open door, to allow these flows of the Spirit through you in many different situations. My beloved, we are not talking about converting people to a particular religion or the ascended masters' teachings. We are not talking about getting them to do outer things. We are talking about giving them some idea, some insight, or maybe even just an infusion of love that somehow shifts their consciousness one step upwards. Maybe they had never experienced it before.

Changing people through the flow

Do you know, my beloved, how many people in the world who have never experienced someone speaking to them without an intent, without wanting to manipulate them or to put them down, or criticize or judge them? Do you realize how many people have never had the kind of interactions and communication that most of you had here today? Do you realize that many people have never, ever met a person who did not judge or criticize them, but who simply radiated love and acceptance to them?

Perhaps by saying one kind remark, you can change a person's life because you give them an experience they have never had before. The experience is real to them, and they experience the reality of the flow of the Spirit coming through you. They cannot deny it and suddenly they have a frame of reference that there is a different way that human beings can interact than what they have experienced so far, where it is all this "fight or flight" and manipulation and unkindness, and all of this human surface interactions.

My beloved, last year I talked about the need to overcome petty problems; but part of this process is overcoming this superficial, derogatory or judgmental conversation that people have so many times. Many times, communication is so superficial because people are so insecure when they meet a stranger that they do not quite know how to talk to somebody, and so they revert back into some kind of pattern that is considered safe in their culture. Often it is to use some kind of humor that is slightly ironic or putting yourself down. While there is not necessarily anything hugely wrong with this, I point out to you that it does not facilitate communication from the heart. It can be sometimes okay to use humor to "break the ice," as they say, but my beloved, what if you do not have any ice in your own being that needs to be broken up? Have you looked at yourself and seen how many times, when you meet a stranger, it is your own insecurity that is talking rather than the security of your higher self? Well, my beloved, some of you have psychological issues. This I fully understand and recognize. Some of you have to resolve those issues before you can talk freely with people you do not know. But for many of you, you have resolved enough of these issues that it really is just a switch in the mind, a turning of the dial of the mind. You recognize that you have had this insecurity, this shyness in yourself, but you no longer need it. In fact, it limits you, and you can make a decision that you will reconnect to your higher being in your heart. You will allow yourself to speak from that level rather than speaking from the level of the outer mind and having to break the ice and feel the other person out before you dare to open up from the heart.

You can actually come to a point where you are always speaking from the heart, or at least very often speaking from the heart when the situation is there for it. Sometimes, I recognize that you have a practical conversation where there is not necessarily any openness for speaking from the heart. You can learn to recognize when that openness is there, and you can speak from the heart from the very beginning without having to go through this little song-and-dance that people outplay where they feel each other out. They try to figure out what it is safe to say to this other person so they do not offend them and get a negative reaction back.

Speaking from the heart is always safe

Well, my beloved, if you speak from the heart, it is always safe. Even if the other person takes offense, as long as you stay in the heart, you will not be offended by their reaction. You will not be put off by it. You will be able to continue speaking from the heart, and as long as you can continue speaking from the heart, there is a possibility that you will help the other person shift out of their focus on the outer mind. They can then reconnect to the heart and then there is a much greater opportunity that you will have a heart-based conversation.

This, my beloved, is not such a far-flung goal for most of you here. It is something that I want you to recognize that you have experienced here and you can and will experience much more in the coming days. When you have experienced it, when you can do it in a safe environment like this, then you can begin to carry that out with you and also experience it in other situations.

My beloved, how many of you who have come to some of these conferences, have experienced that when you travel home from a conference, you suddenly meet a person or you sit next to them in the plane or in the airport or in the train, and suddenly a conversation starts going and you have a deeper, more heart-felt communication with that person than you have ever before had with a stranger? This is because you have been to a conference, and you have had your chakras opened. You have received a lot of light, but you are still in this sense of being in a safe environment, and so you are much more free to share of yourself, and that is why the other person can sometimes sense this and then they open up and suddenly there is that flow.

What I seek to make you aware of is that you can switch the mind so that, in many situations, you can have that openness, that willingness to share something from the heart. Then, you will find that you will attract to you more people who are open to that level of communication, who are actually longing for that level of communication, because many, many people are.

Not everybody is ready for it, surely. People below the 48th level are not open to a heart-felt communication because they have such patterns in their minds that they are always feeling insecure and threatened. They need to have every human interaction follow the pattern that gives them some sense of being in control. If you speak from the heart to them, they will not have experienced this before, they will not know what to do with it in their minds, and therefore often they will close off or give you a negative reaction. Well, in that case, you just move on, but my beloved, many people, and more and more people, are longing for a genuine communication.

A shift in the media

My beloved, look at what has happened to television and radio over the last decade or more. What have you seen happen? You have seen more of what you call reality shows, but you have also seen that interviews on television have, at least in some cases, taken a different turn where there are some interviewers that are able to have a more sincere communication with the guests they invite into their studio. Obviously, not all, for many are still driven by these ego games. But you will see that there are more and more who have discovered that people want something different. Instead of this slick, traditional communication from the media, they want people who are genuine, who dare to be themselves.

This is because there has been a shift in the collective consciousness, especially over the past ten years, where more and more people are looking for something. They may call it "reality." They may say: "I want something real." Or they want something genuine, or they may not know how to put words on it, but they want something that is at the heart level, and they want something that is not controlled by all of these ego mechanisms.

Many people do not see the ego mechanisms. They do not know about the ego, they do not see them clearly. But they are tired of something. They have had enough of something. They are longing for something else and this is the time where you who are the ascended master students can render a great service by shifting into this more sincere form of communication. You can then help raise the collective consciousness, and more and more people will follow. It will filter down so that you will begin to see how this shift will happen and more and more people will be able to have more real, more genuine, interactions.

This is obviously something you can make calls on, but you first of all need to embody it and live it and dare to express it—and each and every one of you has that potential, my beloved. You all have that potential. What I am going to do here is that I am going to take this conversation that is, you might say, at a very personal level, but I am going to connect it to a planetary, even a cosmic perspective.

Are ideas more important than individuals?

Now you see, my beloved, what we have taught you about the fallen beings is that one of the primary ways they manipulate people is by putting out the idea that ideas are more important than the individual. The most extreme expression of this mind-set is that it is justified to kill other human beings because of an idea. In other words, an idea can justify the killing of other human beings. We have talked about it before. I have talked about it in the book on war, but one of the primary shifts that needs to happen before the Golden Age can be manifest, is that the people begin to recognize that this is a lie, this is a manipulation. It is simply out of touch with the higher reality of the spiritual realm, because an idea exists only in the mind. There is no idea in the mind that can justify killing the physical body that a spiritual being is using as its expression on earth.

Physical life on earth is precious because life on earth is an opportunity for growth. The people who embody on earth, being in physical embodiment is their highest opportunity for growth. When you take away the physical body, you take away that opportunity for the soul's growth, and it is therefore the greatest violation of the free will of that being. This is why, when you look at the Old Testament and the command: "Thou shalt not kill," there are no conditions defined under which circumstances it becomes acceptable to kill. Of course, from the very beginning, the priesthood of the Jews defined that there were indeed such conditions. That is why you see in the Old Testament that the Jews could supposedly believe in the ten commandments, and think they honored the ten commandments while they massacred men, women, and children of the tribes who inhabited what the Jews believed was their holy land. This is the fallen beings manipulating the reality of God that physical life is precious into creating conditions where it becomes not only justifiable, but even desirable, that people kill others.

This was done, my beloved, all for the sake of an idea. Now you may say: "But didn't the Jews just simply want the land that these people lived on?" No, because the Jews were motivated by an entire set of ideas that they were God's chosen people, that there was a holy land defined for them, and that therefore it was justified that they went in and took it by force. These were ideas, my beloved, that justified this killing. If you will look at world history, even the recent world wars, you will see that in all wars, ideas played a role. It has always been that way because, as I say in my book on war, you have an instinctive drive not to kill your fellow human beings. You cannot kill another human being without knowing within yourself that this was not right according to some higher standard. You can kill so many people that you have covered over this instinctive knowing, and so you do not notice it anymore, but you still have it, my beloved.

In order to get people to kill each other, the fallen beings have to do one of two things, primarily. They either have to set people in conflicts with each other where two individuals or two groups of people feel that: "If I don't kill them, they will kill me." This, then, is a lower way of getting people to kill each other. It can work sometimes without there being that much of an idea involved but in most cases, there is an aggressor that somehow feels justified in attacking the other group of people. Sometimes the other group of people, who were being attacked, may also have an idea of why the others are wrong and why this justifies that they defend themselves, so you can still have ideas

The other way, the primary way, that the fallen beings get people to kill each other is to define some system of ideas that justifies the killing of particular human beings. In many cases, it is exactly the pattern that you have seen so many times and that you saw in the process that led to the second world war. A group of people somehow feel superior, and they define a scapegoat that is inferior, perhaps even subhuman. Suddenly, for the betterment of some greater good, it is not only justified, but necessary and desirable to kill the scapegoat.

Ideas block genuine communication

My beloved, how does this tie in with the first part of my dictation where I talked about genuine communication from the heart? Well, my beloved, what is it that blocks genuine communication? It is that people are trapped in a matrix of ideas, a set of ideas and beliefs where you are not expressing yourself freely. You have certain ideas in your mind where you think you have to adapt your expression to these ideas. You cannot just be yourself, you have to fulfill some kind of role, and therefore you have to evaluate everything that is being said through you with the outer mind.

When your higher being senses that you are evaluating everything that is being said with the outer mind, it naturally steps back and respects your free will, which you have now centered in the outer mind. You are letting your outer mind run your free will instead of making truly conscious choices and so there will be no free flow. You also, many times, have a set of ideas that says that other people or society expects you to live up to certain criteria, and again this causes you to evaluate everything you do or say: "Is it correct according to the standard?" Then, you have no free flow of communication, my beloved.

How does this tie in with bringing the Golden Age? How does it tie in with the situation here in Europe? Well, as I said, how can there be a Golden Age unless people from different nations, from different groups, different races, different ethnic groups, even the two sexes, men and women, can communicate at the level of the heart? How can there be a Golden Age because what is the Golden Age based on? The Golden Age is based on an inner sense of oneness that transcends all the outer divisions that people have in their outer minds where they identify with their nationality, for example, or their race, ethnic group, sex or whatever.

Let us look at Europe right now. When people come to identify themselves with their nationality and define their nationality being distinctly different from other nationalities, and often in opposition to them or competition with them, well, then their interaction, their communication, will be at that level of the outer mind. Then, how can they come to the point where they have a heart-to-heart talk? What does it mean to have a heart-to-heart talk? It means that you connect to a higher part of your being and you sense that the other person is also connected to the higher part of its being. Then, you sense that it is the same reality you are both connected to. When you know that you are both connected to a higher reality, how can you be fully identified with the outer mind?

The cause of Brexit

My beloved, what caused Brexit? Well, very simply that the British people did not have a heart-to-heart communication with the other nations in Europe. Is that the fault of the British people? Certainly not exclusively. What caused the situation in France where a candidate arose that wanted to take France out of the European community and wanted to go back to a nationalistic state? What has caused the situation in America where you see this nationalism of putting America first? Is it not because people do not have communication at the heart level? What if certain leaders were able to sit down and have a talk where suddenly you are not president this or chancellor that, you are one human talking to another human being and you suddenly connect and realize you are both human beings, and that your peoples are both groups of human beings. All of a sudden, the dynamic shifts completely, and then you are able to have this genuine communication.

Now my beloved, why have you seen this wave of what people call populism where the people are dissatisfied with the political establishment and with politics as usual? What are people tired of? What are they dissatisfied with? Precisely that politics is one big game where everybody has an idea of how things should be, or how they should behave, or how they should talk, and how the other people should talk. They are all just playing this game at the surface level, never connecting at a deeper level. More and more people among the population, as I said, are longing for something genuine. They do not see anything genuine in the arena of politics. If a candidate arises that is not a typical politician, that speaks with a certain conviction, it may be that what he is convinced of is not realistic, but he is convinced and he has conviction, and he is talking about it in a genuine way, and then people think: "Maybe this is what we are looking for." It may not be what they are truly longing for, but it shows you that what people are ready for is a more genuine level of political interaction between nations.

You cannot unite people through ideas

Now my beloved, which part of the world, when you look at the entire planet, is most likely to be able to become the forerunner for this more sincere communication? Well, it is the European continent. I said continent. It is precisely the European nations who have now for decades attempted to create a greater union in Europe. What you need to recognize, my beloved, is that this union must be based on this sense of oneness that only comes when you connect at the heart level. So far, what have the European nations attempted to do with the EU? They have attempted to create a set of ideas saying: "Look at how many wars we have had on the European continent over the centuries. Look how we have fought two world wars. Look how we had the extreme outcome of the Holocaust on our soil. We can never allow this to happen again and therefore we must find a way to cooperate, and therefore we must create a set of ideas that forces us to cooperate."

My beloved, what created the division on the European continent? It was ideas! There was war between the Catholics and the Protestants. There was war between East and West. There was war between Nazis and those who were not Nazis. You have seen so many times that ideas – sets of ideas – were elevated to the status of being more important than the individual human being! You have seen how these ideas have created division, war, conflict. Why does it make sense, *how* does it make sense that creating another set of ideas will resolve the conflict? *It makes no sense,* my beloved.

This is the very idea that I ask you to have in the back of your minds for the rest of this conference. I ask you to make the calls for this, to make the calls that there will be a more genuine communication, and that there will be an awakening and a stepping forward of the many people who are ready for this level of communication. I tell you that in every country, there is a growing number of the population who are ready and longing for this genuine connection with other people. They may not know this consciously, but with a relatively simple and realistic shift in the collective consciousness, many of them will wake up and there will be a new openness and a new willingness to say to your own politicians: "Listen, find a way to talk to other nations, or get out of the way for there are others who are willing to talk at the heart level, to have a genuine conversation, where you are not seeking to dominate the others, you are seeking to reach some understanding that you have not reached before."

This would be a tremendous progress, and this could open the way for so many things where the European nations could get out of this impasse that they are in right now where they all fear for the future. They all fear that suddenly the EU that they have built so carefully over so many decades, is starting to fracture and come apart from within. Well, it is coming apart from within because they have approached it from the same mindset that created the division, and the second law of thermodynamics is doing its work and showing them that it is time to step up to a higher level.

Those, of course, who have been trapped in the bureaucratic mindset, in the political mindset, for decades, they are not the ones who can step up, but the people *can*. The people can elect new representatives, and there can be a new kind of people that come to the forefront in the media who will start talking and communicating in a different way. They simply refuse to play all of the silly games that have so far created nothing but division and misunderstanding.

My beloved, no conflict has ever truly been resolved through the kind of negotiations you have seen so far. It has always been caused by somebody realizing that by continuing the conflict, the consequences would be so severe that they do not want this so they choose the lesser of two evils. In order to avoid a greater evil, they agree to something, but this is not unity. This is not true union.

There have of course been cases where there has been a greater understanding among people and genuine progress has been made. In too many cases it has been this superficial level of communication, and it has been this mindset that in order to avoid the greater calamity of war and conflict, we have to force ourselves into this outer, political, forced union. I tell you, my beloved, that when you have communication at the heart level, you do not need to force yourself or each other into a political or economic union. You will willingly go into it because you experience that this greater union is not a loss, but it is a gain, not politically, economically, or militarily. It is a gain in how you feel about yourself.

The most precious human commodity

Truly, what is the most precious human commodity? Is it gold? Is it diamonds? It is, my beloved, how you feel about yourself. Nothing is more precious than that. Therefore, as Jesus said, when you know the pearl of great price, you willingly sell everything else in order to have it. This means that you willingly give up all aspects of the ego, the outer personality, the wounded personality, in order to come into union with your higher self, come into union with other people, so that you will feel better about who you are.

You will dare to acknowledge who you are: A spiritual being who has nothing to be ashamed of, nothing to feel embarrassed about, nothing to be afraid of, nothing to hide. You have no reason whatsoever to hide who you really are, my beloved. When you recognize that you can be free to share, then you feel the flow from your higher being through your mind and then you feel good about yourself. Truly, I hold the Mother Flame for each one of you. What higher desire could I have than to have each and every one of you feel good about yourselves? I have no higher desire. I am willing to help each and every one of you, if you will ask me, not only during this conference, but if you will ask me wherever and whenever, I will help you. It will require some of you to look at some things you have not looked at before, because they are blocking you feeling good about yourself. Even though it may cause some discomfort and pain to look at this, what you get out of it, in the long run is worth so much more.

Right now, my beloved, for many of you the main focus of your life has been to make other people feel good or to make your ego feel good. I am asking you to make a shift where you are willing to say to yourself: "I don't want to do this anymore. I want to feel good about myself. What will that take?" Then, you are open to the answer that we will find some way to give to you, maybe through a book, a teaching, another person. Maybe from within yourself, from some insight that suddenly comes to you. This, my beloved, is my highest desire. If you will give me some of your attention during these next days, which I know will be a challenge because other masters will give you other things to think about, but if you will give me some of your attention, you may find that I will be able to assist you tremendously in this short time. You may find that I will be able to use other people to give you a thought and insight that you need.

With this, I give you my love. I thank you for coming this long way for many of you, and I thank you, many of you, for coming a very long way in consciousness since you first encountered the teachings of the ascended masters in whatever form you encountered them. I thank you for being willing to move on and listen to the Living Word that is flowing from us today. My heartfelt gratitude and my total acceptance of each and every one of you.

9 | INVOKING GOLDEN AGE COOPERATION

In the name I AM THAT I AM, Jesus Christ, I call to all ascended masters working on manifesting the Golden Age, especially Mother Mary, to radiate into the collective consciousness a new awareness of how to have the true co-operation of the Golden Age. Help people see that we can build a new future by working with the ascended masters and letting go of the old way of looking at life, including...

[Make personal calls.]

Part 1

1. I call for the awakening of people to the fact that we cannot bring a Golden Age if people cannot freely communicate; if they cannot communicate at the level of the heart rather than communicating at the level of the outer mind or the ego.

O blessed Mary, Mother mine,
there is no greater love than thine,
as we are one in heart and mind,
my place in hierarchy I find.

O Mother Mary, generate,
the song that does accelerate,
the earth into a higher state,
all matter does now scintillate.

2. I call for the awakening of people to the many games that are being played and that prevent free and open communication at the heart level. There is always some agenda, there is always some unresolved pattern of psychology that is being outplayed, and this prevents people from connecting at the heart level.

I came to earth from heaven sent,
as I am in embodiment,
I use Divine authority,
commanding you to set earth free.

O Mother Mary, generate,
the song that does accelerate,
the earth into a higher state,
all matter does now scintillate.

3. I call for the awakening of people to experience a more free level of communication that is heart-based rather than being based on the ego or the outer mind.

I call now in God's sacred name,
for you to use your Mother Flame,

to burn all fear-based energy,
restoring sacred harmony.

O Mother Mary, generate,
the song that does accelerate,
the earth into a higher state,
all matter does now scintillate.

4. I call for the awakening of people to see that the sharing from the heart is a flow that comes from the higher part of our beings through the outer mind. Once we establish the flow, it is independent of how other people receive it.

Your sacred name I hereby praise,
collective consciousness you raise,
no more of fear and doubt and shame,
consume it with your Mother Flame.

O Mother Mary, generate,
the song that does accelerate,
the earth into a higher state,
all matter does now scintillate.

5. I call for the awakening of people to switch the mind, to disconnect the flow through the heart from the desire to have a certain reaction from the people with whom we are communicating.

All darkness from the earth you purge,
your light moves as a mighty surge,
no force of darkness can now stop,
the spiral that goes only up.

O Mother Mary, generate,
the song that does accelerate,
the earth into a higher state,
all matter does now scintillate.

6. I call for the awakening of people from the need to change other people or convince them of anything so that the real goal is to establish the flow from our higher beings through the heart and having it be expressed in this world.

All elemental life you bless,
removing from them man-made stress,
the nature spirits are now free,
outpicturing Divine decree.

O Mother Mary, generate,
the song that does accelerate,
the earth into a higher state,
all matter does now scintillate.

7. I call for the awakening of people to find satisfaction, fulfillment and completeness in having the flow go forth from us without having any expectations of what other people's reaction should be, and what kind of a return we will get.

I raise my voice and take my stand,
a stop to war I do command,
no more shall warring scar the earth,
a golden age is given birth.

O Mother Mary, generate,
the song that does accelerate,

the earth into a higher state,
all matter does now scintillate.

8. I call for the awakening of people to be willing to share from the heart no matter what other people's reactions might be. We are not expecting a particular reaction from other people. We are not wanting them to react a certain way. We are not needing them to validate or affirm us.

As Mother Earth is free at last,
disasters belong to the past,
your Mother Light is so intense,
that matter is now far less dense.

O Mother Mary, generate,
the song that does accelerate,
the earth into a higher state,
all matter does now scintillate.

9. I call for the awakening of people to the realization that the best gift we can give on this planet is to be ourselves, to share of ourselves, and to have a flow from our higher beings through our hearts.

In Mother Light the earth is pure,
the upward spiral will endure,
prosperity is now the norm,
God's vision manifest as form.

O Mother Mary, generate,
the song that does accelerate,
the earth into a higher state,
all matter does now scintillate.

Part 2

1. I call forth the judgment of Christ upon the fallen beings who have manipulated us into thinking that when we express ourselves on this planet, we should be concerned about their reactions. Therefore, we should adapt our expression to other people's reactions.

> O blessed Mary, Mother mine,
> there is no greater love than thine,
> as we are one in heart and mind,
> my place in hierarchy I find.

> **O Mother Mary, generate,**
> **the song that does accelerate,**
> **the earth into a higher state,**
> **all matter does now scintillate.**

2. I call forth the judgment of Christ upon the fallen beings who have created a mechanism where they want all people to think that they have to adapt the expression of their hearts to the expectations and standards of the fallen beings.

> I came to earth from heaven sent,
> as I am in embodiment,
> I use Divine authority,
> commanding you to set earth free.

> **O Mother Mary, generate,**
> **the song that does accelerate,**
> **the earth into a higher state,**
> **all matter does now scintillate.**

3. I call forth the judgment of Christ upon the fallen beings who have manipulated us into thinking that we are not allowed to express our higher beings while we are in a physical body on a planet as limited and as dark as earth.

> I call now in God's sacred name,
> for you to use your Mother Flame,
> to burn all fear-based energy,
> restoring sacred harmony.

> **O Mother Mary, generate,**
> **the song that does accelerate,**
> **the earth into a higher state,**
> **all matter does now scintillate.**

4. I call for the awakening of people to the realization that the Spirit bloweth where it listeth. None have a monopoly, none are the exclusive ones, and none are excluded from being the instrument of the Spirit if they are willing.

> Your sacred name I hereby praise,
> collective consciousness you raise,
> no more of fear and doubt and shame,
> consume it with your Mother Flame.

> **O Mother Mary, generate,**
> **the song that does accelerate,**
> **the earth into a higher state,**
> **all matter does now scintillate.**

5. I call for the awakening of people to see that when we have walked the path for some time, we have the potential to help

others. If we have overcome one aspect of the ego, then we can help other people overcome that aspect.

> All darkness from the earth you purge,
> your light moves as a mighty surge,
> no force of darkness can now stop,
> the spiral that goes only up.

> **O Mother Mary, generate,**
> **the song that does accelerate,**
> **the earth into a higher state,**
> **all matter does now scintillate.**

6. I call for the awakening of people to see that by saying one kind remark, we can change a person's life because we give them an experience they have never had before.

> All elemental life you bless,
> removing from them man-made stress,
> the nature spirits are now free,
> outpicturing Divine decree.

> **O Mother Mary, generate,**
> **the song that does accelerate,**
> **the earth into a higher state,**
> **all matter does now scintillate.**

7. I call for the awakening of people to see that we can make a switch in the mind, we can turn the dial of the mind. We can recognize we have had this insecurity, this shyness in ourselves, but we no longer need it.

I raise my voice and take my stand,
a stop to war I do command,
no more shall warring scar the earth,
a golden age is given birth.

**O Mother Mary, generate,
the song that does accelerate,
the earth into a higher state,
all matter does now scintillate.**

8. I call for the awakening of people to see that we can make
a decision that we will reconnect to our higher beings in our
hearts. We will allow ourselves to speak from that level rather
than speaking from the level of the outer mind and having to
break the ice and feel the other person out before we dare to
open up from the heart.

As Mother Earth is free at last,
disasters belong to the past,
your Mother Light is so intense,
that matter is now far less dense.

**O Mother Mary, generate,
the song that does accelerate,
the earth into a higher state,
all matter does now scintillate.**

9. I call for the awakening of people to see that we can come
to a point where we are always speaking from the heart. We
can learn to recognize when the openness is there, and we can
speak from the heart without having to go through these artificial games that most people play.

In Mother Light the earth is pure,
the upward spiral will endure,
prosperity is now the norm,
God's vision manifest as form.

O Mother Mary, generate,
the song that does accelerate,
the earth into a higher state,
all matter does now scintillate.

Part 3

1. I call forth the judgment of Christ upon the fallen beings who manipulate people by projecting that ideas are more important than the individual and that it is justified to kill other human beings because of an idea.

O blessed Mary, Mother mine,
there is no greater love than thine,
as we are one in heart and mind,
my place in hierarchy I find.

O Mother Mary, generate,
the song that does accelerate,
the earth into a higher state,
all matter does now scintillate.

2. I call for people to be cut free to recognize that this is a lie, this is a manipulation. It is out of touch with the higher reality of the spiritual realm, because an idea exists only in the mind.

There is no idea in the mind that can justify killing the physical body that a spiritual being is using as its expression on earth.

> I came to earth from heaven sent,
> as I am in embodiment,
> I use Divine authority,
> commanding you to set earth free.

> **O Mother Mary, generate,**
> **the song that does accelerate,**
> **the earth into a higher state,**
> **all matter does now scintillate.**

3. I call for people to be cut free to see that physical life on earth is precious because it is an opportunity for growth. When you take away the physical body, you take away that opportunity for the soul's growth, and it is therefore the greatest violation of the free will of that being.

> I call now in God's sacred name,
> for you to use your Mother Flame,
> to burn all fear-based energy,
> restoring sacred harmony.

> **O Mother Mary, generate,**
> **the song that does accelerate,**
> **the earth into a higher state,**
> **all matter does now scintillate.**

4. I call forth the judgment of Christ upon the fallen beings who have defined exceptions to the command: "Thou shalt not kill."

Your sacred name I hereby praise,
collective consciousness you raise,
no more of fear and doubt and shame,
consume it with your Mother Flame.

O Mother Mary, generate,
the song that does accelerate,
the earth into a higher state,
all matter does now scintillate.

5. I call forth the judgment of Christ upon the fallen beings
who get people to kill each other by setting people in conflicts
with each other where they feel that: "If I don't kill them, they
will kill me."

All darkness from the earth you purge,
your light moves as a mighty surge,
no force of darkness can now stop,
the spiral that goes only up.

O Mother Mary, generate,
the song that does accelerate,
the earth into a higher state,
all matter does now scintillate.

6. I call forth the judgment of Christ upon the fallen beings
who get people to kill each other by defining some system of
ideas that justifies the killing of particular human beings.

All elemental life you bless,
removing from them man-made stress,
the nature spirits are now free,
outpicturing Divine decree.

**O Mother Mary, generate,
the song that does accelerate,
the earth into a higher state,
all matter does now scintillate.**

7. I call forth the judgment of Christ upon the fallen beings who manipulate a group of people into feeling superior, and they define a scapegoat that is inferior, perhaps even subhuman. For the betterment of some greater good, it is not only justified, but necessary and desirable to kill the scapegoat.

I raise my voice and take my stand,
a stop to war I do command,
no more shall warring scar the earth,
a golden age is given birth.

**O Mother Mary, generate,
the song that does accelerate,
the earth into a higher state,
all matter does now scintillate.**

8. I call for people to be cut free to see that what blocks genuine communication is that people are trapped in a matrix of ideas where they are not expressing themselves freely because they always compare their behavior to some external standard.

As Mother Earth is free at last,
disasters belong to the past,
your Mother Light is so intense,
that matter is now far less dense.

**O Mother Mary, generate,
the song that does accelerate,**

the earth into a higher state,
all matter does now scintillate.

9. I call for people to be cut free to see that there cannot be
a Golden Age unless people from different nations, groups,
races, ethnic groups, and men and women, can communicate
at the level of the heart.

In Mother Light the earth is pure,
the upward spiral will endure,
prosperity is now the norm,
God's vision manifest as form.

O Mother Mary, generate,
the song that does accelerate,
the earth into a higher state,
all matter does now scintillate.

Part 4

1. I call for people to be cut free to see that the Golden Age
is based on an inner sense of oneness that transcends all the
outer divisions that people have in their outer minds where
they identify with their nationality, race, ethnic group or sex.

O blessed Mary, Mother mine,
there is no greater love than thine,
as we are one in heart and mind,
my place in hierarchy I find.

O Mother Mary, generate,
the song that does accelerate,
the earth into a higher state,
all matter does now scintillate.

2. I call forth the judgment of Christ upon the fallen beings who manipulate people to identify themselves with their nationality and define their nationality being distinctly different from other nationalities, and often in opposition to them or competition with them.

I came to earth from heaven sent,
as I am in embodiment,
I use Divine authority,
commanding you to set earth free.

O Mother Mary, generate,
the song that does accelerate,
the earth into a higher state,
all matter does now scintillate.

3. I call for world leaders to be cut free to sit down and have a talk where they are not president this or chancellor that, they connect and realize they are both human beings and that their peoples are groups of human beings. Thereby, the dynamic shifts and they are able to have genuine communication.

I call now in God's sacred name,
for you to use your Mother Flame,
to burn all fear-based energy,
restoring sacred harmony.

O Mother Mary, generate,
the song that does accelerate,
the earth into a higher state,
all matter does now scintillate.

4. I call forth the judgment of Christ upon the fallen beings who have turned politics into a game where everybody has an idea of how things should be. They are all playing this game at the surface level, never connecting at a deeper level.

Your sacred name I hereby praise,
collective consciousness you raise,
no more of fear and doubt and shame,
consume it with your Mother Flame.

O Mother Mary, generate,
the song that does accelerate,
the earth into a higher state,
all matter does now scintillate.

5. I call for people to be cut free to see that they are longing for something genuine in the arena of politics, that they are ready for a more genuine level of political interaction between nations.

All darkness from the earth you purge,
your light moves as a mighty surge,
no force of darkness can now stop,
the spiral that goes only up.

O Mother Mary, generate,
the song that does accelerate,

the earth into a higher state,
all matter does now scintillate.

6. I call for people to be cut free to see that Europe has the potential to become the forerunner for a more sincere communication, because the European nations have for decades attempted to create a greater union in Europe.

All elemental life you bless,
removing from them man-made stress,
the nature spirits are now free,
outpicturing Divine decree.

O Mother Mary, generate,
the song that does accelerate,
the earth into a higher state,
all matter does now scintillate.

7. I call for people to be cut free to see that this union must be based on a sense of oneness that only comes when we connect at the heart level. So far, we have attempted to create a set of ideas of wanting to overcome the wars from the past.

I raise my voice and take my stand,
a stop to war I do command,
no more shall warring scar the earth,
a golden age is given birth.

O Mother Mary, generate,
the song that does accelerate,
the earth into a higher state,
all matter does now scintillate.

8. I call for people to be cut free to see that what created the division on the European continent was ideas! Therefore, it does not make sense that creating another set of ideas will resolve the conflict.

> As Mother Earth is free at last,
> disasters belong to the past,
> your Mother Light is so intense,
> that matter is now far less dense.
>
> **O Mother Mary, generate,**
> **the song that does accelerate,**
> **the earth into a higher state,**
> **all matter does now scintillate.**

9. I call for people to be cut free to step forward and demand and enact a more genuine communication among their leaders so we can truly transcend the divisions of the past.

> In Mother Light the earth is pure,
> the upward spiral will endure,
> prosperity is now the norm,
> God's vision manifest as form.
>
> **O Mother Mary, generate,**
> **the song that does accelerate,**
> **the earth into a higher state,**
> **all matter does now scintillate.**

Part 5

1. I call for people to be cut free to create a shift in the collective consciousness and say to the politicians: "Find a way to talk to other nations, or get out of the way for there are others who are willing to talk at the heart level, to have a genuine conversation, where we are not seeking to dominate the others, we are seeking to reach some understanding that we have not reached before."

> O blessed Mary, Mother mine,
> there is no greater love than thine,
> as we are one in heart and mind,
> my place in hierarchy I find.
>
> **O Mother Mary, generate,**
> **the song that does accelerate,**
> **the earth into a higher state,**
> **all matter does now scintillate.**

2. I call for European leaders to be cut free from the impasse they are in right now where they all fear for the future. They fear that suddenly the EU they have built so carefully over so many decades, is starting to fracture and come apart from within.

> I came to earth from heaven sent,
> as I am in embodiment,
> I use Divine authority,
> commanding you to set earth free.

**O Mother Mary, generate,
the song that does accelerate,
the earth into a higher state,
all matter does now scintillate.**

3. I call for leaders and people to be cut free to see that the EU is coming apart from within because they have approached it from the same mindset that created the division, and the second law of thermodynamics is doing its work and showing them that it is time to step up to a higher level.

I call now in God's sacred name,
for you to use your Mother Flame,
to burn all fear-based energy,
restoring sacred harmony.

**O Mother Mary, generate,
the song that does accelerate,
the earth into a higher state,
all matter does now scintillate.**

4. I call forth the judgment of Christ upon those who have been trapped in the bureaucratic mindset, in the political mindset, for decades.

Your sacred name I hereby praise,
collective consciousness you raise,
no more of fear and doubt and shame,
consume it with your Mother Flame.

**O Mother Mary, generate,
the song that does accelerate,**

the earth into a higher state,
all matter does now scintillate.

5. I call for people to be cut free to elect new representatives.
I call for a new kind of people to come to the forefront in the
media who will start talking and communicating in a different
way. I call for people who refuse to play all of the games that
have so far created nothing but division and misunderstanding.

All darkness from the earth you purge,
your light moves as a mighty surge,
no force of darkness can now stop,
the spiral that goes only up.

O Mother Mary, generate,
the song that does accelerate,
the earth into a higher state,
all matter does now scintillate.

6. I call for people to be cut free to see that so far cooperation has been based on people realizing that by continuing the
conflict, the consequences would be so severe that they do
not want this so they choose the lesser of two evils. In order
to avoid a greater evil, they agree to something, but this is not
unity. This is not true union.

All elemental life you bless,
removing from them man-made stress,
the nature spirits are now free,
outpicturing Divine decree.

O Mother Mary, generate,
the song that does accelerate,

**the earth into a higher state,
all matter does now scintillate.**

7. I call forth the judgment of Christ upon the mindset that in order to avoid the greater calamity of war and conflict, we have to force ourselves into this outer, political, forced union.

I raise my voice and take my stand,
a stop to war I do command,
no more shall warring scar the earth,
a golden age is given birth.

**O Mother Mary, generate,
the song that does accelerate,
the earth into a higher state,
all matter does now scintillate.**

8. I call for people to be cut free to see that when we have communication at the heart level, we do not need to force ourselves or each other into a political or economic union. We will willingly go into it because we experience that this greater union is not a loss, but a gain. It is not a gain politically, economically, or militarily but a gain in how we feel about ourselves.

As Mother Earth is free at last,
disasters belong to the past,
your Mother Light is so intense,
that matter is now far less dense.

**O Mother Mary, generate,
the song that does accelerate,
the earth into a higher state,
all matter does now scintillate.**

9. I call for people to be cut free to see that the most precious human commodity is how we feel about ourselves. Therefore, we will willingly give up all aspects of the ego, the outer personality, the wounded personality, in order to come into union with our higher selves, come into union with other people, so that we will feel better about who we are.

> In Mother Light the earth is pure,
> the upward spiral will endure,
> prosperity is now the norm,
> God's vision manifest as form.
>
> **O Mother Mary, generate,**
> **the song that does accelerate,**
> **the earth into a higher state,**
> **all matter does now scintillate.**

Sealing

In the name of the Divine Mother, I call to all ascended masters for the sealing of myself and all people in my circle of influence in the creative flow of the Divine Mother, the River of Life. I call for the multiplication of my calls by all ascended masters so that we form the perfect figure-eight flow of "As Above, so below." Thus, I accept that this is fully manifest, because the mouth of the Lord, the Divine Mother that I AM, has spoken it. Amen.

10 | KNOWING THE TRUE PURPOSE OF DEMOCRACY

I AM the Ascended Master Saint Germain. It is my privilege and my choice to be the primary ascended master working with earth for these next 2,000 years. My beloved, in my ongoing unfoldment of the vision I hold for the Golden Age, and how the Golden Age can be brought about, I wish to bring to your attention a topic that is of quite large importance.

When people think their government is good enough

Now, one of the primary shifts in consciousness that happened in most democratic nations when they became democracies was that people in general started having more faith in their governments. They started having the sense that their governments were not out to dominate them, to abuse them, to enslave them, to take advantage of them. They started having a sense that they were living in a more benevolent time, a more benevolent society, where there was not the obvious abuse and enslavement that they had known in the past. This of course is a positive and necessary development. There is, however, a downside of everything when it comes to the human consciousness, the consciousness of duality, and its uncanny ability to take everything into an unbalanced state.

What has happened in many, especially of the older democracies, is that there has developed this consciousness that has become very powerful and often takes over the minds of those people who are part of the democratic government, whether they are among the elected representatives, the bureaucracy, the media, the educational system, whatever. This consciousness is that these people, who are the leaders of democratic societies, basically believe that what they are doing now is good enough. They are fulfilling their responsibility towards the people by ensuring a somewhat peaceful and stable society and a stable economy, and so forth and so on. The perception is that as long as a democratic society is functioning reasonably well according to the standard, then the leaders are fulfilling their obligation and their responsibility towards the people.

Now, what is the standard you are using to judge whether a democracy is functioning well? Well, it is often that you look at other democracies. You look at the history of democracy and, of course, you look at societies that do not have a democratic form of government, and they may not have the same freedoms that you supposedly have in a democratic society. Based on this comparison, then people say: "Well, our democracy is doing quite well, isn't it?" And the other people say: "Yes, yes, we are doing quite well compared to how it was before we had democracy and compared to this other nation." You build this sense that what you have done is good enough.

The responsibility to protect the people

What I would like to point out to you is that, when I look at the state of democratic nations, I see very clearly that there is not a single democratic government that is anywhere near to fulfilling its responsibility towards its people. Why is this so, my beloved? It is because it is the responsibility of a government to protect the people. Well, we should say this is *one* of the responsibilities, but it certainly is a primary responsibility.

You think that, if you have some kind of army, if there is not war and the threat of war, if you have a police force, if you have various services in terms of health, and so on, if you have an educational system, this is good enough. But is that truly protecting the people? Well it is, but is it sufficient protection?

We need to step up here and recognize that there has always been two kinds of evil on earth. One is the obvious one that everyone sees and sees as evil. The other is a hidden one that most people do not see. We have the more obvious forms of evil, and most democratic nations think they are protecting their people against those, and many of them *are* to a large degree. How many democratic nations have honestly and openly acknowledged the hidden forces of evil, and have acknowledged that they are not protecting their people against them? How can you protect your people against something that you do not even know exists, and you do not understand the nature of it. Therefore, what chance do you have? How could you protect your people against cholera before you knew that there is a bacteria that creates this disease?

The right to freedom from exploitation

I am not at this point envisioning that most people in the democratic world are ready to step up and consciously acknowledge the teaching that we have on fallen beings and dark forces. Naturally, the gap between the understanding that people have been given, either from materialism or Christianity, is very large. But there are universal aspects of our teachings that certainly can be grasped. If you look at democracy, you see that a very important idea behind democracy is that all people have certain rights. You have a right to happiness, life, liberty.

What has *not* so far been defined in any democratic constitution, but which needs to be defined, is that all human beings have the right to live in freedom from exploitation. You will see that democratic nations have, to some degree, freed their people from the more obvious forms of exploitation. You do not have a dictatorial leader who has a right to kill anyone he wants. There is a rule of law, there is a certain protection against the abuse of power. There is a certain protection against being exploited by other people for various purposes. But these are not the only forms of exploitation. They are only the forms that have been recognized by society or by people at large.

It is necessary for the Golden Age to be manifest that there is a rising awareness that there are many more subtle forms of exploitation that are being imposed upon the people. I will therefore attempt to express this without referring to fallen beings and dark forces, but simply referring to what most people in democratic nations can lock in to, namely that there has throughout history been various power elite groups who have attempted to exploit the people.

Democracy and power elites

It is not so difficult for a critical mass of people to step up and realize that just because you enact a democratic form of government, this does not mean that you automatically get a society that is free from all power elites. This is not difficult to grasp for many, many people who have already started grasping this. What we need to envision, what we need to make calls for, is that they will be raised to a higher vision of this than what they get through the conspiracy theories and various websites that are always trying to be sensationalist. They are often portraying this in such a way that people do not think they can do anything about these hidden elites that are seeking to manipulate and take over society. The reality of the matter is, of course, that people can indeed do something about any power elite group. But they can do it in only one way: through awareness.

The people cannot free themselves from any power elite until they become aware that the power elite exists, that it has certain intentions, that it has certain methods, and that it has used certain ideas to hide from the people and hide its intentions and methods from the people. Naturally, you have seen in history how people in various nations have become aware of a certain power elite, and they have done what has happened so many times: used violence to defeat the power elite. This, of course, will in no way bring the Golden Age. Violence and force cannot bring Saint Germain's Golden Age into manifestation, for it is a Golden Age based on an entirely higher vision. We need to step up and recognize that the key to overcoming the power elite, the key to freeing yourself and the people from exploitation by a power elite, is to raise awareness. Why is this so? Why is it not enough to just know that a power elite is there so you can put them all under the guillotine? Well, it is because if you put one power elite under the guillotine, my beloved, another power elite will immediately start forming. Was that not the lesson you can learn from the French Revolution? Was it not the lesson you can learn from many other situations in history?

What will it take for the people to be free from the power elite? It is that you recognize the influence of consciousness. The power elite can never suppress the people only through violence and force. There must be some mental idea, as Mother Mary explained, that is fooling the people into thinking that they cannot do without the elite, or fooling them into simply not seeing what the elite is doing. There is always a limited awareness in the people that creates the opening for the power elite to step in and exploit the people. Therefore, raising awareness is the key, but the awareness needs to be raised beyond simply knowing about the power elite.

My beloved, this is also the main reason why most conspiracy theories have no constructive role whatsoever. They attempt to raise people's awareness of this or that secret conspiracy, but they never raise the awareness further, even if it is true what they are saying, which it often is not. They never raise the awareness to the point where the people start seeing what is the element of their own consciousness that allows the formation and existence of that elite. This is the vision I am asking you to hold, and of course make the calls that we can enter a spiral where more and more people become willing to reach for this increased awareness.

A benevolent power elite

My beloved, in strictly universal terms, many people can understand that as a free person you need to be free of exploitation. As a citizen in a democratic nation, you have a right to be free of the exploitation of the power elite, or any other group of people that are taking advantage of you. It is not so big of a leap to have these people see that it is actually the responsibility of a democratic government to look at their society and look at whether there is a hidden power elite, and what is the agenda and the methods of that power elite. Until a governmental apparatus has done this, it has not fulfilled its obligation, and this is universally acceptable for a lot of people.

It is also universally acceptable that you need to look at various aspects of society to see how, even in democratic nations, a power elite can form and in some cases, as I have said before, they are not necessarily evil people. They do not necessarily have a malevolent intention, but they have a limited vision. It is a self-centered vision where they tend to see the universe through their personal filter. They are thinking that there is some aspect of the universe that justifies their existence, their superiority, their control and their power.

What is the purpose of democracy?

Many of these power elites in democratic nations still believe that somehow, whether it is by nature or by the hand of God, they are better equipped to rule. They simply are more intelligent and they know better, they have greater power, they know far better than the people how the country should be run. The foundational principle of democracy is that nobody knows better than the people how the country should be run.

This is a surprising statement to many because they will point to examples from history where the people would have voted for something that later would have been disastrous, or where they did vote for something that turned out to be disastrous. Some will point to the election in the United States as an example of this, but I will let that one pass to another time because I want to show you something very, very simple.

What is the purpose of democracy? Well, this is a question that very few people have asked, and certainly no democratic government has asked this question. What is the purpose of democracy? This, you cannot understand without looking at consciousness. Again, in strictly universal terms, it is not so difficult to look at history, especially over the past couple of thousand years, and look at the fact that there has been incredible progress in society, especially in terms of technology, incredible progress compared to the time of Jesus. You know very well that Jesus rode into Jerusalem on a donkey, but you know also that today he would have had a choice of many more sophisticated means of transportation. I am not here going to talk about which one he would have chosen. I will leave that to him, but nevertheless, there has been tremendous progress and it is undeniable.

How has this progress come about? A simple question with a simple answer: raising of awareness. It is not just a matter of knowledge, my beloved. It is a matter of the raising of the awareness. If you would care to look at what the average person knew, thought, understood about life, 2,000 years ago and compare it to the average person today in a democratic nation, you would see that there has been a tremendous raising of the awareness of the people. Tremendous. You can barely imagine today how limited people's consciousness was 2,000 years ago, how limited was their world view, their view of themselves, their ability to even ask questions about what kind of beings they are. There has been a tremendous raising of awareness.

Why has democracy come about? For thousands of years, the dominant form of government has been a dictatorship. Why did democracy suddenly emerge? Well, it can only be because there was a raising of the awareness of the people. It is not so difficult to look at certain discoveries of science and recognize that there must be a collective consciousness. You have many examples of this, even acknowledged and supported by scientific instruments, evidence, and experiments.

It is not impossible or difficult for people to step up and realize that there has been a raising of the collective consciousness, the collective awareness. Then, it is not so difficult to realize that the continuation of progress depends on the continuation of the raising of the collective awareness. How else will progress continue (when it has so far been driven by this raising of awareness) unless we also continue to raise people's awareness? Then, it is not so difficult to look at history and see that in the past there have been various power elites who have been very aggressive in limiting what the people knew, but also limiting the people's awareness.

You have seen in recent history how the communist nations were very strict in censoring what kind of information people were allowed to have because the leaders realized that the only way they could prevent a revolt was that the people in communist nations, in the Soviet Union, did not know how much better life was in the West. If people had known this, they would have rebelled against their station, but they thought they could not have anything better. You know, even today that the Chinese government is censoring the Internet and what people in China can access on the Internet. You know, of course, the

North Korean government is strictly censoring what people are allowed to know about the outside world. You can go back and see how, for over a thousand years, the Catholic church was censoring what people were allowed to know, what books they were allowed to read.

You can quickly step up and realize that the primary weapon of a power elite has always been to attempt to restrict the awareness of the people. You can then take the next step and say that if a democratic government is supposed to guarantee the freedom of its citizens, then this can be achieved in only one way, namely, by making sure that there is not a power elite that is hidden from the people, that is restricting what the people know, whether it be about the power elite or about other topics.

Therefore, it is one of the primary responsibilities of a democratic government to make sure that the people have access to free and complete information about how society works. As a democratic citizen, you have a right to be informed because if you are not informed, how can you make free choices? It cannot be done.

How far can you then take this, once you recognize that it is the responsibility of a democratic government to look at society, to look if there is a hidden power elite that the people do not know about, then to expose that power elite and to also look if there is some kind of mechanism in society that is restricting the knowledge and the awareness of the people. Once you recognize that this is a responsibility, you can begin to make demands about what a government should actually do, what the press should do, what the educational institutions should do.

Exploitation by disinformation

My beloved, this is when you can begin to open up for a consideration of how people on earth have been exploited throughout history by disinformation. Not only a lack of information, but direct disinformation—wrongful, intentionally and maliciously wrongful information. Then, again in strictly universal terms, you can begin to consider what areas of society are influenced by various forms of disinformation. As just one example of how this can be done, you have in most Western democracies a situation where this country was for many, many centuries dominated by the Catholic church first, and some countries then by the Protestant churches for the last five hundred years. Is it unreasonable to consider what kind of disinformation was put upon the people through Catholic and Protestant Christianity?

Then of course, you can see that many Western nations have, for the last two or three hundred years, been dominated by materialistic science, by a materialistic view of life. Again, you can ask the question (and this is a fairly universal, obvious question): "What kind of disinformation has been put upon the people through materialism?" Was there a power elite that took advantage of the Christian religion to program the people and limit the people with disinformation? Well, it does not take a very close look at history to see that of course there was. From the very beginning, there was a power elite around the emperor Constantine who wanted to use Christianity to control his people. This continued until the Catholic church started losing influence over societies. It does not take a genius to see this. It just takes a willingness to ask the right questions and look for the obvious answers. The answers that, as in so many cases, become obvious once you ask the right question.

Is it, then, such a big leap to ask if there is one or several power elite groups who have also taken advantage, not just of science but actually of scientific materialism to again put disinformation on the people? Of course, you can then expand this and look at the economy. Is there a power elite that does not want the people to understand how the money system works? Well, how many people in democratic nations understand how the money system works? Very few. Could this possibly be engineered by a power elite that does not want people to understand how the money system works? If so, why would a power elite not want the people to understand how the money system works? Perhaps it is because there is a power elite that is exploiting the people through the money system, and they know that if the people really understood how the money system works, they would not go along with this?

Well, is it not the responsibility of a democratic government to take a look at how the economy actually works and tell the people how it works, and then let the people decide whether they want to continue the current economy or whether they want to look for a better system? Would it really be beyond the responsibility of a democratic government to do this? I think not.

Public debate about exploitation

I know that there are many, many people in embodiment right now who are coming into that awareness where they also realize that there is a need to take a critical look at society. What I am asking you to do is to make the calls, and also look yourselves so that you could be the forerunners for directing the attention of these people into focusing on the need to be free from exploitation by an elite. If this could be achieved, and it is a realistic goal, it could have a tremendous impact on the public debate in democratic nations.

I am not looking here at any violent uprisings against the power elite, for this is not necessary and it is not my vision. You understand that at the moment a critical mass of people shift their consciousness, then a democratic nation will shift and changes will have to be made. If you look at my efforts to give freedom to humankind, why do you think that I wanted to create a period where most people lived in democratic nations? It is because a democratic nation is far more responsive to the consciousness of the people than a totalitarian form of government. Even a totalitarian form of government is somewhat responsive to the consciousness of the people, but a democratic government is far more responsive. When the consciousness of the people shifts, the government must change its behavior, its laws, its procedures and goals.

This is, of course, all tied in with the greater goal of the Golden Age, which is not, as I have said before, that I am going to drop this Golden Age down upon the people as if I was some almighty god sitting up here, which I am not and which has never been my intention. The Golden Age can only be created when there are people in embodiment who co-create it with me by tuning in to the ideas and by acting upon them. Again, how can you manifest the Golden Age if you do not have the vision, the awareness, of what is even possible?

What is the primary exploitation foisted upon the people by the power elites that you have seen through history? It is precisely that there are so many things on earth that are seen as insurmountable obstacles, as limitations you cannot go beyond: "There is nothing you can do about that. You will run out of oil and there is nothing you can do about it." Well, my beloved, this is one of the most severe forms of exploitation of the people. All of these limitations prevent the people from actually accepting that a better society is possible.

Programmed to accept limitations

Go back just a few hundred years. Look at the fact that in what are now most of the democratic nations, the majority of the population could not read and write. They could not read books that could give them a higher vision. Go back 200 years and take the average person back then. Explain to him what kind of society you have today and he would refuse to believe you. He would label this as complete utopia, complete daydreaming, complete fantasy. Yet, you are experiencing it as a daily reality.

You always have enough food to eat. You do not have to show up at the landowner's land and work for free. You do not have to be afraid of the police. You do not have to work sixteen hours a day just to survive physically. You do not have to walk if you want to get somewhere. You can get into a car and by pushing a button, you are moving forward. Who would believe this 200 years ago? If you are going far away, you get into some machine that takes off into the sky, my beloved. How would they have looked at this? Complete fantasy.

What I am pointing out here is that if you go back 200 years, you can see that with their level of awareness, they could not accept that the society you have today was even possible. What am I seeking to point out with this? It is that most people today cannot accept that the Golden Age that I envision – and that I know is a realistic possibility – these people cannot in any way accept that this Golden Age is truly possible. Even though they have seen so much technological progress in the last hundred years, even though they have seen so many changes in society, they still would not be able to accept my vision of what is possible in the Golden Age. This is an engineered state put upon the people by the power elites of all time who want to restrict their vision and their ability to accept what is possible because if a majority of the people thinks something is impossible, then it will for all practical purposes be impossible.

How can people accept the Golden Age?

I am one of the primary ascended masters who have sponsored the release of most of the technology you see in the modern world. Why have I done this? Because I knew that there was no way that the people of a few hundred years ago could step up in their minds to accept my vision for the Golden Age. Therefore, I needed to bring forth mechanical technology that had visible, undeniable effects that were beyond what people could envision just decades ago. When they saw this technology, and when they saw that here it was demonstrated that what their parents thought was impossible is now possible, well then, it could gradually open their minds to see greater possibilities. This has, to a large degree, happened, but it has not happened to the degree where people can accept the Golden Age as I fully envision it. This is what I look for you to make the calls on, to envision in your minds that people will go even higher.

It is, in fact, not unrealistic that many people will begin to understand that the most subtle and the most dangerous form of exploitation is when a small power elite limits the vision and the awareness of the population. The power elite limits what people believe is possible, what they can even dare to dream about. This of course has only one purpose, and it is easy enough for people to see this. It is that the members of the power elite want to stay in control, they want to stay in power, and in order to do this, they will always try to maintain status quo. How do they maintain status quo? By limiting the people's awareness so the people think that it is not possible to manifest a much better society, a much higher state: "We have pretty much gone as far as we can go."

Have you not seen how even in the modern world this is being programmed into the collective consciousness: "We have gone as high as we can go. We have discovered all there is to discover. We have reached the limits for growth. We are running out of resources." This and that limitation, and the purpose is simply to limit people's ability to envision and accept that there is a much better state waiting in the future. There are also those who say that what we have is good enough and we do not need to go any higher, we just need to maintain the current democracies. There is no need to step up to a higher level with direct democracy, and this and that. All of this has only one purpose: to keep the power elite in power. Millions of people are ready to consciously acknowledge this. They already know it within and when presented to them, it will seem obvious to them.

The real goal of democracy

Now, you will notice that so far I have spoken without talking about the more esoteric aspects of our teachings, such as ascended masters, fallen beings, this or that. These are just universal concepts that people are ready to grasp at some level or other. It is possible to go even a little further because it is possible to look at the fact that whatever progress has been made in society, there has always been an elite who tried to take advantage of it. I have given teachings before that it is obvious to see that there is an established power elite, and at certain times in history you have seen the emergence of an aspiring power elite that have then managed to abuse the people, to exploit the people. They did overthrow the established power elite, but only to the effect that the aspiring power elite now took over and now they became the established power elite.

It is possible to help people see that this is a pattern that has repeated over and over again. "Maybe it is time in our democratic nations that we make an effort to realize that even though the creation of democracies overthrew the established elite of the king or the emperor or the noble class, there has been an aspiring power elite who has attempted to exploit democracy to set themselves up, having power and privileges beyond the population? It is the next logical step for democracy that we expose this, and that we free the people from this condition."

Let me reach back to my earlier statement that many people would be surprised by the statement that the people always know what is best for democracy. Well, why is that so? Can you not see that there is an elite who are more aware and better educated than the general population, and why would not this elite then know better than the people? Well, it is because, as I started saying before I digressed myself into other topics, the goal of democracy is not to manifest a certain outer state.

What is the goal of democracy, really? It is that democracy finds its place in the ongoing raising of the collective awareness. Democracy is a more sophisticated schoolroom for the people than a dictatorship because the people have greater responsibility and greater influence. The primary goal of history is not to create some static society in some ultimate state, but it is the ongoing raising of the awareness of the people. This can be grasped even by people who do not believe in reincarnation, ascended masters or any spiritual purpose. You can just look at history that has been an ongoing raising of the awareness of the people, and why should this not continue? Democracy is a part of that process. Democracy is a form of government that places greater responsibility on the people because they vote, and they can only vote based on what they know. This requires them to raise their awareness so they can make better decisions for their country.

If you recognize that the goal of democracy is not to manifest some ultimate state, but it is actually to raise the awareness of the people, then you see that the people always know best what is right for their country. The purpose of a democracy is to give people the opportunity to have a direct influence on their government, and then to see the result of this. Whether the result is this or that, whether some would call it good or bad, or right or wrong, by the mere fact that the people make a decision and see the consequences, there will be a raising of awareness. That is why, my beloved, the people always know best because they are voting based on their current level of consciousness. What is best for the nation? It is that the people express their current level of consciousness, see the consequences, and therefore are given an opportunity to raise their consciousness.

From a certain perspective, you can say that the people do not know better. From a larger perspective, they actually know better in the sense that what they know or do not know will create consequences that will force them to raise their awareness. When you realize that this is the goal, then you also see why the power elites are not right and are not necessary. What have the power elites always been doing? They have been working against the raising of the awareness of the people because that is the only way they can control them.

Why elites cannot rule

You see, therefore, that the people, in a certain sense, always know best because they are outplaying their current state of consciousness, and when they see the results, they get the maximum opportunity to raise their awareness. The people will not get the maximum opportunity to raise their awareness by a small power elite coming out and saying: "This is the right thing for you." Now, this power elite may be right, my beloved (or an intellectual elite or a political elite). They may be benevolent people. They may have the right vision of which direction the country should go in, but do you see my point? Until the people see it from within themselves, we have not made progress towards the Golden Age because we have not raised awareness. It is not a small elite (even a small elite of educated people or spiritual people) that will bring the Golden Age into manifestation because the bottom line is always the awareness of the people.

You can have certain individuals who, whether they follow the spiritual path in this lifetime or not, have raised their awareness to the point where they could receive an idea from me for a new kind of technology that could bring society forward. I cannot release that technology until the awareness of the people has been raised to a certain level. This is the simple equation. I know that now we are moving beyond what most people can accept from a universal perspective, but I want to give you this perspective. I also want you to hold the vision that many people will be able to again look at the universal perspective.

What kind of beings are we?

Once we recognize that consciousness is important, that there is a collective consciousness, that it has been raised throughout history (especially over the past 2,000 years), then we can start asking a question that has rarely been asked, and that is: "What kind of beings are we?" There are millions of people in embodiment right now who are already grappling with this question. That is why many of them are looking at all of these alternative news, alternative forms of spirituality, New Age forms of spirituality, whatever you have. Why is this? Why are they looking at these? It is simply because they know in some part of their beings that they have not been given an accurate view of who they are through traditional Christianity and scientific materialism.

It is therefore quite possible for you to make the calls and envision that these people will shift their awareness to realize that the next logical step in the raising of the collective awareness is that you come into a greater awareness of the role of consciousness. Human beings are conscious beings; you are conscious first, and human beings second. In other words, your consciousness is not a product of the brain. Your consciousness is beyond the physical body, expresses itself through the physical body, but is more than the body.

Millions of people are already open to this. Millions more are ready to become open to it and embrace these ideas, and therefore say: "It is high time that we use our common sense to go beyond the view of ourselves that we have been given by Christianity that we are sinners, that we are limited beings. It is also high time that we go beyond the view given to us by science that we are evolved apes, that we are material beings, and that our consciousness basically has no capability beyond the physical body. It is high time that we use the tools developed by science to investigate consciousness to find out what kind of beings are we really."

I have said before that, in many of the older democracies, the major challenge that you are facing in the healthcare system is mental illness. What is mental illness? Well, it is again a lack of awareness, and it is a lack of awareness of what kind of beings you are, what consciousness is, what it means to be a conscious being, how you actually function like a conscious being. My beloved, look at medical science and how, over the last hundred years, you have increased your knowledge of how the physical body works, how there are these subtle processes in the physical body, how you need minerals, vitamins, hormones, this and that, in order for the body to function. Is it really so difficult to look at the human psyche and say: "Well it is relatively simple to map physical behavior, but much more complex to map the psychological behavior of human beings, and this must mean that the psyche is far more complex than the physical body. If there are all these processes in the physical body, is it not logical that there is much more to know about the psyche than we have discovered so far. Therefore, it is high time that we start investigating this, and we get rid of these biases of materialism that have held science hostage now for 200 years because there was an aspiring power elite that took over science and wanted to distance themselves from the old power elite that ruled religion."

It is time that we, as a democratic society, as a democratic government, say: "We will have nothing to do with either of these power elites and we want to set the minds of the people free. We want to set the collective mind free so that we can sincerely investigate who we are, what kind of beings we are, what it takes for us to function psychologically."

This is right under the surface, ready to break through where millions of people suddenly see that this is obvious, that this is a logical next step, and that we need to do this. Again, this has nothing to do with ascended masters or a particular spiritual direction or teaching. It is universal. Of course, once you have people starting to objectively look at consciousness, all kinds of avenues can open up. When you discover what kind of beings you truly are, you will realize that you are spiritual beings, that you came from a different realm, a different vibrational spectrum. Then, you can take some of the discoveries of science that have already pointed to the existence of this, and all of a sudden there are many more things that can be opened up.

Universal spirituality that unites people

Therefore, it is not unrealistic that within decades, people will begin more and more to acknowledge the existence of spiritual beings and the spiritual realm. There can be a great shift, not that people suddenly start following one religion or one spiritual teaching, but that there is a universal body of spiritual knowledge that suddenly starts emerging in people's consciousness. Even though they may express it by being members of a particular organization or following a particular teaching, they see that there is so much commonality that it gives them that greater sense of togetherness, oneness and unity. Suddenly, there can be a shift where spirituality no longer divides people but actually brings them together, not in one teaching and one movement, but in the universal awareness that has been talked about previously where they connect in the heart. They realize that even though they may have different outer beliefs and practices and rituals, there is some common knowledge that they are spiritual beings and therefore, we have something in common regardless of how we decide to express it.

This is again fairly universal, but of course it can also lead to a greater recognition of the existence of ascended masters, of the validity of our teachings, and it can bring many more people into looking at those teachings and thereby shifting their consciousness even more. It can even open up for a more widespread recognition of the existence of fallen beings and the need to transcend a certain level of consciousness so they can be removed from the planet. Many things can start happening once you get over that critical hump of recognizing that a democratic nation's primary responsibility is to be dedicated to raising the awareness of the people so that they can make more and more free choices. For only the person who is aware of all options, and the consequences of the options, can make a truly free choice.

The power elites of all time, including the ones in democratic societies, have always wanted the people to sign the contract without reading the fine print. It is time that the people are allowed to read the fine print so they can decide whether they want to sign the contract with the power elite. If they do not, then, of course, it is a responsibility of a democratic government to take the power away from the elite and give it back to the people. What else would be the responsibility? How can it be the responsibility of a democratic government to maintain status quo where the people are dominated and exploited by a power elite?

The most severe form of exploitation

If we return to the topic of exploitation, then the most subtle and severe form of exploitation is that the people have been programmed with disinformation about what kind of beings they are, and what are the true possibilities for their own consciousness, for the collective consciousness, and for creating a better age. This is a very severe, very insidious form of exploitation. Exploitation by disinformation about who you are.

I ask you to be aware of this, to raise your own consciousness, to make the calls, and you will, my beloved, see that there will be breakthroughs in the raising of the collective awareness. Therefore, you will see changes in democratic nations. Much of it can start here in Europe. That is why this dictation is given here. Of course, Europe is not the only place in the world where these breakthroughs can happen, but it is certainly the place where many people are prepared, where many people have embodied. What is the primary requirement for these changes to happen? It is the willingness to openly debate and talk about issues, the state where society no longer has so many taboos that cannot be talked about.

This is another weapon of the power elite: to create a taboo: "We cannot talk about this." You need to see that in a democracy, there is, or there cannot be, there *must* not be, any topic that you cannot talk about. It is precisely behind the topics that you cannot talk about that the power elite can hide, and that is what limits the people. It starts by talking, and that is the opening for the raising of awareness, and the raising of awareness is the direct cause of changes in the physical world. That has always been so. It will always be so. It is, in fact, within the grasp of a large part of the population to recognize this: the role of consciousness in creating and manifesting physical conditions. It is a shift that many people are close to. Many have made it, but many more are close to making that shift.

As we have said, consciousness always comes before the physical manifestation. When you know this, and when you recognize this, and when you take responsibility for your consciousness, that is when you can free yourself from all forms of exploitation. If you will not acknowledge that consciousness precedes physical manifestation, then you cannot free yourself from the exploitation by one power elite or another, even one after another.

I thank you with the sincerity of my heart for being here, for being willing to open your minds and your chakras to be the loudspeakers, so to speak, to radiate my ideas, my vibration, my Being, my Presence, into the collective consciousness. Truly, it has been a powerful release and I am grateful for your willingness to participate. Naturally, I have more to say on the topic of the Golden Age, but it shall be manifest at the right time. So for now, my gratitude and my love.

11 | INVOKING FREEDOM FROM EXPLOITATION

In the name I AM THAT I AM, Jesus Christ, I call to all ascended masters working on manifesting the Golden Age, especially Saint Germain, to radiate into the collective consciousness a new awareness of how we can free ourselves from even subtle forms of exploitation. Help people see that we can build a new future by working with the ascended masters and letting go of the old way of looking at life, including…

[Make personal calls.]

Part 1

1. I call for people to be cut free to see that when a nation becomes a democracy, it is natural for people to develop more faith in their government, so they do not feel it is out to dominate them, to abuse them, to enslave them, to take advantage of them.

O Saint Germain, you do inspire,
my vision raised forever higher,
with you I form a figure-eight,
your Golden Age I co-create.

**O Saint Germain, what love you bring,
it truly makes all matter sing,
your violet flame does all restore,
with you we are becoming more.**

2. I call forth the judgment of Christ upon the consciousness
that has developed in many of the older democracies, where
those who are part of the democratic government believe that
what they are doing now is good enough.

O Saint Germain, what Freedom Flame,
released when we recite your name,
acceleration is your gift,
our planet it will surely lift.

**O Saint Germain, what love you bring,
it truly makes all matter sing,
your violet flame does all restore,
with you we are becoming more.**

3. I call forth the judgment of Christ upon the consciousness
that leaders are fulfilling their responsibility towards the people by ensuring a somewhat peaceful and stable society and
economy.

O Saint Germain, in love we claim,
our right to bring your violet flame,

from you Above, to us below,
it is an all-transforming flow.

O Saint Germain, what love you bring,
it truly makes all matter sing,
your violet flame does all restore,
with you we are becoming more.

4. I call forth the judgment of Christ upon the perception that as long as a democratic society is functioning reasonably well according to its own standard, then the leaders are fulfilling their obligation and their responsibility towards the people.

O Saint Germain, I love you so,
my aura filled with violet glow,
my chakras filled with violet fire,
I am your cosmic amplifier.

O Saint Germain, what love you bring,
it truly makes all matter sing,
your violet flame does all restore,
with you we are becoming more.

5. I call for people to be cut free to see that it is not enough to compare a democracy to other democracies or to non-democratic nations and use this to evaluate how well a nation is doing.

O Saint Germain, I am now free,
your violet flame is therapy,
transform all hang-ups in my mind,
as inner peace I surely find.

O Saint Germain, what love you bring,
it truly makes all matter sing,
your violet flame does all restore,
with you we are becoming more.

6. I call for people to be cut free to see that there is not a single democratic government that is anywhere near to fulfilling its responsibility to protect the people from exploitation.

O Saint Germain, my body pure,
your violet flame for all is cure,
consume the cause of all disease,
and therefore I am all at ease.

O Saint Germain, what love you bring,
it truly makes all matter sing,
your violet flame does all restore,
with you we are becoming more.

7. I call for people to be cut free to see that there has always been two kinds of evil on earth. One is the obvious one that everyone sees and sees as evil. The other is a hidden one that most people do not see.

O Saint Germain, I'm karma-free,
the past no longer burdens me,
a brand new opportunity,
I am in Christic unity.

O Saint Germain, what love you bring,
it truly makes all matter sing,
your violet flame does all restore,
with you we are becoming more.

8. I call for people to be cut free to see that most democratic nations are protecting their people against the obvious forms of evil, but they have not honestly and openly acknowledged the hidden forces of evil. Therefore, they have not seen that they are not protecting their people against them.

> O Saint Germain, we are now one,
> I am for you a violet sun,
> as we transform this planet earth,
> your Golden Age is given birth.

> **O Saint Germain, what love you bring,**
> **it truly makes all matter sing,**
> **your violet flame does all restore,**
> **with you we are becoming more.**

9. I call for people to be cut free to see that what needs to be defined in any democratic constitution, is that all human beings have the right to live in freedom from exploitation.

> O Saint Germain, the earth is free,
> from burden of duality,
> in oneness we bring what is best,
> your Golden Age is manifest.

> **O Saint Germain, what love you bring,**
> **it truly makes all matter sing,**
> **your violet flame does all restore,**
> **with you we are becoming more.**

Part 2

1. I call for people to be cut free to see that democratic nations have, to some degree, freed their people from the more obvious forms of exploitation. But there are more subtle forms of exploitation because throughout history various power elite groups have attempted to exploit the people.

> O Saint Germain, you do inspire,
> my vision raised forever higher,
> with you I form a figure-eight,
> your Golden Age I co-create.

> **O Saint Germain, what love you bring,**
> **it truly makes all matter sing,**
> **your violet flame does all restore,**
> **with you we are becoming more.**

2. I call for people to be cut free to see that enacting a democratic form of government does not mean that we automatically get a society that is free from all power elites.

> O Saint Germain, what Freedom Flame,
> released when we recite your name,
> acceleration is your gift,
> our planet it will surely lift.

> **O Saint Germain, what love you bring,**
> **it truly makes all matter sing,**
> **your violet flame does all restore,**
> **with you we are becoming more.**

3. I call for people to be cut free to see that we can do something about any power elite group, but we can do it only through awareness. We cannot free ourselves from any power elite until we become aware that the power elite exists, that it has certain intentions and methods, and that it has used certain ideas to hide from us.

O Saint Germain, in love we claim,
our right to bring your violet flame,
from you Above, to us below,
it is an all-transforming flow.

**O Saint Germain, what love you bring,
it truly makes all matter sing,
your violet flame does all restore,
with you we are becoming more.**

4. I call for people to be cut free to see that using violence to defeat the power elite will not bring the Golden Age. Violence and force cannot bring Saint Germain's Golden Age into manifestation, for it is a Golden Age based on an entirely higher vision.

O Saint Germain, I love you so,
my aura filled with violet glow,
my chakras filled with violet fire,
I am your cosmic amplifier.

**O Saint Germain, what love you bring,
it truly makes all matter sing,
your violet flame does all restore,
with you we are becoming more.**

5. I call for people to be cut free to see that the key to overcoming the power elite, the key to freeing ourselves and the people from exploitation by a power elite, is to raise awareness. If we put one power elite under the guillotine, another power elite will immediately start forming.

O Saint Germain, I am now free,
your violet flame is therapy,
transform all hang-ups in my mind,
as inner peace I surely find.

O Saint Germain, what love you bring,
it truly makes all matter sing,
your violet flame does all restore,
with you we are becoming more.

6. I call for people to be cut free to see that in order to be free from the power elite, we need to recognize the influence of consciousness. The power elite can never suppress us only through violence and force. There must be some mental idea that is fooling us into thinking that we cannot do without the elite.

O Saint Germain, my body pure,
your violet flame for all is cure,
consume the cause of all disease,
and therefore I am all at ease.

O Saint Germain, what love you bring,
it truly makes all matter sing,
your violet flame does all restore,
with you we are becoming more.

7. I call for people to be cut free to see that there is always a limited awareness in the people that creates the opening for the power elite to step in and exploit us. Raising awareness is the key, but the awareness needs to be raised beyond simply knowing about the power elite.

O Saint Germain, I'm karma-free,
the past no longer burdens me,
a brand new opportunity,
I am in Christic unity.

O Saint Germain, what love you bring,
it truly makes all matter sing,
your violet flame does all restore,
with you we are becoming more.

8. I call for people to be cut free to see that we need to raise awareness to the point where we start seeing what is the element of our own consciousness that allows the formation and existence of an elite.

O Saint Germain, we are now one,
I am for you a violet sun,
as we transform this planet earth,
your Golden Age is given birth.

O Saint Germain, what love you bring,
it truly makes all matter sing,
your violet flame does all restore,
with you we are becoming more.

9. I call for people to be cut free to enter a spiral where more and more people become willing to reach for this increased awareness.

> O Saint Germain, the earth is free,
> from burden of duality,
> in oneness we bring what is best,
> your Golden Age is manifest.

> **O Saint Germain, what love you bring,**
> **it truly makes all matter sing,**
> **your violet flame does all restore,**
> **with you we are becoming more.**

Part 3

1. I call for people to be cut free to see that it is the responsibility of a democratic government to look at their society and look at whether there is a hidden power elite, and what is the agenda and the methods of that power elite. Until a governmental apparatus has done this, it has not fulfilled its obligation to its people.

> O Saint Germain, you do inspire,
> my vision raised forever higher,
> with you I form a figure-eight,
> your Golden Age I co-create.

> **O Saint Germain, what love you bring,**
> **it truly makes all matter sing,**

**your violet flame does all restore,
with you we are becoming more.**

2. I call for people to be cut free to see that members of a power elite are not necessarily evil people. They do not necessarily have a malevolent intention, but they have a limited vision.

O Saint Germain, what Freedom Flame,
released when we recite your name,
acceleration is your gift,
our planet it will surely lift.

**O Saint Germain, what love you bring,
it truly makes all matter sing,
your violet flame does all restore,
with you we are becoming more.**

3. I call for people to be cut free to see that members of a benevolent power elite have a self-centered vision. They think that there is some aspect of the universe that justifies their existence, their superiority, their control, and their power.

O Saint Germain, in love we claim,
our right to bring your violet flame,
from you Above, to us below,
it is an all-transforming flow.

**O Saint Germain, what love you bring,
it truly makes all matter sing,
your violet flame does all restore,
with you we are becoming more.**

4. I call for people to be cut free to see that members of power elites in democratic nations believe that somehow, whether it is by nature or by the hand of God, they are better equipped to rule. They are more intelligent, and they know better, they have greater power, they know far better than the people how the country should be run.

> O Saint Germain, I love you so,
> my aura filled with violet glow,
> my chakras filled with violet fire,
> I am your cosmic amplifier.

> **O Saint Germain, what love you bring,**
> **it truly makes all matter sing,**
> **your violet flame does all restore,**
> **with you we are becoming more.**

5. I call for people to be cut free to see that the foundational principle of democracy is that nobody knows better than the people how the country should be run. The purpose of democracy is the raising of the consciousness of the people.

> O Saint Germain, I am now free,
> your violet flame is therapy,
> transform all hang-ups in my mind,
> as inner peace I surely find.

> **O Saint Germain, what love you bring,**
> **it truly makes all matter sing,**
> **your violet flame does all restore,**
> **with you we are becoming more.**

6. I call for people to be cut free to see that democracy emerged because there was a raising of the awareness of the people, there was a raising of the collective consciousness, the collective awareness.

> O Saint Germain, my body pure,
> your violet flame for all is cure,
> consume the cause of all disease,
> and therefore I am all at ease.

> **O Saint Germain, what love you bring,**
> **it truly makes all matter sing,**
> **your violet flame does all restore,**
> **with you we are becoming more.**

7. I call for people to be cut free to see that the continuation of progress depends on the raising of the collective awareness. In the past, various power elites have been very aggressive in limiting what the people knew, but also limiting the people's awareness.

> O Saint Germain, I'm karma-free,
> the past no longer burdens me,
> a brand new opportunity,
> I am in Christic unity.

> **O Saint Germain, what love you bring,**
> **it truly makes all matter sing,**
> **your violet flame does all restore,**
> **with you we are becoming more.**

8. I call for people to be cut free to see that the primary weapon of a power elite has always been to attempt to restrict the

awareness of the people. If a democratic government is supposed to guarantee the freedom of its citizens, then this can be achieved only by making sure that no power elite is restricting what the people know.

> O Saint Germain, we are now one,
> I am for you a violet sun,
> as we transform this planet earth,
> your Golden Age is given birth.

> **O Saint Germain, what love you bring,**
> **it truly makes all matter sing,**
> **your violet flame does all restore,**
> **with you we are becoming more.**

9. I call for people to be cut free to see that it is one of the primary responsibilities of a democratic government to make sure that the people have access to free and complete information about how society works. As democratic citizens, we have a right to be informed because if we are not informed, how can we make free choices?

> O Saint Germain, the earth is free,
> from burden of duality,
> in oneness we bring what is best,
> your Golden Age is manifest.

> **O Saint Germain, what love you bring,**
> **it truly makes all matter sing,**
> **your violet flame does all restore,**
> **with you we are becoming more.**

Part 4

1. I call for people to be cut free to see that it is the responsibility of a democratic government to look if there is a hidden power elite, then to expose that power elite and to also look if there is a mechanism in society that is restricting the knowledge and the awareness of the people.

> O Saint Germain, you do inspire,
> my vision raised forever higher,
> with you I form a figure-eight,
> your Golden Age I co-create.

> **O Saint Germain, what love you bring,**
> **it truly makes all matter sing,**
> **your violet flame does all restore,**
> **with you we are becoming more.**

2. I call for people to be cut free to see that we have been exploited throughout history by disinformation. Not only a lack of information, but direct disinformation—intentionally and maliciously wrongful information.

> O Saint Germain, what Freedom Flame,
> released when we recite your name,
> acceleration is your gift,
> our planet it will surely lift.

> **O Saint Germain, what love you bring,**
> **it truly makes all matter sing,**
> **your violet flame does all restore,**
> **with you we are becoming more.**

3. I call for people to be cut free to see that we need to consider what kind of disinformation was put upon us through Catholic and Protestant Christianity.

> O Saint Germain, in love we claim,
> our right to bring your violet flame,
> from you Above, to us below,
> it is an all-transforming flow.
>
> **O Saint Germain, what love you bring,**
> **it truly makes all matter sing,**
> **your violet flame does all restore,**
> **with you we are becoming more.**

4. I call for people to be cut free to see that we need to consider what kind of disinformation has been put upon us through materialism.

> O Saint Germain, I love you so,
> my aura filled with violet glow,
> my chakras filled with violet fire,
> I am your cosmic amplifier.
>
> **O Saint Germain, what love you bring,**
> **it truly makes all matter sing,**
> **your violet flame does all restore,**
> **with you we are becoming more.**

5. I call forth the judgment of Christ upon the power elite that took advantage of the Christian religion to program the people and limit the people with disinformation.

O Saint Germain, I am now free,
your violet flame is therapy,
transform all hang-ups in my mind,
as inner peace I surely find.

**O Saint Germain, what love you bring,
it truly makes all matter sing,
your violet flame does all restore,
with you we are becoming more.**

6. I call forth the judgment of Christ upon the power elite that used Christianity to control people until the Catholic church started losing influence over societies.

O Saint Germain, my body pure,
your violet flame for all is cure,
consume the cause of all disease,
and therefore I am all at ease.

**O Saint Germain, what love you bring,
it truly makes all matter sing,
your violet flame does all restore,
with you we are becoming more.**

7. I call forth the judgment of Christ upon the power elite that has used scientific materialism to put disinformation on the people.

O Saint Germain, I'm karma-free,
the past no longer burdens me,
a brand new opportunity,
I am in Christic unity.

**O Saint Germain, what love you bring,
it truly makes all matter sing,
your violet flame does all restore,
with you we are becoming more.**

8. I call forth the judgment of Christ upon the power elite that does not want the people to understand how the money system works.

O Saint Germain, we are now one,
I am for you a violet sun,
as we transform this planet earth,
your Golden Age is given birth.

**O Saint Germain, what love you bring,
it truly makes all matter sing,
your violet flame does all restore,
with you we are becoming more.**

9. I call forth the judgment of Christ upon the power elite that is exploiting the people through the money system, and who know that if the people really understood how the money system works, they would not go along with this.

O Saint Germain, the earth is free,
from burden of duality,
in oneness we bring what is best,
your Golden Age is manifest.

**O Saint Germain, what love you bring,
it truly makes all matter sing,
your violet flame does all restore,
with you we are becoming more.**

Part 5

1. I call for people to be cut free to see that it is the responsibility of a democratic government to take a look at how the economy actually works and tell the people how it works, and then let the people decide whether they want to continue the current economy or whether they want to look for a better system.

O Saint Germain, you do inspire,
my vision raised forever higher,
with you I form a figure-eight,
your Golden Age I co-create.

O Saint Germain, what love you bring,
it truly makes all matter sing,
your violet flame does all restore,
with you we are becoming more.

2. I call for people to be cut free to be the forerunners for directing the attention of the general population into focusing on the need to be free from exploitation by an elite.

O Saint Germain, what Freedom Flame,
released when we recite your name,
acceleration is your gift,
our planet it will surely lift.

O Saint Germain, what love you bring,
it truly makes all matter sing,
your violet flame does all restore,
with you we are becoming more.

3. I call for people to be cut free to see that the moment a critical mass of people shift their consciousness, then a democratic nation will shift and changes will have to be made. A democratic nation is far more responsive to the consciousness of the people than a totalitarian form of government.

> O Saint Germain, in love we claim,
> our right to bring your violet flame,
> from you Above, to us below,
> it is an all-transforming flow.

> **O Saint Germain, what love you bring,**
> **it truly makes all matter sing,**
> **your violet flame does all restore,**
> **with you we are becoming more.**

4. I call for people to be cut free to see that the Golden Age can only be created when there are people in embodiment who co-create it with Saint Germain by tuning in to his ideas and by acting upon them.

> O Saint Germain, I love you so,
> my aura filled with violet glow,
> my chakras filled with violet fire,
> I am your cosmic amplifier.

> **O Saint Germain, what love you bring,**
> **it truly makes all matter sing,**
> **your violet flame does all restore,**
> **with you we are becoming more.**

5. I call for people to be cut free to see that the primary exploitation foisted upon the people by the power elites is that

there are so many things on earth that are seen as limitations we cannot go beyond. All of these limitations prevent us from actually accepting that a better society is possible.

O Saint Germain, I am now free,
your violet flame is therapy,
transform all hang-ups in my mind,
as inner peace I surely find.

O Saint Germain, what love you bring,
it truly makes all matter sing,
your violet flame does all restore,
with you we are becoming more.

6. I call for people to be cut free so they can accept that the Golden Age envisioned by Saint Germain is truly possible.

O Saint Germain, my body pure,
your violet flame for all is cure,
consume the cause of all disease,
and therefore I am all at ease.

O Saint Germain, what love you bring,
it truly makes all matter sing,
your violet flame does all restore,
with you we are becoming more.

7. I call forth the judgment of Christ upon the power elites of all time who want to restrict the people's vision and their ability to accept what is possible because if a majority of the people think something is impossible, then it will for all practical purposes be impossible.

O Saint Germain, I'm karma-free,
the past no longer burdens me,
a brand new opportunity,
I am in Christic unity.

**O Saint Germain, what love you bring,
it truly makes all matter sing,
your violet flame does all restore,
with you we are becoming more.**

8. I call for people to be cut free to see that technology has demonstrated that what their parents thought was impossible is now possible, and thus they need to open their minds to see greater possibilities.

O Saint Germain, we are now one,
I am for you a violet sun,
as we transform this planet earth,
your Golden Age is given birth.

**O Saint Germain, what love you bring,
it truly makes all matter sing,
your violet flame does all restore,
with you we are becoming more.**

9. I call for people to be cut free to see that the most subtle and the most dangerous form of exploitation is when a small power elite limits the vision and the awareness of the population. The power elite limits what people believe is possible, what they can even dare to dream about and thus prevent us from accepting Saint Germain's Golden Age.

O Saint Germain, the earth is free,
from burden of duality,
in oneness we bring what is best,
your Golden Age is manifest.

O Saint Germain, what love you bring,
it truly makes all matter sing,
your violet flame does all restore,
with you we are becoming more.

Sealing

In the name of the Divine Mother, I call to all ascended masters for the sealing of myself and all people in my circle of influence in the creative flow of the Divine Mother, the River of Life. I call for the multiplication of my calls by all ascended masters so that we form the perfect figure-eight flow of "As Above, so below." Thus, I accept that this is fully manifest, because the mouth of the Lord, the Divine Mother that I AM, has spoken it. Amen.

12 | INVOKING THE TRUE PURPOSE OF DEMOCRACY

In the name I AM THAT I AM, Jesus Christ, I call to all ascended masters working on manifesting the Golden Age, especially Saint Germain, to radiate into the collective consciousness a new awareness of the higher purpose of democracy. Help people see that we can build a new future by working with the ascended masters and letting go of the old way of looking at life, including…

[Make personal calls.]

Part 1

1. I call forth the judgment of Christ upon the members of the power elite who want to stay in control, and in order to do this, they are trying to maintain status quo by limiting the people's awareness so the people think that it is not possible to manifest a better society.

O Saint Germain, you do inspire,
my vision raised forever higher,
with you I form a figure-eight,
your Golden Age I co-create.

O Saint Germain, what love you bring,
it truly makes all matter sing,
your violet flame does all restore,
with you we are becoming more.

2. I call forth the judgment of Christ upon the power elite that
has programmed into the collective consciousness: "We have
gone as high as we can go. We have discovered all there is to
discover. We have reached the limits for growth. We are running out of resources."

O Saint Germain, what Freedom Flame,
released when we recite your name,
acceleration is your gift,
our planet it will surely lift.

O Saint Germain, what love you bring,
it truly makes all matter sing,
your violet flame does all restore,
with you we are becoming more.

3. I call forth the judgment of Christ upon the power elite that
is limiting people's ability to envision and accept that there is a
much better state waiting in the future, or make them believe
that what we have is good enough.

O Saint Germain, in love we claim,
our right to bring your violet flame,

from you Above, to us below,
it is an all-transforming flow.

**O Saint Germain, what love you bring,
it truly makes all matter sing,
your violet flame does all restore,
with you we are becoming more.**

4. I call for people to be cut free to see that whatever progress has been made in society, there has always been an elite who tried to take advantage of it. There is an established power elite, and at certain times there is the emergence of an aspiring power elite that takes over and now becomes the established power elite.

O Saint Germain, I love you so,
my aura filled with violet glow,
my chakras filled with violet fire,
I am your cosmic amplifier.

**O Saint Germain, what love you bring,
it truly makes all matter sing,
your violet flame does all restore,
with you we are becoming more.**

5. I call for people to be cut free to see that this pattern has repeated over and over again, and even though the creation of democracies overthrew the established elite of the king, the emperor or the noble class, there has been an aspiring power elite who has attempted to exploit democracy to get power and privileges beyond the population.

O Saint Germain, I am now free,
your violet flame is therapy,
transform all hang-ups in my mind,
as inner peace I surely find.

**O Saint Germain, what love you bring,
it truly makes all matter sing,
your violet flame does all restore,
with you we are becoming more.**

6. I call for people to be cut free to see that the next logical step for democracy is that we expose this power elite, and that we free the people from their exploitation.

O Saint Germain, my body pure,
your violet flame for all is cure,
consume the cause of all disease,
and therefore I am all at ease.

**O Saint Germain, what love you bring,
it truly makes all matter sing,
your violet flame does all restore,
with you we are becoming more.**

7. I call for people to be cut free to see that even thought there is always an elite who is better educated and may seem more powerful, no one knows better than the people how a country should be run.

O Saint Germain, I'm karma-free,
the past no longer burdens me,
a brand new opportunity,
I am in Christic unity.

**O Saint Germain, what love you bring,
it truly makes all matter sing,
your violet flame does all restore,
with you we are becoming more.**

8. I call for people to be cut free to see that the real goal is not
to manifest some perfect society. The goal is that democracy
finds its place in the ongoing raising of the collective awareness.

O Saint Germain, we are now one,
I am for you a violet sun,
as we transform this planet earth,
your Golden Age is given birth.

**O Saint Germain, what love you bring,
it truly makes all matter sing,
your violet flame does all restore,
with you we are becoming more.**

9. I call for people to be cut free to see that democracy is a
more sophisticated schoolroom for the people than a dictatorship because the people have greater responsibility and greater
influence. The primary goal of history is not to create some
static society in some ultimate state, but it is the ongoing raising of the awareness of the people.

O Saint Germain, the earth is free,
from burden of duality,
in oneness we bring what is best,
your Golden Age is manifest.

**O Saint Germain, what love you bring,
it truly makes all matter sing,**

**your violet flame does all restore,
with you we are becoming more.**

Part 2

1. I call for people to be cut free to see that there has been an ongoing raising of the awareness of the people and this will continue. Democracy is part of that process because it is a form of government that places greater responsibility on the people.

O Saint Germain, you do inspire,
my vision raised forever higher,
with you I form a figure-eight,
your Golden Age I co-create.

**O Saint Germain, what love you bring,
it truly makes all matter sing,
your violet flame does all restore,
with you we are becoming more.**

2. I call for people to be cut free to see that people can only vote based on what they know. This requires them to raise their awareness so they can make better decisions for their country.

O Saint Germain, what Freedom Flame,
released when we recite your name,
acceleration is your gift,
our planet it will surely lift.

**O Saint Germain, what love you bring,
it truly makes all matter sing,
your violet flame does all restore,
with you we are becoming more.**

3. I call for people to be cut free to see that because the goal of democracy is not to manifest some ultimate state, but to raise the awareness of the people, then the people always know best what is right for their country.

O Saint Germain, in love we claim,
our right to bring your violet flame,
from you Above, to us below,
it is an all-transforming flow.

**O Saint Germain, what love you bring,
it truly makes all matter sing,
your violet flame does all restore,
with you we are becoming more.**

4. I call for people to be cut free to see that the purpose of a democracy is to give people the opportunity to have a direct influence on their government, and then to see the result of this. Whether the result is this or that, by the mere fact that the people make a decision and see the consequences, there will be a raising of awareness.

O Saint Germain, I love you so,
my aura filled with violet glow,
my chakras filled with violet fire,
I am your cosmic amplifier.

O Saint Germain, what love you bring,
it truly makes all matter sing,
your violet flame does all restore,
with you we are becoming more.

5. I call for people to be cut free to see that the people always know best because they are voting based on their current level of consciousness. What is best for the nation is that the people express their current level of consciousness, see the consequences, and therefore are given an opportunity to raise their consciousness.

O Saint Germain, I am now free,
your violet flame is therapy,
transform all hang-ups in my mind,
as inner peace I surely find.

O Saint Germain, what love you bring,
it truly makes all matter sing,
your violet flame does all restore,
with you we are becoming more.

6. I call for people to be cut free to see that the people know better in the sense that what they know or do not know will create consequences that will force them to raise their awareness. When we realize that this is the goal, we see why the power elites are not right and are not necessary.

O Saint Germain, my body pure,
your violet flame for all is cure,
consume the cause of all disease,
and therefore I am all at ease.

**O Saint Germain, what love you bring,
it truly makes all matter sing,
your violet flame does all restore,
with you we are becoming more.**

7. I call forth the judgment of Christ upon the power elites that have been working against the raising of the awareness of the people because that is the only way they can control them.

O Saint Germain, I'm karma-free,
the past no longer burdens me,
a brand new opportunity,
I am in Christic unity.

**O Saint Germain, what love you bring,
it truly makes all matter sing,
your violet flame does all restore,
with you we are becoming more.**

8. I call for people to be cut free to see that we, the people always know best because we are outplaying our current state of consciousness. When we see the results, we get the maximum opportunity to raise our awareness. We will not get the maximum opportunity to raise our awareness by a small power elite making decisions for us.

O Saint Germain, we are now one,
I am for you a violet sun,
as we transform this planet earth,
your Golden Age is given birth.

**O Saint Germain, what love you bring,
it truly makes all matter sing,**

**your violet flame does all restore,
with you we are becoming more.**

9. I call for people to be cut free to see that until we see it from within ourselves, we have not made progress towards the Golden Age because we have not raised awareness. It is not a small elite that will bring the Golden Age into manifestation because the bottom line is always the awareness of the people.

O Saint Germain, the earth is free,
from burden of duality,
in oneness we bring what is best,
your Golden Age is manifest.

**O Saint Germain, what love you bring,
it truly makes all matter sing,
your violet flame does all restore,
with you we are becoming more.**

Part 3

1. I call for people to be cut free to see that Saint Germain cannot release new technology until the awareness of the people has been raised to a certain level. This is the simple equation.

O Saint Germain, you do inspire,
my vision raised forever higher,
with you I form a figure-eight,
your Golden Age I co-create.

**O Saint Germain, what love you bring,
it truly makes all matter sing,
your violet flame does all restore,
with you we are becoming more.**

2. I call for people to be cut free to see that we have not been given an accurate view of who we are through traditional Christianity and scientific materialism.

O Saint Germain, what Freedom Flame,
released when we recite your name,
acceleration is your gift,
our planet it will surely lift.

**O Saint Germain, what love you bring,
it truly makes all matter sing,
your violet flame does all restore,
with you we are becoming more.**

3. I call for people to be cut free to see that the next logical step in the raising of the collective awareness is that we come into a greater awareness of the role of consciousness. Human beings are conscious beings; we are conscious first and human beings second.

O Saint Germain, in love we claim,
our right to bring your violet flame,
from you Above, to us below,
it is an all-transforming flow.

**O Saint Germain, what love you bring,
it truly makes all matter sing,**

your violet flame does all restore,
with you we are becoming more.

4. I call for people to be cut free to see that our consciousness is not a product of the brain. Our consciousness is beyond the physical body, expresses itself through the physical body, but is more than the body.

O Saint Germain, I love you so,
my aura filled with violet glow,
my chakras filled with violet fire,
I am your cosmic amplifier.

O Saint Germain, what love you bring,
it truly makes all matter sing,
your violet flame does all restore,
with you we are becoming more.

5. I call for people to be cut free to see that it is high time that we use our common sense to go beyond the view of ourselves that we have been given by Christianity that we are sinners, that we are limited beings. It is also high time that we go beyond the view given to us by science that we are evolved apes, that we are material beings, and that our consciousness has no capability beyond the physical body.

O Saint Germain, I am now free,
your violet flame is therapy,
transform all hang-ups in my mind,
as inner peace I surely find.

O Saint Germain, what love you bring,
it truly makes all matter sing,

**your violet flame does all restore,
with you we are becoming more.**

6. I call for people to be cut free to see that it is high time that
we use the tools developed by science to investigate consciousness to find out what kind of beings we really are.

O Saint Germain, my body pure,
your violet flame for all is cure,
consume the cause of all disease,
and therefore I am all at ease.

**O Saint Germain, what love you bring,
it truly makes all matter sing,
your violet flame does all restore,
with you we are becoming more.**

7. I call for people to be cut free to see that mental illness is
a lack of awareness, and it is a lack of awareness of what kind
of beings we are, what consciousness is, what it means to be
a conscious being, how we actually function like a conscious
being.

O Saint Germain, I'm karma-free,
the past no longer burdens me,
a brand new opportunity,
I am in Christic unity.

**O Saint Germain, what love you bring,
it truly makes all matter sing,
your violet flame does all restore,
with you we are becoming more.**

8. I call for people to be cut free to see that the psyche is far more complex than the physical body. There is much more to know about the psyche than we have discovered so far.

> O Saint Germain, we are now one,
> I am for you a violet sun,
> as we transform this planet earth,
> your Golden Age is given birth.
>
> **O Saint Germain, what love you bring,**
> **it truly makes all matter sing,**
> **your violet flame does all restore,**
> **with you we are becoming more.**

9. I call forth the judgment of Christ upon the consciousness and the dark forces behind materialism that have held science hostage for 200 years because there was an aspiring power elite that took over science and wanted to distance themselves from the old power elite that ruled religion.

> O Saint Germain, the earth is free,
> from burden of duality,
> in oneness we bring what is best,
> your Golden Age is manifest.
>
> **O Saint Germain, what love you bring,**
> **it truly makes all matter sing,**
> **your violet flame does all restore,**
> **with you we are becoming more.**

Part 4

1. I call for people to be cut free to see that it is time that we, as a democratic society, as a democratic government, say: "We will have nothing to do with either of these power elites and we want to set the minds of the people free. We want to set the collective mind free so that we can sincerely investigate who we are, what kind of beings we are, what it takes for us to function psychologically."

> O Saint Germain, you do inspire,
> my vision raised forever higher,
> with you I form a figure-eight,
> your Golden Age I co-create.

> **O Saint Germain, what love you bring,**
> **it truly makes all matter sing,**
> **your violet flame does all restore,**
> **with you we are becoming more.**

2. I call for people to be cut free to acknowledge the existence of spiritual beings and the spiritual realm so that a universal body of spiritual knowledge will emerge in people's consciousness.

> O Saint Germain, what Freedom Flame,
> released when we recite your name,
> acceleration is your gift,
> our planet it will surely lift.

> **O Saint Germain, what love you bring,**
> **it truly makes all matter sing,**

> **your violet flame does all restore,**
> **with you we are becoming more.**

3. I call for people to be cut free to see beyond particular teachings and find the commonality that gives us a greater sense of unity, so that spirituality no longer divides us but brings us together, not in one teaching and one movement, but in the universal awareness where we connect in the heart.

> O Saint Germain, in love we claim,
> our right to bring your violet flame,
> from you Above, to us below,
> it is an all-transforming flow.

> **O Saint Germain, what love you bring,**
> **it truly makes all matter sing,**
> **your violet flame does all restore,**
> **with you we are becoming more.**

4. I call for people to be cut free to see that even though we may have different outer beliefs, practices and rituals, there is a common knowledge that we are spiritual beings and therefore, we have something in common regardless of how we decide to express it.

> O Saint Germain, I love you so,
> my aura filled with violet glow,
> my chakras filled with violet fire,
> I am your cosmic amplifier.

> **O Saint Germain, what love you bring,**
> **it truly makes all matter sing,**

your violet flame does all restore,
with you we are becoming more.

5. I call for people to be cut free to recognize the existence of ascended masters, looking at the teachings and shifting their consciousness even more.

O Saint Germain, I am now free,
your violet flame is therapy,
transform all hang-ups in my mind,
as inner peace I surely find.

O Saint Germain, what love you bring,
it truly makes all matter sing,
your violet flame does all restore,
with you we are becoming more.

6. I call for people to be cut free to recognize the existence of fallen beings and the need to transcend a certain level of consciousness so they can be removed from the planet.

O Saint Germain, my body pure,
your violet flame for all is cure,
consume the cause of all disease,
and therefore I am all at ease.

O Saint Germain, what love you bring,
it truly makes all matter sing,
your violet flame does all restore,
with you we are becoming more.

7. I call for people to be cut free to see that a democratic nation's primary responsibility is to raise the awareness of the

people so that they can make more and more free choices. For only the person who is aware of all options, and the consequences of the options, can make a truly free choice.

> O Saint Germain, I'm karma-free,
> the past no longer burdens me,
> a brand new opportunity,
> I am in Christic unity.

> **O Saint Germain, what love you bring,**
> **it truly makes all matter sing,**
> **your violet flame does all restore,**
> **with you we are becoming more.**

8. I call for people to be cut free to see that the power elites of all time, including the ones in democratic societies, have always wanted us to sign the contract without reading the fine print. It is time we read the fine print so we can decide whether we want to sign the contract with the power elite.

> O Saint Germain, we are now one,
> I am for you a violet sun,
> as we transform this planet earth,
> your Golden Age is given birth.

> **O Saint Germain, what love you bring,**
> **it truly makes all matter sing,**
> **your violet flame does all restore,**
> **with you we are becoming more.**

9. I call for people to be cut free to see that it is the responsibility of a democratic government to take the power away from the elite and give it back to the people. It cannot be the

responsibility of a democratic government to maintain status quo where the people are dominated and exploited by a power elite.

O Saint Germain, the earth is free,
from burden of duality,
in oneness we bring what is best,
your Golden Age is manifest.

**O Saint Germain, what love you bring,
it truly makes all matter sing,
your violet flame does all restore,
with you we are becoming more.**

Part 5

1. I call for people to be cut free to see that the most subtle and severe form of exploitation is that the people have been programmed with disinformation about what kind of beings we are, and what are the true possibilities for our own consciousness, for the collective consciousness, and for creating a better age.

O Saint Germain, you do inspire,
my vision raised forever higher,
with you I form a figure-eight,
your Golden Age I co-create.

**O Saint Germain, what love you bring,
it truly makes all matter sing,**

your violet flame does all restore,
with you we are becoming more.

2. I call forth a breakthrough in the raising of the collective awareness that will bring changes in democratic nations, starting in Europe.

O Saint Germain, what Freedom Flame,
released when we recite your name,
acceleration is your gift,
our planet it will surely lift.

O Saint Germain, what love you bring,
it truly makes all matter sing,
your violet flame does all restore,
with you we are becoming more.

3. I call for people to be cut free to see that we need an open debate about issues, so that society no longer has so many taboos that cannot be talked about.

O Saint Germain, in love we claim,
our right to bring your violet flame,
from you Above, to us below,
it is an all-transforming flow.

O Saint Germain, what love you bring,
it truly makes all matter sing,
your violet flame does all restore,
with you we are becoming more.

4. I call for people to be cut free to see that another weapon of the power elite is to create a taboo that people cannot talk about.

O Saint Germain, I love you so,
my aura filled with violet glow,
my chakras filled with violet fire,
I am your cosmic amplifier.

O Saint Germain, what love you bring,
it truly makes all matter sing,
your violet flame does all restore,
with you we are becoming more.

5. I call for people to be cut free to see that in a democracy, there cannot be, there *must* not be, any topic that we cannot talk about. It is precisely behind the topics that we cannot talk about that the power elite can hide, and that is what limits the people.

O Saint Germain, I am now free,
your violet flame is therapy,
transform all hang-ups in my mind,
as inner peace I surely find.

O Saint Germain, what love you bring,
it truly makes all matter sing,
your violet flame does all restore,
with you we are becoming more.

6. I call for people to be cut free to see that change starts by talking about issues. This is the opening for the raising of awareness, and the raising of awareness is the direct cause of

changes in the physical world. It has always been so. It will always be so.

> O Saint Germain, my body pure,
> your violet flame for all is cure,
> consume the cause of all disease,
> and therefore I am all at ease.

> **O Saint Germain, what love you bring,**
> **it truly makes all matter sing,**
> **your violet flame does all restore,**
> **with you we are becoming more.**

7. I call for people to be cut free to see the role of consciousness in creating and manifesting physical conditions. Consciousness always comes before the physical manifestation.

> O Saint Germain, I'm karma-free,
> the past no longer burdens me,
> a brand new opportunity,
> I am in Christic unity.

> **O Saint Germain, what love you bring,**
> **it truly makes all matter sing,**
> **your violet flame does all restore,**
> **with you we are becoming more.**

8. I call for people to be cut free to see that when we know this, and when we take responsibility for our consciousness, that is when we can free ourselves from all forms of exploitation.

> O Saint Germain, we are now one,
> I am for you a violet sun,

as we transform this planet earth,
your Golden Age is given birth.

O Saint Germain, what love you bring,
it truly makes all matter sing,
your violet flame does all restore,
with you we are becoming more.

9. I call for people to be cut free to see that if we will not acknowledge that consciousness precedes physical manifestation, then we cannot free ourselves from the exploitation by one power elite or another, even one after another. Therefore, we will not be able to receive and accept Saint Germain's Golden Age.

O Saint Germain, the earth is free,
from burden of duality,
in oneness we bring what is best,
your Golden Age is manifest.

O Saint Germain, what love you bring,
it truly makes all matter sing,
your violet flame does all restore,
with you we are becoming more.

Sealing

In the name of the Divine Mother, I call to all ascended masters for the sealing of myself and all people in my circle of influence in the creative flow of the Divine Mother, the River of Life. I call for the multiplication of my calls by all ascended masters so that we form the perfect figure-eight flow of "As

Above, so below." Thus, I accept that this is fully manifest, because the mouth of the Lord, the Divine Mother that I AM, has spoken it. Amen.

13 | ACCELERATING DEMOCRACY TO A NEW LEVEL

I AM the Ascended Master Astrea, Elohim of the Fourth Ray, often called the ray of purity but also the ray of acceleration. Naturally, building on Saint Germain's discourse, we need to accelerate democracies. We need to accelerate the sense of what is the responsibility of a democratic government and the governmental apparatus.

The responsibility of a democratic society

What is actually the responsibility of a democratic society as a whole? Well, my beloved, let us go back and look at history. You can go back to different eras and see that there have been eras of almost complete chaos where there was no rule of law and where the people never knew when they might be attacked by an outside enemy and their lives might be destroyed in an instant. You may ask yourselves today why people so willingly submitted to the Catholic church, to the feudal system, to the kings of the Middle Ages.

You can barely understand (in the modern, western world) that these people had for a long time lived in societies where the ordinary person had very little protection against either bands of robbers or even bigger invasions from various forces. They gave up their freedom in order to be protected and have the kind of stability that you, after all, did have in many periods. There were, of course, also periods where neither the church nor the feudal lords could guarantee people's safety. But people still thought that the safety was so important that they saw no other option than submitting themselves to the elite.

This, of course, is something we have transcended with democracy, but my aim is to show you that there have been different stages in the evolution of society. You can go back to a point where the main issue was physical protection, physical survival. Then you can see that, beginning with the industrial revolution and forward, it was not so much physical survival or physical protection; it was more having the material needs fulfilled (those who are beyond the need for protection and survival). What you naturally see is that now many of the more affluent, many of the older, democracies have reached a new stage, but they have not become aware that they have reached that new stage, and that is why the democratic governments are not living up to their responsibility towards their citizens.

If you employ the pyramid of needs defined by Maslow, you can see that the highest of all needs is the need for self-actualization. We could also say in a more universal way that there are many people in democratic nations who are not quite ready for self-actualization, but they are ready to step up to a level that is beyond this quest for material affluence and security.

Democracies must fulfill people's higher needs

Many of you can go back to your parents' or grandparents' generation who lived in the difficult years during the 1930's or during the Second World War. You will see that, for them, poverty was such an issue that the main vision and dream they had in life was to have enough food, have a place to live, and even have money left over to do something more enjoyable. This need, in many nations, gradually became fulfilled during the 50's and 60's. Then, people went into desiring not only the necessities of life fulfilled, but having more affluence so they could also have a certain luxury of material goods. Again, this can be seen as a natural stage.

Now, in many of the older democracies, people have had such affluence for so long that they begin to take it for granted. When the people begin to take something for granted, it is no longer promoting growth, it is no longer helping them raise the collective consciousness. On the contrary, it can actually cause a lowering of the collective consciousness in the sense that when people take something for granted, they go into a blind alley in their spiritual growth and they are no longer appreciating what they have. If you do not appreciate what you have, you cannot actually multiply it. That is, in fact, one of the reasons why, in some of these nations, you have seen the economy starting to contract. It is again because people are simply not appreciating it and they are not willing to step up to the next level so there cannot be an acceleration.

When you have the knowledge that you are not going to be killed by some war or an invasion by barbarian tribes, when you have your material needs fulfilled or even when you have enough money to buy various kinds of luxuries, what is the next step up? Well, ultimately it is self-actualization but many people have to go through a phase before that because they are not quite ready and consciously engaging in a spiritual path of systematically and consciously raising their consciousness. The intermediate stage that, in universal terms, people are ready to lock in to is that the next natural step is that people come to feel good about themselves, not about their outer situation or their society but about themselves as an individual, as a conscious being. This is something that many, many people are ready to see. It is very simply that we have now been focused on material welfare for decades and the next natural step in the evolution of democracy is that we focus on psychological welfare.

Psychological welfare as the next step

We have talked about it before, but I wish to go even further with this topic. What will it take then to promote psychological, mental welfare among the people in a free democratic nation who have more material affluence than they actually know what to do with? Well, it will take, as Saint Germain also mentioned, that you begin a discussion of what kind of beings you actually are. More than that, it will actually take that people begin to question the approach that we have had so far to understanding reality, understanding the universe, understanding ourselves.

Now, I know that most people are not familiar with philosophy so I wish to give you a very quick crash course in western philosophy. Most of you know that about twenty-five hundred years ago there were some philosophers in Greece, in Athens. You have probably heard about Socrates and Plato and Aristotle. What most of you do not know, because very few people actually realize this, even most philosophy professors, is that the two main philosophers of the Greek era, Plato and Aristotle, actually represent two different approaches. I am not trying to say here that one was completely in alignment with the ascended masters and one was completely out of alignment. Nevertheless, the approach and the main philosophy of Plato was that beyond the material universe is a realm where there exists ideal forms. These ideal forms are what have manifested all of the physical forms we see at this level.

You will see, of course, that this is quite similar to what we have taught you, only we have gone into more detail that there are four levels of the material universe and that the conditions you see at the physical level are actually created at the three higher levels: identity, mental, emotional. Plato was open to the existence of a realm beyond, and his main approach to philosophy was that if we wanted to understand the physical world, we had to understand the realm of ideal forms and how they had manifested the forms we see in the physical.

His own student, Aristotle, took philosophy in a different direction by focusing on the material world and actually saying that it should be possible to explain and understand everything in the material world by only looking at the material world. It was not necessary to look beyond to some realm that we could not directly perceive with our senses. Aristotle thought that we can understand the world through what we can see or perceive through the senses. Plato said that the soul comes into embodiment with certain knowledge and ideas into it. Aristotle said that the soul is a blank slate, and as the child grows and receives sensory impressions, then the soul starts gaining content. Again, you can see that Plato obviously was more in alignment with ascended master teachings about reincarnation, and that the soul already comes in with much knowledge and psychological patterns from past lives.

Naturally, for many, many years, even centuries, the Greek philosophers had relatively little influence on the rest of the world. There was even a time where they were forcefully suppressed by the Catholic church because it was seen as incompatible with Christianity. Then, there came a point where a philosopher, Thomas Aquinas, started to study Aristotle and created a new philosophical system where he sought to unify Aristotle and Catholic Christianity. This then, brought the awareness of Aristotle to the western world, and when scientists began to have conflict with religion, then the people who took over science and set the stage for scientific philosophy, they built on Aristotle and the idea that you can understand the material world by looking only at the material world.

The very foundation for science since then has been precisely this: To study only the material world and to actually believe that it is possible to come up with what they call a "theory of everything" where you find some material condition that can explain everything that is happening in the universe. This my beloved, is a philosophical and scientific blind alley, and there are many, many people in embodiment who are actually ready to see this—to awaken from this illusion. Just like you see in the fairy tale where they all believe the emperor was wearing these fanciful clothes until the little boy cried out: "But the emperor has nothing on."

The emperors of scientific materialism truly have nothing on. This becomes very, very clear when you realize a very simple fact. The focus on material welfare has not automatically brought psychological welfare. No matter how much material affluence people have, it does not automatically make them feel good about themselves. It does not automatically make them happy.

Helping people feel good about themselves

You can see then that if you are a truly responsible, democratic society, if you want to do what is best for your own citizens, you need to step up to where you can focus on psychological welfare and helping all people feel good about themselves. This is not some far-flung spiritual goal about reaching higher states of consciousness. It is quite universal for people to realize that why shouldn't people feel good about themselves?

Then, you can of course look at the fact that in most of the affluent democracies, there has been an increase in the frequency of mental illness. Many people are unhappy, many people are dissatisfied. In fact, it seems like the more affluent people get, the more dissatisfied they become. You can start simply asking why this is so. Therefore, you can recognize a very simple fact: that people are not material beings. If they were, then once they had the affluent material conditions, they should automatically be happy and feel good about themselves. The very fact that the affluence materially does not lead to them feeling good, shows that people have needs that are not material. This then, leads to the recognition that human beings are conscious beings and that how you feel about yourself, whether you are happy or not, is determined by consciousness.

You will see that as there has been a rise in mental illness, depression or unhappiness, pharmaceutical companies have been frantically trying to create this wonder drug where you just take a pill and then you are happy. They have not been able to come up with one, and more and more healthcare professionals are beginning to realize that we cannot use drugs to overcome mental illness and the rise in mental illness. This shows you that there is no material mechanism in the physical body that guarantees that you feel good about yourself. Feeling good about yourself is a condition that exists in consciousness and therefore must be brought about at the level of your consciousness—not at the level of your physical body.

This can lead on to a critical examination of another platform, another principle, brought out by Aristotle and adopted by materialistic science. It is simply this: every thing in the world can be broken down into smaller, more basic components. If we understand the basic components out of which a thing is made, then we can understand the thing. In other words, for every whole, this whole is made up of smaller components. If we understand those components and how they work, then we can understand the whole.

The whole is not a physical thing

This is why scientists have been studying the physical brain in order to find out how the human psyche works. They think that consciousness is produced by the brain. The brain has smaller components. If we find out how those components work, then we must understand how consciousness works and what makes people happy and what does not. It is not a big leap to take this experience that you have and realize that the very fact that people are not happy proves that you cannot understand a human being by looking at the material components in the brain. You can expand this to recognize that you actually can never understand a whole by looking only at the individual, smaller components. You cannot understand the entire universe by looking at atoms and sub-atomic particles. There is no smallest possible particle that you can find that will allow you to understand the totality of the universe—because the universe is a whole.

Now my beloved, where does a "whole" exist? It exists only in consciousness. You can look at all of the cells, all of the neurons, all of the connections in the physical brain of a human being but they will not in themselves make up the totality – the whole – of a person. You can look at all of the components of the universe and they do not make up the totality of the universe. Therefore, it is very, very realistic, and it is a very small switch for people, to actually realize that our attempt to understand the whole by looking only at the components is flawed from the beginning. It will never take us to an understanding of the whole. We need to step up and look at the whole and we can do this because we are conscious beings.

We have the capacity of consciousness to understand the whole but we cannot do this through the current scientific methods. We cannot do this through the analytical, intellectual mind, which is designed to look at the details, and categorize the details, and organize the details. In the process of doing so, the analytical mind loses the whole. We can only look at the whole through what is popularly called intuition, but which is actually a much more multi-faceted ability. It is ultimately what we have said: the Conscious You's ability to step outside of the four lower bodies and look at the world from a different perspective. The essence of the Conscious You, as we have described it, is its ability to look at a whole, its ability to put two things together and see a whole.

Now, you can understand this from a very simple analogy. If you take an old-fashioned newspaper photograph as many of you probably did as children, you can take a magnifying glass and you can see that these are individual black dots that make up the photograph. If you imagine being very close to the photograph, all you see are the black dots. When you step back far enough, then you see that the individual black dots form a picture. Now my beloved, if you take a picture of a rose, and if scientists go in and look at the black dots, and analyze each and every black dot, tell me, my beloved: If they could not see the whole picture, could they by looking at the individual black dots ever construe that they make up the image of a rose? You cannot, by looking at the components, see the totality, see the whole.

From physical to psychological needs

This is the approach that democratic nations have so far had to serving their citizens: You are trying to look at the individual components of a human being, the material, physical components. You can do this very well for material needs. You can look at the body and what it needs in terms of nutrition and exercise and this and that, and you can come up with a whole list of this. When it comes to psychological welfare, you cannot promote psychological welfare without looking at the whole, without understanding the whole of what is a human being and how does it function.

This is something you can envision, you can make the calls for, namely that society will wake up and realize that the next step for democracy is to make people feel good about themselves. We can only do this when we adopt what we might call a more holistic approach and look at human beings as more than the components of their physical brains. Truly, if this shift can happen, or rather *when* it will happen, then it opens up so many perspectives for how society can begin to redefine what is truly the goal of a democratic society.

To again tie in to Saint Germain and that you have a right to be free of exploitation, well, you can see that this very tendency to look at the details and to ignore the whole is actually something that is put upon people and put upon societies by a small elite. They may not necessarily be malicious when you look at the people, but they have a very, very limited vision. At the same time, they also have a very, very big pride and sense that they know better because they are the intellectual elite who are able to decide that God does not exist. Therefore, society should move away from any form of religion and spirituality, and society should be entirely materialistic because that is just the way the world is.

They feel they are capable of deciding on behalf of society and so you need to look at the fact here that there has formed this intellectual power elite. Although there are other power elites who have more clandestine intentions, this power elite – on the surface – they have benign intentions. The fact of the matter is that they are not so benign because they are willing to ignore the well-being of all people in society in order to promote their materialistic ideology. They do not care about the fact that people are dissatisfied, that people are becoming depressed, that there are more and more psychological problems, or that people are not feeling good about themselves. They are so fanatically promoting their materialistic idea that they do not care about human beings because, as we have said before, the idea has become more important than the individual. This is a very, very insidious form of exploitation.

Materialism is an exploitative ideology

When you have an entire society that is based on an idea, and when this idea is more important than the individual, be it the physical survival of the individual or the psychological well-being of the individual, then you have an abusive, exploitative society. Then, the population is being abused. Naturally, you can see societies where, if the people did not agree with a communist ideology, they would be sent to Siberia. Or if they did not agree with a Nazi ideology, they would be sent to a concentration camp. This is a more extreme form, but my beloved, are you not realizing that most of the people in democratic nations who claim to be free (and *of* the people, *by* the people and *for* the people), these people are being held hostage by a small intellectual elite who are fanatically promoting the idea of materialism and ignoring the fact that this does not promote the well-being of the population. These people are so fanatical that they are willing to actually exploit the people, abuse the people, in order to promote an ideology. This is very abusive and it is something that a democratic government has a responsibility to protect its citizens from. When you begin to recognize this, you can see the need to rethink the way we approach society.

You can even realize that it is not a matter of thinking we have done wrong so far. It is a matter of realizing that the next logical step in this process of raising the collective awareness, as Saint Germain described, is that we step up and promote psychological welfare. In order to do this, we, of course, have to understand the psychology. In order to understand the psychology better, we have to overcome the unwillingness of materialistic science to seriously study consciousness, and to seriously consider how consciousness influences not only every aspect of our individual lives, but how the collective consciousness influences society as a whole. We must even explore the possibility that the collective consciousness may influence the physical, material universe.

The hidden superstructure

These are very, very important topics because, by a subtle shift in the mindset, society can be free from the current stalemate and suddenly make leaps and bounds forward, also in the field of science. First of all, progress can be made in the field of psychology, of understanding what kind of beings you are, and what actually makes a person feel good about himself or herself. This can lead to so many things, but what I need you, who are ascended master students, to make calls on is to realize that behind this intellectual power elite that wants to promote materialism and behind the other power elites that seek power or economic control, there are always forces in the three other realms.

There are powerful demons and fallen beings behind all of this and we need you to make the calls to authorize us to step in and bind and consume some of this entire superstructure that has been built. There is a very, very powerful collective beast that has been built, going all the way back to Aristotle, up through the Catholic era and into the scientific age where people do not want to look at the whole. It is a powerful set of demons that are trying to prevent people from looking at the whole, either shutting down their minds or fanatically focusing on understanding certain details and thinking that we do not have to understand the whole, or it is too big for us to understand. They are trying to get people to focus on the material world so they never have time to step back and ask these bigger questions, ask these questions of: "Why are we doing this, why are we continuing to do this even though we see that it is not working?" They are trying to prevent people from actually coming to this recognition where they say: "Now we have been doing this for some time, let us just step back and see what are the actual consequences? What is actually happening as a result of this approach to science and reality? Have we really gotten closer to understanding the universe by looking at the details?"

Opening for scientific progress

If you are honest, you will recognize that since the advent of quantum physics, there has not been decisive progress in the field of science, and this should show you that science is focused in the wrong direction. You can also step back and say: "Have we actually achieved anything in terms of promoting welfare and happiness by all of our focus on details and technology and the material world? Have we made people happier by seeking a material explanation for everything?" It is not difficult to see that we have not, and thus could there be something missing in our approach?

You see my beloved, I am not here talking about saying that science is completely wrong for focusing on details. I am simply saying that focusing on details is the omega aspect of doing science, and focusing on greater structures, focusing on the whole, focusing on patterns, is the alpha aspect of doing science. What these dark forces and fallen beings have managed to make people do is to forget about the alpha aspect of science by saying that this falls under the area of religion and all you get through your intuition is just superstition, it cannot be proven.

You see, my beloved, if you go back to my analogy of the picture of the rose, by looking at the individual dots, you cannot prove that they make up a rose. By looking at sub-atomic particles alone, you cannot prove that they make up a universe. Yet you observe with your consciousness that there is a universe. There is a whole but you cannot prove this by looking at the details.

All people have the ability to look at a whole, and this is in fact the entire purpose of doing science: not to understand every detail, but to understand the whole. You cannot understand the whole by looking only at the details. You must step back, you must use the intuitive abilities to look at patterns, to put them together and to see the whole.

Now, of course, the ability to look at the whole can also be manipulated by the fallen beings and that is what they attempt to do by creating these ideologies. What is the purpose of most of the ideologies you have seen in this world? They all claim that the purpose is to bring forth some ultimate truth about how the universe works. This is complete propaganda. This has nothing to do with reality. The purpose of the fallen beings is to actually present a false theory, a false whole, and say this is how the universe should work, this is how the universe works, and then get people to focus on the idea instead of using their ability to look at how do things actually work. Does the economy work like the capitalists say or like the communists say? Or does the economy work in and entirely different way? Well, it is the same with everything, my beloved.

What needs to truly happen in society, and what is close to actually beginning to happen, is that more and more people need to step forward and question and say: "Why have we taken the approach that we first create a theory of how we think the world works and then we attempt to prove or disprove the theory? This might have been useful at the time where we had more primitive scientific tools than we have today, but today, we can actually make a leap where we shift into not focusing on the theory, but we focus on observation of how things actually work. We do not observe only the details, we also look at the whole, at the connections, at the bigger picture."

The time of ideology is over

This is the shift that some of the most advanced scientists and philosophers have already made, but more and more people – millions of people – are becoming ready to embrace this and to demand that it not only be made in the scientific field but that it be made in society at large so that societies realize that the time of ideology is over. The time of having theories is over. The time of having political parties that say that society should work this way is over. It is time to just look at: "Who are we? How do we work? What works for us? What makes us feel good? What makes people happy? Then, this is what we base our society on. Not on some fanciful theory about how we *should* work or how the universe *should* work."

This would be a quantum leap beyond what you have seen in the past several thousand years. Even the Greek philosophers could be said to be trapped in this desire to create a theory in the mind of how the world works. Many, many philosophers throughout the ages, many political ideologists, have been trapped in this tendency that we have actually called the consciousness of Satan, of thinking that you can look at the material world and, based on the conditions you see in the material world, you can make up a theory about how the universe works, including whether there is a spiritual world. If you say that there is, then you can make up a theory about how that spiritual world works.

You could say that we are, in our teachings, presenting you with another theory. The difference is, my beloved, that we are giving you a theory that we do not claim to be an absolute truth, but we are giving it for the purpose of raising your awareness. We are making you aware that, at the current level of awareness collectively, it is not possible to understand how the spiritual world works because you are still trapped in the linear consciousness. The spiritual world is not linear, and therefore you cannot understand it with a linear awareness. We are trying to give you an understanding that can help you free yourself from this entire consciousness of Satan that thinks you can take current conditions in the material world and use them to explain how the universe works.

Why is this such a detrimental theory? Well, in terms of the Golden Age, what is the goal of Saint Germain? It is to manifest a Golden Age where the material conditions, the material affluence, is so much higher than what you have today. How can you ever manifest that age by looking at current conditions and thinking that these conditions can explain how the universe works? You need to come to the recognition that current conditions were not created by God and are not defined by the laws of nature. They are not inevitable. They are not insurmountable.

They are created through the collective consciousness. By raising the collective consciousness, you can change many of the material conditions that today you think cannot be changed. Do you see, my beloved, that when you want to explain the universe based on current conditions, you shut your mind to the vision that could take you and the earth beyond current conditions and help you create a better age?

If, my beloved, you had been completely focused that the only way to produce any kind of mechanical work was to use an animal that is dragging an ox cart or walking around in one of these devices where it turns a wheel that pumps water, how would you have created the modern age? It only happened because there was a leap in consciousness where some people were willing to look beyond current conditions and say: "Something better is possible. It is possible to go beyond these conditions and create a different society."

My beloved, how was it possible for people to invent the airplane? You take an airplane, you look at all of the components of the airplane. All of them are heavier than air. None of them can fly on their own, but when you put them all together and look at the whole, you see that there are certain conditions that actually allow an airplane that weighs several tons to fly into the air. This is holistic thinking, not details. Again, somebody made the leap and said: "It must be possible to fly, even with a device that is heavier than air."

There are so many of these limitations that have been programmed into people's minds, and they are preventing the manifestation of the Golden Age for the simple reason that people cannot even accept that it is possible. If you cannot accept that something is possible, if a critical mass of people cannot accept this, then by the Law of Free Will, by the Law of Plausible Deniability, Saint Germain cannot bring forth these ideas. He cannot release them, he cannot bring forth the technology that will take society to a higher level.

The unrecognized potential of consciousness

The reality is, my beloved, that when you start looking at what does it take for people to feel good about themselves, then you end up investigating the role of consciousness and the potential of consciousness. When people start honestly looking at the potential of consciousness, you will sooner or later end up with the realization that this potential is far greater than anyone has seen before. You will come to the conclusion that it is possible to raise a person's consciousness to a distinctly higher level than what most people have today. You will even scientifically discover that there is a systematic process whereby people can raise their consciousness to higher and higher levels.

This will open up for the fact that you can now begin to realize that what really makes you feel good in the long run is that you work on actualizing yourself and manifesting a higher state of consciousness. However, in the short run what makes you feel good is a very simple thing: that you are not manipulated by any force outside yourself. There are, of course, inside forces, namely your own ego. The first level of realization that needs to come is that society begins to realize that for people to feel good about themselves (and I am not talking here about just an emotional feeling, but also a mental and identity level feeling of feeling at peace with who you are and your life), this will require that people are not exploited by any external force. This can actually open up for the recognition that if we are to explain the more severe forms of mental illness, we need to recognize that there are certain energies or beings that are not material but that can still influence the human psyche.

In the beginning, it will be difficult for scientists to put words on this, but they can actually gradually develop a universal language where they can explain that there are certain forces that are not in the material realm, but they can influence human psychology and manipulate people in various ways. This will first be discovered by looking at mental illness, and the more severe cases of mental illness that are all caused by the person being open to these forces. Once society begins to recognize this, it begins to recognize that if we are to overcome mental illness, and actually overcome the epidemic of mental illness, then we need to start looking at this and finding ways to help people overcome this and protect themselves from it. This is, again, what may seem like a far-flung development but it is actually quite realistic, quite within the range of what can happen in a matter of a few decades. Of course, many people around the world have already started recognizing this, many psychologists, many healthcare professionals. We are, again, asking you to make the calls that they will be cut free, that they will be emboldened to step forward and say that we need a new approach to mental illness because our present approach is not helping people.

Again, what is the goal? Find out what works. Find out what helps people. Find out what makes them feel better about themselves and their lives. This is the ultimate responsibility of a democratic society and a democratic form of government. It is the ultimate responsibility of the people in democratic nations to hold their governments accountable because who else will do it? You cannot expect that the government itself would hold itself accountable. This is the job of the people whether you have representative democracy or direct democracy.

The significance of a conference

My beloved, I am quite aware that time is moving on, and your bodies and your chakras are reaching a certain maximum capacity of what you can handle in one sitting. I thank you again, as we have all done, for being willing to be here and be the open doors for multiplying our releases that we may send an even more powerful impulse into the collective conscious-ness. Truly, I do not think that with your outer minds you fully recognize the significance of what you are doing when you come together at a conference.

It is naturally very significant when you sit individually or in small groups and give the invocations and study the teachings. When you come together in a group, the bigger the group, the bigger the multiplication factor, and the more powerful of an impulse we can release through you. As always, you have actually done a far greater work than you are aware of with your conscious minds, and it is not that you need to consciously understand everything you are doing and all the ramifications and see how it is all working out there.

Nevertheless, we still want you to understand something very, very simple. We understand fully that when you are in physical embodiment, you are always dealing with an immediate situation. You may have your psychology you are dealing with, you may have issues with your physical body, you may have issues with your family situation, with your work situation, your financial situation. You have all of these worries and concerns, but why are you ascended master students? You are because you have been able to stop identifying yourself fully with your material situation so you could realize there is more to life. You want more and therefore, you have found our teachings and you have decided to apply them. What we want you to understand is that even though you are sitting here, maybe feeling a bit tired, the consequences of what you are doing are very, very significant. We want to give you this impetus that even walking the spiritual path, raising your consciousness, has significance that goes beyond your own life. This gives you a different perspective on the path, it gives you a different perspective on your daily lives where you can sort of depersonalize your daily lives, not be so identified with it, not be so caught up in it.

The decision on the path

I tell you, my beloved, that when it comes to the spiritual path, we have all talked about resolving certain psychological issues, but there is also a certain element of making spiritual progress that requires you to make a decision. You cannot make this decision when you are not ready for it, but when you have given invocations for a certain issue, when you have increased your understanding, there can come a point where you simply need to decide that you are no longer putting your attention on this issue. In this case, it can be a great help to actually say to yourself: "But I'm not in physical embodiment just to live a material life, I'm here to help raise the consciousness of the planet. This particular issue in my personal life, I will not allow it to stand in the way of my spiritual progress and my helping the ascended masters, and therefore I will simply take my attention away from it and focus on other things."

In making this shift, this can often be the very last step in overcoming a certain issue because there will always be an element of ego, a certain internal spirit, a certain element of the outer self that will want to keep you continually trapped in seeing yourself as defined by a certain issue. It may be something that has happened in your past, it may be something that is happening now. It may be something that has not happened but that you think should happen. You create a self that is defined by this issue, and you may give your decrees and invocations and resolve the energy that feeds the self. You may come to a greater understanding of the mechanism but you still have not decided to step back, look at this self and say: "Now I see that there is a whole self created here that is tying me in to this issue and I no longer want it, I no longer need it and I am simply refusing to give it my attention and my energy." Then you can very quickly come to the point where it simply fades away and it no more has any pull on you. What you will find is that you will feel better about yourself by letting go of this limited self.

I am giving you the sense of how important your work is in order to make it easier for you to let go of these lesser selves because, after all, you are not here to live a normal life. You know that you cannot be happy by living a normal life. You are here to work on your self-actualization, which is another word for Christhood. You know that ultimately you will only be happy, you will only be fulfilled, by manifesting higher and higher degrees of Christhood. What does it mean to manifest higher degrees of Christhood? Well, it means to let those lesser selves die so you can follow Christ higher on the path. Those who are willing to lose their lives for my sake, they are worthy to be the disciples of the Living Christ, and to become the living Christ themselves.

With these remarks, I again express my gratitude, and I commend you for your willingness to come together, and for your willingness to interact in such an open and free way. Truly, it is our joy to observe you, my beloved, and to even feel one with you, as we truly feel even if you may not always feel it. You can, if you are willing, feel that oneness with the ascended masters. If you can experience it during a conference, you can take it with you when you go to your homes and know that we are not limited by time and space. That is the real reason why Jesus said: "I am with you always, even unto the end of the world," meaning not that the world is destroyed, but that the world is accelerated to a higher level. Then, of course, we will be with you at that higher level as well.

14 | INVOKING A HIGHER LEVEL OF DEMOCRACY

In the name I AM THAT I AM, Jesus Christ, I call to all ascended masters working on manifesting the Golden Age, especially Astrea, to radiate into the collective consciousness a new awareness of how to take democracy to a higher level. Help people see that we can build a new future by working with the ascended masters and letting go of the old way of looking at life, including…

[Make personal calls.]

Part 1

1. I call for people to be cut free to see that democratic governments are not living up to their responsibility towards their citizens because they have not seen that the highest of all needs is the need for self-actualization.

Beloved Astrea, your heart is so true,
your Circle and Sword of white and blue,
cut all life free from dramas unwise,
on wings of Purity our planet will rise.

Beloved Astrea, in oneness with you,
your circle and sword of electric blue,
with Purity's Light cutting right through,
raising the earth into all that is true.

2. I call for people to be cut free to see that when we have our material needs fulfilled, the next step up is self-actualization, but many people have to go through a phase of coming to feel good about themselves, not about their outer situation or their society but about themselves as individuals, as conscious beings.

Beloved Astrea, in God Purity,
accelerate all of our life energy,
we're rising beyond every impurity,
as Purity's Light forever we see.

Beloved Astrea, in oneness with you,
your circle and sword of electric blue,
with Purity's Light cutting right through,
raising the earth into all that is true.

3. I call for people to be cut free to see that we have been focused on material welfare for decades and the next natural step in the evolution of democracy is that we focus on psychological welfare.

Beloved Astrea, from Purity's Ray,
send forth deliverance to all life today,
acceleration to Purity, we are now free
from all that is less than love's Purity.

**Beloved Astrea, in oneness with you,
your circle and sword of electric blue,
with Purity's Light cutting right through,
raising the earth into all that is true.**

4. I call for people to be cut free to see that in order to promote psychological, mental welfare in a free democratic nation, we need to have a discussion of what kind of beings we actually are.

Beloved Astrea, accelerate us all,
as for your deliverance we fervently call,
set all life free from vision impure
beyond fear and doubt, we're rising for sure.

**Beloved Astrea, in oneness with you,
your circle and sword of electric blue,
with Purity's Light cutting right through,
raising the earth into all that is true.**

5. I call for people to be cut free to question the approach that we have had so far to understanding reality, understanding the universe, understanding ourselves.

Beloved Astrea, we're willing to see,
all of the lies that keep us unfree,
we surrender all lies causing the fall,
forever affirming the oneness of All.

**Beloved Astrea, in oneness with you,
your circle and sword of electric blue,
with Purity's Light cutting right through,
raising the earth into all that is true.**

6. I call for people to be cut free to see that the foundation for science has been to study only the material world and to believe that it is possible to come up with a "theory of everything" where material conditions can explain everything that is happening in the universe.

Beloved Astrea, accelerate life
beyond all duality's struggle and strife,
consume all division between God and man,
accelerate fulfillment of God's perfect plan.

**Beloved Astrea, in oneness with you,
your circle and sword of electric blue,
with Purity's Light cutting right through,
raising the earth into all that is true.**

7. I call for people to be cut free to see that this is a philosophical and scientific blind alley because the focus on material welfare has not automatically brought psychological welfare. No matter how much material affluence we have, it does not automatically make us feel good about ourselves.

Beloved Astrea, we lovingly call,
break down separation's invisible wall,
raising our minds into true unity
with the Masters of love in Infinity.

**Beloved Astrea, in oneness with you,
your circle and sword of electric blue,
with Purity's Light cutting right through,
raising the earth into all that is true.**

8. I call for people to be cut free to see that if a truly responsible, democratic society wants to do what is best for its own
citizens, we need to step up to where we can focus on psychological welfare and helping all people feel good about
themselves.

Beloved Astrea, help all of us find,
the secret that we create with the mind,
and thus what in ignorance we decreate,
in knowledge we easily can recreate.

**Beloved Astrea, in oneness with you,
your circle and sword of electric blue,
with Purity's Light cutting right through,
raising the earth into all that is true.**

9. I call for people to be cut free to see that in most of the
affluent democracies it seems that the more affluent people
get, the more dissatisfied they become. This proves that we are
not material beings.

Beloved Astrea, we all do aspire,
to learning to use your purity's fire,
to raise every form in infamy sown,
as Saint Germain makes this planet his own.

**Beloved Astrea, in oneness with you,
your circle and sword of electric blue,**

with Purity's Light cutting right through,
raising the earth into all that is true.

Part 2

1. I call for people to be cut free to see that the very fact that material affluence does not automatically make us happy, shows that we have needs that are not material.

Beloved Astrea, your heart is so true,
your Circle and Sword of white and blue,
cut all life free from dramas unwise,
on wings of Purity our planet will rise.

Beloved Astrea, in oneness with you,
your circle and sword of electric blue,
with Purity's Light cutting right through,
raising the earth into all that is true.

2. I call for people to be cut free to see that human beings are conscious beings and that how we feel about ourselves, whether we are happy or not, is determined by consciousness.

Beloved Astrea, in God Purity,
accelerate all of our life energy,
we're rising beyond every impurity,
as Purity's Light forever we see.

Beloved Astrea, in oneness with you,
your circle and sword of electric blue,

**with Purity's Light cutting right through,
raising the earth into all that is true.**

3. I call for people to be cut free to see that we cannot use drugs to overcome mental illness and the rise in mental illness. There is no material mechanism in the physical body that guarantees that we feel good about ourselves.

Beloved Astrea, from Purity's Ray,
send forth deliverance to all life today,
acceleration to Purity, we are now free
from all that is less than love's Purity.

**Beloved Astrea, in oneness with you,
your circle and sword of electric blue,
with Purity's Light cutting right through,
raising the earth into all that is true.**

4. I call for people to be cut free to see that feeling good about ourselves is a condition that exists in consciousness and therefore must be brought about at the level of consciousness—not at the level of the physical body.

Beloved Astrea, accelerate us all,
as for your deliverance we fervently call,
set all life free from vision impure
beyond fear and doubt, we're rising for sure.

**Beloved Astrea, in oneness with you,
your circle and sword of electric blue,
with Purity's Light cutting right through,
raising the earth into all that is true.**

5. I call for people to be cut free to see that the very fact that people are not happy proves that we cannot understand a human being by looking at the material components in the brain. We can never understand a whole by looking only at the individual components.

> Beloved Astrea, we're willing to see,
> all of the lies that keep us unfree,
> we surrender all lies causing the fall,
> forever affirming the oneness of All.

> **Beloved Astrea, in oneness with you,**
> **your circle and sword of electric blue,**
> **with Purity's Light cutting right through,**
> **raising the earth into all that is true.**

6. I call for people to be cut free to see that a "whole" exists only in consciousness. The cells, the neurons, the connections in the physical brain of a human being do not in themselves make up the totality – the whole – of a person.

> Beloved Astrea, accelerate life
> beyond all duality's struggle and strife,
> consume all division between God and man,
> accelerate fulfillment of God's perfect plan.

> **Beloved Astrea, in oneness with you,**
> **your circle and sword of electric blue,**
> **with Purity's Light cutting right through,**
> **raising the earth into all that is true.**

7. I call for people to be cut free to see that our attempt to understand the whole by looking only at the components is

flawed from the beginning. It will never take us to an understanding of the whole. We need to step up and look at the whole and we can do this because we are conscious beings.

> Beloved Astrea, we lovingly call,
> break down separation's invisible wall,
> raising our minds into true unity
> with the Masters of love in Infinity.

> **Beloved Astrea, in oneness with you,**
> **your circle and sword of electric blue,**
> **with Purity's Light cutting right through,**
> **raising the earth into all that is true.**

8. I call for people to be cut free to see that we have the capacity of consciousness to understand the whole but we cannot do this through the current scientific methods. We cannot do this through the analytical, intellectual mind, which is designed to look at and organize the details. In the process of doing so, the analytical mind loses the whole.

> Beloved Astrea, help all of us find,
> the secret that we create with the mind,
> and thus what in ignorance we decreate,
> in knowledge we easily can recreate.

> **Beloved Astrea, in oneness with you,**
> **your circle and sword of electric blue,**
> **with Purity's Light cutting right through,**
> **raising the earth into all that is true.**

9. I call for people to be cut free to see that we can only look at the whole through intuition, which is our ability to step outside

our normal awareness and look at the world from a different perspective.

> Beloved Astrea, we all do aspire,
> to learning to use your purity's fire,
> to raise every form in infamy sown,
> as Saint Germain makes this planet his own.

> **Beloved Astrea, in oneness with you,**
> **your circle and sword of electric blue,**
> **with Purity's Light cutting right through,**
> **raising the earth into all that is true.**

Part 3

1. I call for people to be cut free to see that we cannot promote psychological welfare without looking at the whole, without understanding the whole of what is a human being and how we function.

> Beloved Astrea, your heart is so true,
> your Circle and Sword of white and blue,
> cut all life free from dramas unwise,
> on wings of Purity our planet will rise.

> **Beloved Astrea, in oneness with you,**
> **your circle and sword of electric blue,**
> **with Purity's Light cutting right through,**
> **raising the earth into all that is true.**

2. I call for society to wake up and realize that the next step for democracy is to make people feel good about themselves. We can only do this when we adopt a more holistic approach and look at human beings as more than the components of our physical brains.

> Beloved Astrea, in God Purity,
> accelerate all of our life energy,
> we're rising beyond every impurity,
> as Purity's Light forever we see.
>
> **Beloved Astrea, in oneness with you,**
> **your circle and sword of electric blue,**
> **with Purity's Light cutting right through,**
> **raising the earth into all that is true.**

3. I call for people to be cut free to see that the tendency to look at the details and to ignore the whole is put upon people and societies by a small elite who have a limited vision but a big pride.

> Beloved Astrea, from Purity's Ray,
> send forth deliverance to all life today,
> acceleration to Purity, we are now free
> from all that is less than love's Purity.
>
> **Beloved Astrea, in oneness with you,**
> **your circle and sword of electric blue,**
> **with Purity's Light cutting right through,**
> **raising the earth into all that is true.**

4. I call forth the judgment of Christ upon those who have a sense that they know better because they are the intellectual

elite who are able to decide that God does not exist. They think society should move away from any form of religion and spirituality and be entirely materialistic because that is just the way the world is.

> Beloved Astrea, accelerate us all,
> as for your deliverance we fervently call,
> set all life free from vision impure
> beyond fear and doubt, we're rising for sure.

> **Beloved Astrea, in oneness with you,**
> **your circle and sword of electric blue,**
> **with Purity's Light cutting right through,**
> **raising the earth into all that is true.**

5. I call forth the judgment of Christ upon those who feel they are capable of deciding on behalf of society and have formed this intellectual power elite.

> Beloved Astrea, we're willing to see,
> all of the lies that keep us unfree,
> we surrender all lies causing the fall,
> forever affirming the oneness of All.

> **Beloved Astrea, in oneness with you,**
> **your circle and sword of electric blue,**
> **with Purity's Light cutting right through,**
> **raising the earth into all that is true.**

6. I call forth the judgment of Christ upon the intellectual elite who claim to be benign, but who are willing to ignore the well-being of all people in society in order to promote their materialistic ideology.

Beloved Astrea, accelerate life
beyond all duality's struggle and strife,
consume all division between God and man,
accelerate fulfillment of God's perfect plan.

Beloved Astrea, in oneness with you,
your circle and sword of electric blue,
with Purity's Light cutting right through,
raising the earth into all that is true.

7. I call forth the judgment of Christ upon those who do not care about the fact that people are dissatisfied, that people are becoming depressed, that there are more and more psychological problems, or that people are not feeling good about themselves.

Beloved Astrea, we lovingly call,
break down separation's invisible wall,
raising our minds into true unity
with the Masters of love in Infinity.

Beloved Astrea, in oneness with you,
your circle and sword of electric blue,
with Purity's Light cutting right through,
raising the earth into all that is true.

8. I call forth the judgment of Christ upon those who are so fanatically promoting their materialistic idea that they do not care about human beings because the idea has become more important than the individual.

Beloved Astrea, help all of us find,
the secret that we create with the mind,

and thus what in ignorance we decreate,
in knowledge we easily can recreate.

**Beloved Astrea, in oneness with you,
your circle and sword of electric blue,
with Purity's Light cutting right through,
raising the earth into all that is true.**

9. I call for people to be cut free to see that when we have a society that is based on an idea that is more important than the individual and the psychological well-being of the individual, then we have an exploitative society where the population is being abused.

Beloved Astrea, we all do aspire,
to learning to use your purity's fire,
to raise every form in infamy sown,
as Saint Germain makes this planet his own.

**Beloved Astrea, in oneness with you,
your circle and sword of electric blue,
with Purity's Light cutting right through,
raising the earth into all that is true.**

Part 4

1. I call for people to be cut free to see that we are being held hostage by a small intellectual elite who are fanatically promoting the idea of materialism and ignoring the fact that this does not promote the well-being of the population.

Beloved Astrea, your heart is so true,
your Circle and Sword of white and blue,
cut all life free from dramas unwise,
on wings of Purity our planet will rise.

**Beloved Astrea, in oneness with you,
your circle and sword of electric blue,
with Purity's Light cutting right through,
raising the earth into all that is true.**

2. I call forth the judgment of Christ upon those who are so fanatical that they are willing to exploit the people, abuse the people, in order to promote an ideology.

Beloved Astrea, in God Purity,
accelerate all of our life energy,
we're rising beyond every impurity,
as Purity's Light forever we see.

**Beloved Astrea, in oneness with you,
your circle and sword of electric blue,
with Purity's Light cutting right through,
raising the earth into all that is true.**

3. I call for people to be cut free to see that this is very abusive and it is something that a democratic government has a responsibility to protect its citizens from.

Beloved Astrea, from Purity's Ray,
send forth deliverance to all life today,
acceleration to Purity, we are now free
from all that is less than love's Purity.

**Beloved Astrea, in oneness with you,
your circle and sword of electric blue,
with Purity's Light cutting right through,
raising the earth into all that is true.**

4. I call for people to be cut free to see that we need to rethink the way we approach society because the next logical step in the process of raising the collective awareness is that we step up and promote psychological welfare.

Beloved Astrea, accelerate us all,
as for your deliverance we fervently call,
set all life free from vision impure
beyond fear and doubt, we're rising for sure.

**Beloved Astrea, in oneness with you,
your circle and sword of electric blue,
with Purity's Light cutting right through,
raising the earth into all that is true.**

5. I call for people to be cut free to see that in order to do this, we have to understand psychology. In order to understand psychology better, we have to overcome the unwillingness of materialistic science to seriously study consciousness.

Beloved Astrea, we're willing to see,
all of the lies that keep us unfree,
we surrender all lies causing the fall,
forever affirming the oneness of All.

**Beloved Astrea, in oneness with you,
your circle and sword of electric blue,**

**with Purity's Light cutting right through,
raising the earth into all that is true.**

6. I call for people to be cut free to see that we need to study how consciousness influences not only every aspect of our individual lives, but how the collective consciousness influences society as a whole.

Beloved Astrea, accelerate life
beyond all duality's struggle and strife,
consume all division between God and man,
accelerate fulfillment of God's perfect plan.

**Beloved Astrea, in oneness with you,
your circle and sword of electric blue,
with Purity's Light cutting right through,
raising the earth into all that is true.**

7. I call for society to be cut free from the current stalemate and make progress in the field of psychology, of understanding what kind of beings we are and what actually makes a person feel good about himself or herself.

Beloved Astrea, we lovingly call,
break down separation's invisible wall,
raising our minds into true unity
with the Masters of love in Infinity.

**Beloved Astrea, in oneness with you,
your circle and sword of electric blue,
with Purity's Light cutting right through,
raising the earth into all that is true.**

8. I call for Astrea to bind the demons and fallen beings behind the intellectual power elite that wants to promote materialism.

> Beloved Astrea, help all of us find,
> the secret that we create with the mind,
> and thus what in ignorance we decreate,
> in knowledge we easily can recreate.

> **Beloved Astrea, in oneness with you,**
> **your circle and sword of electric blue,**
> **with Purity's Light cutting right through,**
> **raising the earth into all that is true.**

9. I call for Astrea to bind the demons and fallen beings behind the power elites that seek power or economic control. Astrea, I authorize you to step in and bind and consume the entire superstructure that has been built.

> Beloved Astrea, we all do aspire,
> to learning to use your purity's fire,
> to raise every form in infamy sown,
> as Saint Germain makes this planet his own.

> **Beloved Astrea, in oneness with you,**
> **your circle and sword of electric blue,**
> **with Purity's Light cutting right through,**
> **raising the earth into all that is true.**

Part 5

1. I call for Astrea to bind the collective beast that has been built, going all the way back to Aristotle, up through the Catholic era and into the scientific age where people do not want to look at the whole.

> Beloved Astrea, your heart is so true,
> your Circle and Sword of white and blue,
> cut all life free from dramas unwise,
> on wings of Purity our planet will rise.
>
> **Beloved Astrea, in oneness with you,**
> **your circle and sword of electric blue,**
> **with Purity's Light cutting right through,**
> **raising the earth into all that is true.**

2. I call for Astrea to bind the set of demons that are trying to prevent people from looking at the whole, either shutting down their minds or fanatically focusing on understanding certain details and thinking that we do not have to understand the whole, or it is too big for us to understand.

> Beloved Astrea, in God Purity,
> accelerate all of our life energy,
> we're rising beyond every impurity,
> as Purity's Light forever we see.
>
> **Beloved Astrea, in oneness with you,**
> **your circle and sword of electric blue,**
> **with Purity's Light cutting right through,**
> **raising the earth into all that is true.**

3. I call for Astrea to bind the demons that are trying to get people to focus on the material world so they never have time to step back and ask: "Why are we doing this, why are we continuing to do this even though we see that it is not working?"

> Beloved Astrea, from Purity's Ray,
> send forth deliverance to all life today,
> acceleration to Purity, we are now free
> from all that is less than love's Purity.

> **Beloved Astrea, in oneness with you,**
> **your circle and sword of electric blue,**
> **with Purity's Light cutting right through,**
> **raising the earth into all that is true.**

4. I call for people to be cut free to say: "Now we have been doing this for some time, let us just step back and see what are the actual consequences. What is actually happening as a result of this approach to science and reality? Have we really gotten closer to understanding the universe by looking at the details?"

> Beloved Astrea, accelerate us all,
> as for your deliverance we fervently call,
> set all life free from vision impure
> beyond fear and doubt, we're rising for sure.

> **Beloved Astrea, in oneness with you,**
> **your circle and sword of electric blue,**
> **with Purity's Light cutting right through,**
> **raising the earth into all that is true.**

5. I call for people to be cut free to say: "Have we actually achieved anything in terms of promoting welfare and happiness

by all of our focus on details and technology and the material world? Have we made people happier by seeking a material explanation for everything?"

> Beloved Astrea, we're willing to see,
> all of the lies that keep us unfree,
> we surrender all lies causing the fall,
> forever affirming the oneness of All.

> **Beloved Astrea, in oneness with you,**
> **your circle and sword of electric blue,**
> **with Purity's Light cutting right through,**
> **raising the earth into all that is true.**

6. I call for people to be cut free to see that focusing on details is the omega aspect of doing science, and focusing on greater structures, focusing on the whole, focusing on patterns, is the alpha aspect of doing science.

> Beloved Astrea, accelerate life
> beyond all duality's struggle and strife,
> consume all division between God and man,
> accelerate fulfillment of God's perfect plan.

> **Beloved Astrea, in oneness with you,**
> **your circle and sword of electric blue,**
> **with Purity's Light cutting right through,**
> **raising the earth into all that is true.**

7. I call for Astrea to bind the dark forces and fallen beings that have made people forget about the alpha aspect of science by saying that this falls under the area of religion and all we get through our intuition is superstition that cannot be proven.

Beloved Astrea, we lovingly call,
break down separation's invisible wall,
raising our minds into true unity
with the Masters of love in Infinity.

**Beloved Astrea, in oneness with you,
your circle and sword of electric blue,
with Purity's Light cutting right through,
raising the earth into all that is true.**

8. I call for people to be cut free to see that the entire purpose of doing science is not to understand every detail, but to understand the whole. We cannot understand the whole by looking only at the details. We must step back, we must use the intuitive abilities to look at patterns, to put them together and to see the whole.

Beloved Astrea, help all of us find,
the secret that we create with the mind,
and thus what in ignorance we decreate,
in knowledge we easily can recreate.

**Beloved Astrea, in oneness with you,
your circle and sword of electric blue,
with Purity's Light cutting right through,
raising the earth into all that is true.**

9. I call for Astrea to bind the fallen beings who are manipulating our ability to look at the whole by creating ideologies that claim they have some ultimate truth about how the universe works.

Beloved Astrea, we all do aspire,
to learning to use your purity's fire,
to raise every form in infamy sown,
as Saint Germain makes this planet his own.

Beloved Astrea, in oneness with you,
your circle and sword of electric blue,
with Purity's Light cutting right through,
raising the earth into all that is true.

Part 6

1. I call for Astrea to bind the fallen beings who present a false theory, a false whole, and say this is how the universe should work and then get people to focus on the idea instead of using our ability to look at how things actually work.

Beloved Astrea, your heart is so true,
your Circle and Sword of white and blue,
cut all life free from dramas unwise,
on wings of Purity our planet will rise.

Beloved Astrea, in oneness with you,
your circle and sword of electric blue,
with Purity's Light cutting right through,
raising the earth into all that is true.

2. I call for people to be cut free to step forward and say: "Why have we taken the approach that we first create a theory of how we think the world works and then we attempt to prove or disprove the theory? Why don't we shift into not focusing on

the theory, but we focus on observation of how things actually work. We do not observe only the details, we also look at the whole, at the connections, at the bigger picture."

> Beloved Astrea, in God Purity,
> accelerate all of our life energy,
> we're rising beyond every impurity,
> as Purity's Light forever we see.

> **Beloved Astrea, in oneness with you,**
> **your circle and sword of electric blue,**
> **with Purity's Light cutting right through,**
> **raising the earth into all that is true.**

3. I call for the cutting free of scientists and philosophers and millions of people to embrace this shift and to demand that it not only be made in the scientific field but that it be made in society at large so that societies realize that the time of ideology is over.

> Beloved Astrea, from Purity's Ray,
> send forth deliverance to all life today,
> acceleration to Purity, we are now free
> from all that is less than love's Purity.

> **Beloved Astrea, in oneness with you,**
> **your circle and sword of electric blue,**
> **with Purity's Light cutting right through,**
> **raising the earth into all that is true.**

4. I call for people to be cut free to see that the time of having theories is over. The time of having political parties that say that society should work this way is over.

Beloved Astrea, accelerate us all,
as for your deliverance we fervently call,
set all life free from vision impure
beyond fear and doubt, we're rising for sure.

Beloved Astrea, in oneness with you,
your circle and sword of electric blue,
with Purity's Light cutting right through,
raising the earth into all that is true.

5. I call for people to be cut free to look at: "Who are we? How do we work? What works for us? What makes us feel good? What makes people happy? Then, this is what we base our society on. Not on some fanciful theory about how we should work or how the universe should work."

Beloved Astrea, we're willing to see,
all of the lies that keep us unfree,
we surrender all lies causing the fall,
forever affirming the oneness of All.

Beloved Astrea, in oneness with you,
your circle and sword of electric blue,
with Purity's Light cutting right through,
raising the earth into all that is true.

6. I call for people to be cut free to make this quantum leap and rise above the consciousness of Satan, of thinking that we can look at the material world and, based on the conditions we see in the material world, we can make up a theory about how the universe works, including whether there is a spiritual world.

Beloved Astrea, accelerate life
beyond all duality's struggle and strife,
consume all division between God and man,
accelerate fulfillment of God's perfect plan.

Beloved Astrea, in oneness with you,
your circle and sword of electric blue,
with Purity's Light cutting right through,
raising the earth into all that is true.

7. I call for people to be cut free to see that the goal of Saint Germain is to manifest a Golden Age where the material conditions, the material affluence, is so much higher than what we have today. How can we ever manifest that age by looking at current conditions and thinking that these conditions can explain how the universe works?

Beloved Astrea, we lovingly call,
break down separation's invisible wall,
raising our minds into true unity
with the Masters of love in Infinity.

Beloved Astrea, in oneness with you,
your circle and sword of electric blue,
with Purity's Light cutting right through,
raising the earth into all that is true.

8. I call for people to be cut free to see that current conditions were not created by God and are not defined by the laws of nature. They are not inevitable. They are not insurmountable. They are created through the collective consciousness and by raising the collective consciousness, we can change many of the material conditions that we think cannot be changed.

Beloved Astrea, help all of us find,
the secret that we create with the mind,
and thus what in ignorance we decreate,
in knowledge we easily can recreate.

**Beloved Astrea, in oneness with you,
your circle and sword of electric blue,
with Purity's Light cutting right through,
raising the earth into all that is true.**

9. I call for people to be cut free to see that when we want to explain the universe based on current conditions, we shut your minds to the vision that could take us and the earth beyond current conditions and help us create a better age.

Beloved Astrea, we all do aspire,
to learning to use your purity's fire,
to raise every form in infamy sown,
as Saint Germain makes this planet his own.

**Beloved Astrea, in oneness with you,
your circle and sword of electric blue,
with Purity's Light cutting right through,
raising the earth into all that is true.**

Part 7

1. I call for people to be cut free to see that progress only happens because there is a leap in consciousness where some people are willing to look beyond current conditions and say:

"Something better is possible. It is possible to go beyond these conditions and create a different society."

> Beloved Astrea, your heart is so true,
> your Circle and Sword of white and blue,
> cut all life free from dramas unwise,
> on wings of Purity our planet will rise.

> **Beloved Astrea, in oneness with you,**
> **your circle and sword of electric blue,**
> **with Purity's Light cutting right through,**
> **raising the earth into all that is true.**

2. I call for people to be cut free to see that there are so many limitations that have been programmed into our minds, and they are preventing the manifestation of the Golden Age for the simple reason that we cannot even accept that it is possible.

> Beloved Astrea, in God Purity,
> accelerate all of our life energy,
> we're rising beyond every impurity,
> as Purity's Light forever we see.

> **Beloved Astrea, in oneness with you,**
> **your circle and sword of electric blue,**
> **with Purity's Light cutting right through,**
> **raising the earth into all that is true.**

3. I call for people to be cut free to see that if we cannot accept that something is possible, if a critical mass of people cannot accept this, then by the Law of Free Will, by the Law of Plausible Deniability, Saint Germain cannot bring forth these ideas.

He cannot release them, he cannot bring forth the technology that will take society to a higher level.

> Beloved Astrea, from Purity's Ray,
> send forth deliverance to all life today,
> acceleration to Purity, we are now free
> from all that is less than love's Purity.

> **Beloved Astrea, in oneness with you,**
> **your circle and sword of electric blue,**
> **with Purity's Light cutting right through,**
> **raising the earth into all that is true.**

4. I call for people to be cut free to see that the potential of consciousness is far greater than anyone has seen before. It is possible to raise a person's consciousness to a distinctly higher level than what most people have today. There is a systematic process whereby we can raise our consciousness to higher and higher levels.

> Beloved Astrea, accelerate us all,
> as for your deliverance we fervently call,
> set all life free from vision impure
> beyond fear and doubt, we're rising for sure.

> **Beloved Astrea, in oneness with you,**
> **your circle and sword of electric blue,**
> **with Purity's Light cutting right through,**
> **raising the earth into all that is true.**

5. I call for people to be cut free to see that what really makes us feel good in the long run is that we work on actualizing ourselves and manifesting a higher state of consciousness. In the

short run, what makes us feel good is that we are not manipulated by any force outside ourselves.

> Beloved Astrea, we're willing to see,
> all of the lies that keep us unfree,
> we surrender all lies causing the fall,
> forever affirming the oneness of All.

> **Beloved Astrea, in oneness with you,**
> **your circle and sword of electric blue,**
> **with Purity's Light cutting right through,**
> **raising the earth into all that is true.**

6. I call for society to be cut free to realize that for people to feel good about themselves, we must not be exploited by any external force.

> Beloved Astrea, accelerate life
> beyond all duality's struggle and strife,
> consume all division between God and man,
> accelerate fulfillment of God's perfect plan.

> **Beloved Astrea, in oneness with you,**
> **your circle and sword of electric blue,**
> **with Purity's Light cutting right through,**
> **raising the earth into all that is true.**

7. I call for people to be cut free to see that if we are to explain the more severe forms of mental illness, we need to recognize that there are certain energies or beings that are not material but that can still influence the human psyche.

Beloved Astrea, we lovingly call,
break down separation's invisible wall,
raising our minds into true unity
with the Masters of love in Infinity.

Beloved Astrea, in oneness with you,
your circle and sword of electric blue,
with Purity's Light cutting right through,
raising the earth into all that is true.

8. I call for people to be cut free to see that there are certain forces that are not in the material realm, but they can influence human psychology and manipulate people in various ways. I call for the cutting free of the psychologists and healthcare professionals to be emboldened to step forward and say that we need a new approach to mental illness because our present approach is not helping people.

Beloved Astrea, help all of us find,
the secret that we create with the mind,
and thus what in ignorance we decreate,
in knowledge we easily can recreate.

Beloved Astrea, in oneness with you,
your circle and sword of electric blue,
with Purity's Light cutting right through,
raising the earth into all that is true.

9. I call for people to be cut free to see that it is the ultimate responsibility of the people in democratic nations to hold their governments accountable because who else will do it? We cannot expect that the government itself would hold itself

accountable. This is the job of the people whether we have representative democracy or direct democracy.

Beloved Astrea, we all do aspire,
to learning to use your purity's fire,
to raise every form in infamy sown,
as Saint Germain makes this planet his own.

Beloved Astrea, in oneness with you,
your circle and sword of electric blue,
with Purity's Light cutting right through,
raising the earth into all that is true.

Sealing

In the name of the Divine Mother, I call to all ascended masters for the sealing of myself and all people in my circle of influence in the creative flow of the Divine Mother, the River of Life. I call for the multiplication of my calls by all ascended masters so that we form the perfect figure-eight flow of "As Above, so below." Thus, I accept that this is fully manifest, because the mouth of the Lord, the Divine Mother that I AM, has spoken it. Amen.

15 | A POSITIVE VISION OF THE GOLDEN AGE

I AM the Ascended Master Saint Germain, and I wish to give you a slightly different take on the Golden Age. Now, you may look at the discourses that I have given so far, that we gave last year, that other masters have given about the Golden Age and you could say that we are focusing a lot on all of the problems that need to be overcome for the Golden Age to be manifest.

Now, my beloved, there are some spiritual people on earth who would look at this and say: "These cannot be the real ascended masters because we should not focus on anything negative because we magnify it with our consciousness and the real masters would never ask us to do this. They would give us a positive vision and have us focus on that." Well, my beloved, while these people are well-meaning, they are also not very well informed because they are not willing to recognize the existence of dark forces and fallen beings. You simply cannot, on a planet like earth, bring forth a new age, let alone a Golden Age, by only focusing on the positive and ignoring the not-so-positive.

Why we need to look at issues

It is necessary for you to be aware of certain issues. It is necessary to make precise calls on these issues because only when those in embodiment make these calls, can we of the ascended masters step in and deal with the issues and the dark forces behind them. If you do not do this, you simply will not manifest a better age. It cannot be done.

Naturally we are not asking you to focus on these problems with fear, and that is why we give you such a large overall teaching that, when you understand it, you realize that we are not giving you a fear-based teaching where you feel completely overwhelmed and pacified and feel like you cannot do anything about all these problems or dark forces. We are giving you an empowering teaching whereby you realize that you can actually do something. You can make the calls and this authorizes us to step in. While *you* may not have the power to overcome the dark forces, *we* do. We simply need the authority.

If you are not willing to look at various issues, you cannot solve them and why is that, my beloved? It is very simple. The earth is an educational institution. How do people learn? Well, they learn by the push-pull of immersing yourself and identifying yourself in the material realm and then awakening yourself from that identification. The awakening process is a twofold process where you both come to see the issues that are limiting you, that have caused you to be identified with the material realm, and you also come to see that you are much more. You are a spiritual being and there is a positive vision of a higher society and a higher state on earth.

If you will not look at the issues that have limited you, my beloved, how can you then free yourself from them and consciously separate yourself from them? It is precisely in separating yourself from the limitations that you expand your consciousness, that you raise your consciousness to a new level. There are many new-age people who have lulled themselves into, or have been lulled into by the fallen beings, a state where they think they are so peaceful, they are so harmonious, they are so focused on the positive that surely they are helping to radiate good vibrations that will transform the earth. The reality is that many of these people are not growing whatsoever. They are not raising their consciousness beyond that level because they are not willing to look at the fact that they have an ego, they have internal spirits, they have ties to the fallen beings. They are not willing to look at the fact that the reason why they feel so peaceful and calm is that the fallen beings are leaving them alone for the simple reason that they are not a threat. As long as you are not a threat to the fallen beings, they will often leave you alone—unless you get sucked into one of their more overall schemes, like for example, a war or some of the other exploitations that we have talked to you about that affect many people.

We are not asking you to focus on these issues with fear but actually with a love-based approach where you realize that we are simply bringing this to your attention so you can make the calls that allow us to step in. Now, that being said, I do want to give you a sort of more positive, you might say, vision of the process of moving the earth into the Golden Age.

We are also ignorant today

Now, I am not here going to go too far beyond the present time and the more immediate future because the long-term perspectives of what can happen in the Golden Age over the next 2,000 years will indeed take us so far beyond what most people on earth can even imagine. What I would like to do is to begin with the fact that there was a time in history that you today look back at and call the "Dark Ages." Why do you call them the Dark Ages? Because you see today that you know so much more than people knew back then, and therefore they were living in a state of ignorance that you then associate with darkness.

Yet the time you are talking about was not necessarily completely dark. For example, all of the great cathedrals of Europe were built during that time. Buildings that you would find it rather difficult to duplicate today even with modern technology because you simply would not have the knowledge of geometry that these buildings are based on. There are other examples you could mention and, of course, many of the productions of that time – the art, the history, the culture – may seem primitive compared to today but it was not necessarily that people were so ignorant.

The reason I am bringing this up is that if you actually project into the future a hundred or two hundred years, they will look back at your time and consider that you were in the Dark Ages because they know so much more about the world than you know today, at least at the official level. What you need to recognize here is that even though you know much in the modern age, even though science has discovered much about the material universe, there is still a certain level of ignorance and it will, of course, be overcome as you move into the Golden Age. This overcoming of ignorance is a gradual process.

I have already in my previous discourses, as has Astrea, given you some perspectives on the changes in consciousness that need to happen so that you can gradually move out of the mindset that is so prevalent in western nations. This mindset is a peculiar form of ignorance where you know an awful lot about the external world but you, as a society and as most people, know very little about the internal world of the psyche, of what consciousness is, how it works, what is the potential of consciousness. As a result of this ignorance, you are actually bringing up your children (as you yourselves were brought up) in a state of ignorance about who you are, what your real potential is. This means that most people today have been brought up without having one of their basic needs fulfilled.

The need for a sense of purpose

We have talked before about the fact that one of the basic human needs is a sense of purpose. You need to have a sense of purpose in life or you are very likely to go into a state of depression, mental illness, substance abuse, any form of escapism that you can mention. This, of course, is not going to make you feel good about yourself and about life. It is not going to make you feel fulfilled in your life.

As we move further into the Golden Age, and here we are not necessarily talking a very long timespan, there will be a shift where suddenly a critical mass of people have come to accept that we must be more than material beings. We have a need for a sense of purpose, and in fact, society should bring up children to have some knowledge of who they are, how the psychology works, what the potential for human consciousness is. It actually should bring up children with a sense that there is a purpose in life, there is a direction in life.

This means that there can – relatively quickly – come a shift so that people in greater numbers begin to accept some of the ideas that we are teaching you today. Now, as we are teaching you these ideas, my beloved, they may seem to you to be far ahead. They may even seem to you to be spiritual, but as we have attempted to show you in this conference, it is, in fact, possible to express many of the ideas we have given you in a universal way so that they are not tied to any particular religion, spiritual philosophy and not even tied to ascended masters.

We do not need society at large to recognize the existence of ascended masters for the foreseeable future. Naturally, at some point in the Golden Age, societies will recognize this. Those who recognize it and openly and consciously cooperate with us, will prosper and those who do not will fall behind. For the foreseeable future, it is not necessary that society recognizes us, but it is necessary that people begin to recognize and accepts some of these universal ideas.

Consciousness can be expanded

A very universal idea is that human consciousness is something that can be expanded, something that can have different levels. It is not difficult to even look at this today and look at people and see that they have different levels of consciousness. Look at historical persons, and you see that they have had different levels of consciousness. If you compare Hitler to Gandhi, anyone who is willing to take an objective look can see they were clearly at two different levels of consciousness. If you take a criminal, a serial killer or whatever, and compare it to a person who is working selflessly to help others (or even to the average person), you can see that there are clearly different levels of consciousness here.

It is not that far away that this will begin to be recognized. Of course, it has already been recognized by some psychologists and other thinkers that do not know about ascended masters but they recognize that this must simply be the only way to explain that there can be such a difference in human behavior.

These people have also begun to see that it is actually possible for a human being to spend an entire lifetime consciously seeking to raise its level of consciousness. It is therefore not a big leap to the point where people begin to realize that if all children were brought up with this awareness (and with some fairly universal, fairly basic, knowledge of how the psyche works and how consciousness works, and how it can be expanded), then this can give the vast majority of people a new sense of purpose and direction in their lives.

It is not necessary to give children at an early age a very sophisticated understanding of where they might be able to take their consciousness. You need not necessarily go into details about the higher levels of consciousness and what it means. By simply showing them that there is a way to raise their consciousness, giving them the tools, you put them on the path. Although they may not be able to see where this is going (as many of you could not see where it was going when you first started the spiritual path) it means that if they continue the process throughout their lives, they will reach higher levels of consciousness and then their vision will be expanded.

Even though as children they may have a sense that the purpose of life is so and so, as they rise in the levels of consciousness, they will get a more sophisticated understanding of what the purpose of their personal lives really is. It will then mean that as they grow in age, they become more and more fulfilled. They have more and more of a sense of being at peace with themselves, at peace with life and feeling good about themselves, being who they are, being in embodiment on earth and making a positive contribution to society. Can you see, my beloved, how this relatively simple change would have an incredible impact on society?

Freeing up people's creativity

Look at society today. Look how many people have grown up without a sense of purpose. What does it mean? Well, even in childhood it means that there are some children that simply do not know that there is any kind of purpose to life and therefore they are acting out all kinds of self-destructive behavior. Often, they rebel against their parents so that there is a generation gap created in the early teenage years. As they grow up through the teenage years, they may get into drugs, alcohol, any kind of escapism. They may decide that what is the point in getting an education because it does not seem like the goal of life can be to make money. You have all kinds of these behaviors that come up, that are really not constructive for the individual but also have a large-scale negative impact on society. Not only do resources have to be spent on dealing with the problems of these children and teenagers, but there is also the loss of creativity and productivity that these children could bring to society if they were able to live a more constructive life.

Then you see, of course, when you go to the later ages and people get into their twenties and beyond, you see that there are many people today who cannot feel fulfilled in their relationships. We end up having divorces that leave children without two parents and it creates all kinds of conflicts between the parents, creates conflicts in the minds of the children, and it also impacts society and ties up resources. You have those who become alcoholics or drug addicts and this ties up resources. You have those who go into crime and end up tying up resources in the police, the welfare system, the prison system and so on. You have those who become depressed and go into various forms of mental illness.

Just imagine, my beloved, how big a portion of the economical resources in most modern democracies are tied up in these issues. Then begin to imagine that these resources were freed so that society could spend that money on other areas. Imagine how much more could be done if the billions and billions of dollars spent on these problems could be redirected into building something constructive. It could be anything you can imagine, but just imagine that this was freed up. Imagine also how much happier people would be, not only the people who are having the problems but also the people who have it as their daily job to deal with these people who are having all these problems, and therefore often are very burdened by this.

You see that all of a sudden there could be such an increase in productivity, an increase in creativity, because, as we have said many times those who get into various forms of mental illness and depression are precisely the children that came in to make a positive contribution to society. Because they were not taught this from an early age, because they found there was no outlet for how they could do this, they then go into the negative spiral.

Imagine that they did not and now they are making a positive contribution to society. Suddenly, everyone has a purpose. A society might even develop a purpose for how we can help other nations. Imagine, just as a historical example, that at the fall of Communism the nations in Western Europe had said: "We are each, or maybe 2 or 3 nations going together, going to pick a nation in Eastern Europe and we are going to focus all of our national resources and creativity on helping that nation come up to a higher level of material affluence."

What is to stop you from doing the same today? It may not be so needed in Eastern Europe but certainly there are other parts of the world where it is needed. Would it not be a tremendous shift in how nations relate to each other if you could make these decisions?

Multiplication of resources and wealth

Now, imagine a little bit further and see how actually there is a collective consciousness and there is an awareness of the collective consciousness. Suddenly, you have all of these people who instead of dragging down the collective consciousness are now raising up the collective consciousness. This can lead to a shift in a nation so that the nation decides to actually engage in helping others.

What these nations, who would do this, will find is that not only will they get a sense of purpose as a nation, but they would actually gain more affluence. The moment a nation begins to spend resources on selflessly helping others, then we of the ascended masters can, of course, multiply that effort and the nation will have more abundance. Something will be brought forth, some kind of way that the nation can manifest more abundance and prosper.

Education in the Golden Age

Now imagine, my beloved, what would happen if you could overcome this stranglehold of religion, especially Christianity and materialism, scientific materialism. Imagine what would happen to the educational systems. Now, you have a situation where precisely because of the unresolved conflict between science and religion, most modern democracies feel that they cannot teach their children the kind of things I am talking about because they have too much of a religious connotation. Imagine you could transcend this and decide that in schools you would not only teach children about their psychology but you would teach children many other things about how life works, how the universe works, how the psyche works. Suddenly, you would have a form of education that is much more directly related to people's personal lives.

Today, you are coming into a school day with a stack of books on your back, focused on different topics, and then going from one short class to another short class where you are taught history, you are taught math, you are taught this, you are taught that and they seem to have no connection to each other. Instead of this, you would come to school and you would be taught topics that are directly related to your personal life, how you see the world, how the world works. You would be taught this in a way that is not broken up in separate topics but it is tied together. You would be taught it in a way that is not passive but is interactive where you are participating. All of a sudden, all of these topics become alive because instead of learning something without knowing why or learning something for the sake of learning it, instead of being forced to learn something and therefore reacting against this by not really wanting to put your mind on this, you would now have a motivation for learning.

You would see that the more you actually know, the more you can raise your own consciousness, the more you can find a sense of purpose, the more you can further your own creativity, your own creative expression throughout your life. Suddenly, there would be a totally different motivation for educating yourself. As this is carried into the higher levels of education, you can see that there are these people who will come out in their twenties with an education that is very, very different from the university degrees you get today. Instead of being so completely focused on one particular topic, you have a much more holistic awareness of how life works. You have a sense of connection between what you have been learning and how society works. You would also have a much more direct con-nection between what you are learning at school and what you are actually going to do after school. Whether it be in a work situation or in some other field. There will even be the possibility that children can be educated not to simply find a position in some kind of job, be it for a private company or the state. They can actually be educated into sustaining themselves with some creative endeavor; starting their own company, inventing something, going into music, going into art, going into philosophy, creativity, writing, this or that.

If you then have the situation where all people have the right to have a basic income, you can see that there a people who from an early age can go through their educational process and educate themselves to go into some creative field. They may not be able to make money perhaps for many years, perhaps not ever, but they know from an early age that they have the economic basis for pursuing and expressing their creativity.

My beloved, I can assure you that those nations who will allow this to happen, they will find that they will attract some extremely advanced and creative souls to take embodiment there. These souls will bring forth new ideas, new inventions, that will have a very positive impact on those nations.

What you will actually see is that in the beginning there will be somewhat of a contrast between the nations who can implement some of these ideas and those who cannot. Those who implement these new ideas, will have such a burst of creativity after some time that they will actually leap ahead of the nations who are not willing to shift into a new paradigm, a new way of approaching life.

Religion in the Golden Age

What will happen in the field of religion as we move further into the Golden Age? Well, actually religion (when you look at official religion, such as the Catholic church or Islam) will continue its decline as we move into the Golden Age. There is very little realistic possibility that the Catholic church or Islam or any other of these large religions will be willing and able to reform themselves.

As people become more and more aware of the possibility of raising consciousness, they will see that these religions have very little to offer in this field and they will simply withdraw from them. These religions will go into an even greater decline than they have gone into and they will simply, as they say, "fade away." They will fade into insignificance and the simple reason for this is that when you know that the purpose of your life is to raise your consciousness to a higher level, you do not need an external religion that tells you what to believe about life.

You see, my beloved, the only way to raise your level of consciousness (not to raise your knowledge because this can be done intellectually) is to expand your intuitive faculties. Well, when you expand your intuitive faculties, what happens? You look at life, you look at some of the questions you have about life, and two things will happen. Firstly, you will attract to yourself a mystical teaching that can give you some answers. Secondly, you will begin to get answers from inside yourself. When you can get answers from inside yourself, why do you need a traditional religion that instead of giving you answers gives you doctrines and dogmas and tells you to have blind faith or you will go to hell? This kind of approach to religion will simply have no meaning for people and they will not need to listen to some Pope or potentate or Imam who will tell them what to believe; and so the religions will fade away.

Now, what will begin to happen is that people will in much greater numbers than you see today seek a more mystical explanation and do this on an individual level. As we have said before, and which has surprised and even disappointed some ascended master students, we are not looking to create one main religion that will dominate the Golden Age. We are not even looking for the teachings of the ascended masters to form such a religion. We are looking at people finding this in a much more individual way and the advantage of this is very, very simple. You have seen in past societies, and you see it even today, how one of these big monolithic religions cannot simply help themselves from trying to have a direct influence on society and the political process. You have seen the very unfortunate effects of this throughout history.

You have seen that in most democratic constitutions it is written in that there should be religious freedom in the country. Some countries in Europe have chosen to have a state-sponsored religion while America, for example, took the revolutionary leap at the time of having no one state-sponsored religion but allowing this to be up to the choices of the people. What you see here is that it is necessary for the functioning of a democracy, the full functioning of a democracy, that there is not one religion that dominates that society. It simply is not possible to have a truly free democracy if the thinking is dominated by one religion. You might say: "Am I not saying that these ideas that people will be accepting about the possibility to raise consciousness, am I not saying this is religious or at least spiritual?" Well is it really, my beloved? Is it really?

The science of psychology in the Golden Age

What has been one of the major contributions of science? If you actually go back to the society you had before the advent of science, you will see something that you often do not think about in today's day and age. You have grown up with the concept promoted by science that it is possible to explain certain things in a universal, objective manner that is not affected by human beliefs or superstitions or by a particular religious interpretation. Yes, it is ironic that this same science has been hijacked by materialism, which has the exact same approach as the religions have of defining how the universe *should* work, wanting to force people to accept this, wanting to force the universe to fit into their thought system. Nevertheless, science has still introduced the concept that it is possible to look at: "How does the universe actually work" instead of having a theory and seeking to impose that theory upon the universe, therefore forcing the results of science to conform to the theory.

Again, you can say: "Isn't that what science is doing today where many scientists are wanting their results to conform to materialism?" Yes it is, my beloved, but still you have the concept that it is possible to make observations and experiments and look at the results and look at what that says about how things actually work, and therefore we can discard the theories that we cannot support through these observations. Well, it is possible to take this exact approach to the human psyche, to the concept of consciousness, and it is possible to investigate consciousness. You can look at how does the psyche actually work, what works, what does not work. You can conduct observations, conduct experiments and then you can come up with something that we are giving you today as a mystical philosophy. You can actually come up with it as something that is completely based on experience and experiment.

Therefore, you can come up with an entirely new view of the psyche that when it is developed, will not be seen as religious or even spiritual.

It will be seen as simply a natural, objective, neutral realization, a higher awareness and a natural element in the evolution of humanity, a higher awareness of how the human psyche works, what a human being is, what our potential really is. When you come to this point, you are so to speak de-mystifying the topic and therefore it is not a religious approach because you are not actually asked to believe this, you are asked to test it out yourself.

Can you raise your consciousness? Can you feel a difference? Well, then it obviously works for you, does it not? Does following this path make you feel better about yourself? Well, then it must work. As more and more people begin to actually demonstrate that it works, there will be that shift where now it is not a matter of calling it religious, it is not a matter of belief or not belief. It has simply become the new norm, the newly accepted truth.

Do you realize, my beloved, that if you go back just a hundred or two hundred years and look at the average person, they had virtually no concept of the psyche; what the psyche is, how it functions. Modern science (and in part credited to Sigmund Freud who although he took this in a slightly unfortunate direction, still broke new ground and made psychology a more accepted science) has produced an increase in the awareness of the psyche. Most people in the more developed part of the world have an awareness that there is something called the human psyche and it has a great impact on their lives.

There can be psychological problems, psychological illness, and if you go back just a few decades, you would see how there was an incredible social trauma associated with seeking help with psychological problems. Psychological illness was a taboo that most people did not even dare to acknowledge for themselves. They certainly did not dare to seek help because it was considered as socially unacceptable in many circles.

Of course, it still is today in some, but you can clearly see that in many nations that trauma has gone away. The stigma has gone away and more and more people are seeking help with depression or other mental illnesses. They are going to psychologists, other forms of therapy and this is a development that you could scarcely have foreseen just a few decades ago.

What has shifted here is that the awareness of the psyche (that it has a great impact on your life and that it is necessary for human beings sometimes to do something about their psyche) has now become accepted. It has now become normal and it is not a big leap to go to the point that instead of waiting for a mental illness to occur, it is better to have an ounce of prevention. You then teach the children from an early age how to avoid mental illness by actually looking at how society can help children function better and help their citizens function better and come to feel good about themselves. This is not religious, it is not spiritual, it is not mystical. It is only a matter of time before it comes to be seen that this is absolutely natural and absolutely self-evident. People will look back and can scarcely understand that there was a time where individuals and societies resisted this, which now seems so self-evident.

As a result of this, these religions that give you answers from without and demand that you will believe in these answers even if they do not make sense, will clearly fade away. This does not mean that people will not have questions about the spiritual aspects of life and naturally these questions will not be answered by some state-defined religion. They will not be answered as people go to school and get an education because this will be focused on the universal aspects of the psyche.

People will naturally pursue this on an individual basis. Again, I do not actually look at the emergence of one dominant religious, spiritual or mystical teaching or philosophy even though I, of course, look to the fact that ascended masters will become more known, will become more accepted and that more and more people will study our teachings on an individual basis.

There always will be room for other spiritual teachings, other directions. There will be room for many different kind of spiritual communities. Maybe they will not even be called spiritual communities because they will be seen as a form of community where people can come together and support each other in the raising of consciousness, in the answering of their questions about life and fulfilling that basic human need that most people have and that more people will become aware of, namely that you need to have some understanding of who you are, how the world works and how you fit into the world.

Of course, there are many different levels. I do not look to this process as coming to a point where, when you have gone through the educational system, everybody is at the same level of consciousness. Naturally, people will come into embodiment at many different levels and so there will still be many different levels of consciousness in society. In fact, there will always be 144 possible levels of consciousness on earth even if the scale shifts upwards. Therefore, these people will need different things, different explanations, different practices because there will be a greater awareness of the need to practice some form of technique in order to raise your awareness. Again, there will not be one that will be sponsored or acknowledged officially by society. It will be up to people to choose this individually. My beloved, there will still be much diversity in the Golden Age. In fact, there will be more diversity in the Golden Age than you have right now in the field of spirituality—and, of course, in many other fields as well. Now, is this all idyllic, is this all wonderful, does it mean that all problems will fade away? Well, of course it does not because there will come a point (or rather there will always be a point, there will always be a process) where there are people who are lagging behind.

Crime in the Golden Age

Naturally, there will come a point (as we move much further into the Golden Age) where crime will simply disappear. If you have a basic income that allows you to sustain yourself materially and if you have a sense of purpose and direction and you have freedom to express yourself creatively (or for that matter have the freedom to sit under a tree and do nothing), then why would you need to steal from anyone else?

If you have a healthy knowledge about psychology, then why would you need the escapism of drugs? Just imagine, my beloved, how drugs and the drug trade tie up incredible amounts of resources in the justice systems of the world: How many people are in prison because of this, how much this costs society, how much it costs to treat the people who are addicted and so on. Imagine that this all fades away. This will, of course, happen. In the beginning stages, certainly in the coming decades, there will be some crime. How will then society deal with this?

Well, why will there be crime? Actually it will be because it will take some time to implement a new educational system that will teach children about the psyche. There will be many adults who have not received this education and you cannot expect that they will all want to educate themselves in this. There will still be some that are in a lower state of consciousness where they see crime as the only way to get what they want. This, of course, will mean that there will have to be a police force. These people will be captured by the police and they will be put into the justice system.

How will this system work? Well, you will (within a relatively short period of time when these changes I am talking about are implemented) see a shift where the justice system will shift away from punishment because what is actually the point of punishing? Well, is it not a rather desperate attempt to scare other people away from going into crime, and making society feel better so that the citizens who are not committing crime can feel that those who do are at least being punished. When you shift away from this, you realize that naturally people have their free will and if they are not interested in working on their psychology, then society cannot force them to do so as long as they live within the law.

When a person breaks the law and therefore harms the whole with what is clearly anti-social behavior, then society has a right to say that you cannot now escape looking at your own psychology and doing whatever is needed to overcome the state of consciousness that caused you to commit a crime. You will see that there will be, in the beginning, a certain force of forcing criminals into going into psychological treatment. Gradually, there will be less and less need to force because they will simply be given a choice. Will they have a traditional form of punishment where they sit in a prison cell with nothing to do or will they go into a more positive process that can actually help them get out more quickly and therefore lead a more constructive life?

Naturally, it will be so that instead of saying that people have to spend ten years in jail, you will say that people have to enter this treatment process. When the people in charge of this process judge that a person is ready to re-enter society, then the person will naturally be let out and will actually be given help to re-integrate into society or to find a positive way to sustain itself.

Perhaps even the enactment of the basic payment will prevent many people from going into crime, or at least making it easier for them to go out of crime because they can come out of prison or the treatment process and maybe actually decide to go into an education instead of being out on the street with no job and no ability to get a job because nobody will hire somebody who has been to prison. Now there can be this shift where society actually sees that people who have gone into crime and have gone through the treatment process deserve a second chance. Suddenly, many people might be willing to help these people get on a constructive track with their lives and so this can bring very, very profound changes in society.

Business in the Golden Age

Now, what will happen in the business field? Well, gradually there can be a shift where you begin to realize that the old-fashioned capitalist model of businesses has become completely and utterly obsolete. When you recognize that we are not material beings and we are, in fact, all beings who have the potential to expand our awareness and grow, all of a sudden there will be this shift. Business will shift away from the current capitalistic model where it is the more aggressive businesses that survive and thrive, where businesses are seeking to out-compete each other, they are seeking to destroy the competition, they are seeking to gain a monopoly.

Instead, there will be a shift and it will be demonstrated, as it is to some degree already, that those businesses who have the greatest creativity will prosper because they are the ones who will come up with the new ideas. They are the ones who will invent, or rather be the instrument for receiving from me, entire new industries that the old-fashioned capitalists could not even envision or could not take seriously.

My beloved, some of you have seen the program where there was a large American company, which is now not so large, called Xerox. They had a small research branch that were given some freedom of creativity, and in the infancy of the computer age they had invented the computer mouse. The executives of Xerox were presented this little gadget and they were saying: "Do you seriously expect Xerox to promote a device called a mouse?" They completely rejected the technology, which was then discovered by the founder of Apple computer who saw the potential and all of a sudden an entirely new industry was developed that the old-fashioned capitalists could not even fathom. Still, there are some of these die-hard capitalists who cannot fathom what happened with the computer industry. They are actually waiting for the point where the computer industry will decline and lose its importance and we will get back to the old ways of doing business.

This is, of course, like the dinosaurs that refused to die but eventually became extinct. In the new age, in the not too distant future, there will be this shift where at first, of course, many business leaders will go into denial and attempt to continue business as usual. Yet more and more will see, and more and more new leaders will come up who see that the real key to the future is creativity. Therefore, there will also be this shift where you see that well, what is creativity?

How can we actually expand creativity? How can we promote creativity? Well, is it not logical that when people raise their awareness, their level of consciousness, they free their creative resources, they become more creative? These business leaders will start promoting this in their businesses, they will start demanding that society does this on a large scale. All of a sudden there can be this shift where you shift away from the more aggressive forms of doing business and you shift into a focus on creativity.

This can also cause a shift where people see that there has been a certain cycle in the evolution of many businesses. First, a business starts up in a new field. It is in an expansive phase. There may, in fact, be some room for creativity, but then a business grows to a certain size where now it dominates either the entire industry or it dominates a certain country. Suddenly, there is a shift where the business now becomes more concerned about maintaining its market share, its markets position, rather than expanding, rather than being creative, rather than finding new fields. This actually has caused many businesses to stagnate or go into a decline. Many businesses have even disappeared because they could not re-invent themselves. Instead, some other company came up that was more in tune with the times, more in tune with the new opportunities, more in tune with the needs of the people and suddenly they took over the market.

Business leaders will become more aware of how to avoid this and that they do want to avoid this. Now there will also be a shift where business leaders begin to realize that in order to attract truly creative people, truly dedicated people, truly balanced people that have the psychological wholeness to actually carry out their tasks, they need to find a new ownership model. It is simply is not enough that one person or a small group of shareholders own the business and most of the employees work for it for a salary without ever getting a sense of ownership or physical ownership of the business.

As the consciousness is raised and as there comes to be more of an awareness, as we have said many times, of the power elite (which again is not beyond what people are ready to acknowledge), then it will be acknowledged that businesses

– the businesses that are most creative – cannot allow themselves to be taken over by a financial power elite who are simply shareholders. They go out and when a company becomes big enough or seems to have a growth potential, they buy the shares so that they can make the profit when a company grows. Otherwise, they absolutely do not care about the business or the people working there and if it comes to it, they are willing to sell their shares, sell the business, merge the business into others, have it be taken over by bigger companies or whatever.

These new business leaders will see that what needs to be created is an ownership model where the people who are working in the company are the ones who own the business and are reaping the rewards of its success, instead of having some shareholders that have not contributed to the business but are simply extracting money from it. In the process, they are willing to kill the business if they can make a bigger profit on that in the short term.

There will be various ways of implementing this new ownership model and this will, of course, give the people who work in the business a greater sense of purpose, a greater sense of personal involvement and ownership, a greater sense they are a part of something. They are allowed to be creative and allowed to make a contribution. Again, it will be seen that these businesses are the ones who will prosper and they will begin to take over the economy in many nations.

The money system in the Golden Age

Naturally, you will also within the not so distant future see that there will be a breakthrough of awareness of the power elite and how the power elite has manipulated the economy and the money system. This his will lead many nations to come to that truly revolutionary shift in consciousness where they realize that it is, in fact, one of the primary responsibilities of a democratic government to make sure that the economy of their country and even the economy of the world cannot be dominated and controlled by a small power elite who do not have the interests of the people at heart or for that matter have the interests of the people anywhere else at heart. They have no concern whatsoever for the people and only look at them as slaves that they can make work for them and they can reap the rewards of the people's labor.

This, of course, is not democracy, this is not freedom and it is the responsibility of a democratic government to make sure that this does not happen. There will be this awareness that we need to rethink how the money system works, we need to get out of a debt-based economy. We cannot allow a small power elite to create money and reap the profit from lending it with interest. This is something that the state needs to take on, and the state needs to be in control of the money system so that only the state benefits and thereby the people benefit. If the state makes money off of money, people do not have to pay so much taxes.

It needs to be seen that the only institution in society that has a right to make money off of money is the state. The state, of course, cannot go into the many forms of schemes that the capitalists have come up with in order to manipulate the economy because the state has no interest in manipulating the economy. It simply has an interest in creating a money system that allows for the greatest amount of creativity, movability of the money, the greatest ability to finance new businesses. This will promote a growth in the economy, and the more the economy grows, the more it is in the interest of all of the people and also, of course, in the interest of the state. These are very, very dramatic shifts compared to what you have today but they are not so unrealistic that they are so far off. It can come to that point where there is such an awareness of the existence of power elites that they will very quickly be put out of commission by the democratic nations. There will be either a raised awareness of how the power elites work and how anti-democratic it is, or there would be an awareness that if we do not reform the money system, then our economies, our debt-based economies, are going to collapse. The debt has reached such proportions that no country can pay it back and it is, in fact, in no way democratic, in no way in accordance with the democratic ideals, that the population of an entire country are enslaved financially so that for the next many decades a majority of their resources will go to pay back the interest to a small power elite. How is this democracy? How is this freedom? How is this allowable in a democratic nation, in a democratic world?

Naturally, again this ties in with exploitation where, as the people begin to realize how the economy is being exploited by a small elite, it will be seen that we cannot allow this to happen and therefore we will create a new money system. Now, the new money system can be implemented in a variety of ways but the main thing here is that when you do not concentrate or allow the concentration of wealth in the hands of a small percentage of the population, but instead spread it out over the entire population, then what you will see is that spending, consumer spending as it is often called, will increase. This means that there will be a need to produce all of these goods that people want to buy and this will create a tremendous growth in the economy.

If you look at a very, very simple fact, my beloved, if you have 2% of the population of the United States who controls 90% of the wealth, well those 2% have the money to buy all the luxury yachts they want but how many luxury yachts can you actually use? If you instead took some of that money and gave it out to the population, then many more people would want to buy, not a luxury yacht, but maybe a nice boat. All of a sudden, there would be a much bigger demand for boats than there is today for luxury yachts that it would create a tremendous growth in the economy.

This is just a very simple example but there are so many other shifts that will happen when you free up the money so that it is not tied up in these investment schemes that really have only the purpose of creating greater and greater numbers on certain peoples financial accounts so that they can feel that they are richer and richer. They have long ago gone beyond the point where they can actually spend the money but they have this insatiable need because they have been sucked into being controlled by the fallen beings. They have an insatiable need to accumulate more and more money. When this is not allowed to happen, the money will now no longer be tied up, it will become liquefied. Therefore, it will be freed up to be invested into new businesses, new ventures and all of a sudden again there will be a tremendous growth in the economy.

Unfathomable economic growth

The simple fact is, my beloved, that if you look at a country like the United States today, this country prides itself and loves to promote itself as the richest nation in the world. How is it the richest nation when 2% of the people control 90% of the wealth? The United States is the richest exclusive, elitist club in the world but it is not the richest nation because it cannot even afford to give basic health care to all of its citizens, which most nations in Europe can afford. You will see that if these changes could happen so that the United States would see that it is their responsibility as a democratic government to prevent that 90%

of the wealth is concentrated in the hands of 2% of the people, then there would be such a freeing up of resources that the economy in a matter of a couple of decades could grow.

The national economy could grow to ten times its current size and if that money was spent to benefit all of the people, then you could say that the United States is the richest nation in the world. The United States has to be very careful that it is not overtaken by some of the other nations that also have a large population because I tell you, my beloved, that if a nation with as large a population as India could implement some of these ideas, then simply because they have so many more people and they currently have such a low standard of living materially and would like to come up to a higher standard, then the Indian economy could quickly become larger than the economy of the United States—unless the United States really allows tremendous new growth to happen.

You see my beloved, those countries who are willing to implement these principles will be the ones who prosper the most. The question is: "Will it be the countries who today are affluent but are often controlled by a small power elite or will it be the countries who are not so affluent and who have perhaps a greater willingness to increase the economy in order to allow their people to reach a higher standard of living?" China, of course, could also become a very, very rich country if they could throw away the last remnants of the communist mindset and certain other aspects of the national psyche of always wanting to isolate itself, standing apart from the rest of the world in order to feel superior.

You see here that the potential for economic growth is simply unfathomable to most people. Now, if you go back to the 1800's and if you had taken people back then, for example people who knew something about the economy, and if you had transported them into the modern age and shown them how the economy has grown in 150 years, they would scarcely believe their eyes. They would scarcely believe that such an incredible increase in wealth was possible. I tell you that when some of these ideas begin to break through and are implemented, then the economy can grow much faster than it has done in the last 50 or 100 years. There can be a growth in the economy that even the most advanced economist today would scarcely be able or willing to accept because they would think, as they are programmed to think, that this would simply lead to such inflation that the economies would overheat and collapse. But my beloved, the inflationary cycle is a product of the power elite and the debt-based economy.

When you transcend this, you can create an economy that can grow much faster without producing inflation. When you have a better money system, there will be no inflationary factor built into the money system. Therefore, there is no limit to how the economy can grow without creating an inflationary spiral. A free economy cannot overheat because in a free economy you do not create money artificially. You create money only to pay for goods and services. If the money is backed by something that has real value, how can there be inflation, how can the economy overheat?

Equality among nations

When you envision this tremendous economic growth, you can begin to think about what ramifications this will have on societies. For example, you can see that right now there is such an unequal distribution of wealth in the world that it is scarcely fathomable to us that people can actually live with this. We understand, of course, as we have said, that you cannot be concerned about every issue going on on the planet. I am not talking about you individually but I am talking about the more developed nations of how they can accept this. As the economy begins to grow, you come to a point where you simply have no excuse for not raising the standard of living in other nations. In fact, you can come to a situation where new ideas will be released in the nations that need it the most rather than the ones who no longer need it.

You can come to a situation here where very quickly the rest of the world will be brought up to a material standard of living that is closer to what the most affluent nations have today. This, of course, does not mean that the affluent nations will stagnate. They will also grow but there will still come that point where there is less of a distance between the rich and the not so rich nations. This will change so many things that you see in the world, my beloved. There will be less disease. There will be no starvation. How could you even accept, in a matter of a few decades, that there are children dying of starvation every year? There will come a point where the world will simply wake up and say: "How could we ever accept this? We certainly cannot accept this anymore." And many other things like this.

What you will see is that there will be such a shift in the focus, in the sense of purpose. Why are we here on earth? Why are we actually here on this planet? Is it just to fight with each other and destroy ourselves in either a war or some environmental collapse or do we have a higher purpose? Well, when you begin to see that you have a higher purpose individually, you can, of course, see that you have a higher purpose as a whole, as the human race. Suddenly, you begin to see that at least in the short term one of these purposes is to give all people equal opportunity to raise their awareness and live a fulfilled life where they feel good about themselves. Think about how many people in the world live in such poor material conditions that the concept of feeling good about yourself just seems like a complete pipe dream, as a luxury they could not even imagine. When you are hungry, what does it matter whether you feel good about yourself or not? There will come that point where it is seen that it is our collective responsibility to create a planet where people have this opportunity.

War and conflict in the Golden Age

Now, of course, my beloved, you may say: "Well what happens to war and conflict and terrorism and all of these things?" Well, when you actually have this shift in consciousness where people begin to see that you are not material beings, they begin to understand the basic dynamic of the power elite, then you will see that within a matter of a few decades, the world will move to a point where it is not that warfare will be forcefully eradicated. It is simply that the world will transcend the consciousness where warfare is seen as a solution to any kind of problem.

This will mean that there will be some nations who will dare to take the step to abandon the military, as I talked about before. There will actually come a point where all nations will have either no military or a very small military that has many other tasks than actually killing other human beings. You can have a situation where some nations will say that the money we are now spending on the military we will spend on creating a force that can go into other countries and in the short term help with natural disasters or starvation but in the long term help build that country, build the infrastructure, build a better economy, give the people a better standard of living. What you today see as the help to third world countries as a form of charity is now seen as a major task for the country, and instead of spending money on the military you are spending it on building other countries.

All of a sudden, there can be this shift where you recognize that if you are not a material being and you have the opportunity to raise your consciousness, as you raise consciousness you will begin to feel that you have a basic humanity within you. You have a certain worth as a human being. You will begin to connect to the basic humanity in other people and you will begin to see that these national divisions and other kinds of divisions will begin to fade away. Suddenly, there can be this greater cooperation, this greater sense of community.

There could be nations who decide to merge because what is the point of having national boundaries? There can be the emergence of these greater regions where armed conflicts simply becomes obsolete, unthinkable. This will take a little bit of time because some nations will lag behind. The question will always be when can the more evolved, the more peaceful nations abandon the military as a deterrent to those nations who are still at a lower state of collective consciousness and therefore could potentially commit aggressive actions?

Still, within a matter of a few decades it is possible to reach this state where war becomes more and more of a remote possibility; it becomes a more and more of a remote occurrence. Suddenly, there comes this shift where people in many nations will stop feeling threatened. In fact, we were already close to this in many European nations before the situation with Russia invading Crimea and the turmoil in Ukraine made the countries of Europe go backwards and think now they need to increase military spending. Of course, the United States is also lagging behind on this, thinking that it needs to maintain the biggest military in the world.

How can it be, my beloved, that the country that in many ways considers itself to be the most developed and sophisticated country in the world is still so afraid that it needs to maintain the biggest military in the world? Does this make any sense to anyone—certainly, not to me. You will come to that point where it is not that terrorism will be eradicated or that rogue nations will be eradicated forcefully. It is simply that the consciousness will be raised. Certain fallen beings will be taken out of the four levels of matter by the ascended masters, and all of a sudden warfare will fade away as a realistic risk. More and more nations will begin to see the need to step into an entirely different approach to life. It will also be seen that those who can do this, will again prosper financially. They will prosper in terms of the peoples' wellbeing and the increase in creativity.

Focusing on possibilities rather than problems

There are so many things here that can and will happen as the consciousness goes through this series of shifts that I envision that it can be difficult for most people to even fathom that such changes can happen. This is actually one reason why we have so far focused on giving you an awareness of the problem because many people are still so focused on the problems that they are able to grasp that: "Yes, if there is to be a better age, we need to overcome this and that and the next problem."

There will be a shift, that is perhaps more subtle than any of the others, and it is that people will begin to shift their focus away from the problems and shift onto the possibilities, the potential. Suddenly, it will be seen that right now many people think that the problems are real and the potential is a fantasy or at least very unlikely. There can be a shift where people begin to realize that, in a sense, (from a certain perspective) it is the problems that are unreal and it is the potential that has reality to it. It is the possibilities that are real and this can lead to a shift, which has already happened in many nations. There have been these gradual shifts up throughout the last century where the material affluence has been increased. People have without realizing this shifted into a more positive view of life, into a more trusting view of life. They have felt that perhaps they live in a more friendly universe than their grandparents did, and certainly a more friendly world.

This can cause this shift where people begin to actually accept that the material realm, the mother realm, wants to nurture them and give them everything they need in the material so that they can pursue the raising of consciousness. This is again a very subtle shift that can have incredibly widespread impact on how people feel about themselves, how they feel about the world, how they feel about each other, how they relate to each other. Suddenly, if you do not distrust the universe, why do you need to distrust your neighbor, especially when you experience that basic humanity in both yourself and your neighbor.

You will see that neighboring nations who have had conflicts in previous centuries, maybe even previous decades, nations who have had distrust of each other, suddenly this will dissolve and they can scarcely understand how they used to look at each other with this distrust. They realize that: "Really, why shouldn't we trust each other, after all we are so alike?"

One of the areas where this potentially could happen is among the three Scandinavian countries: Norway, Sweden and Denmark. They are so alike in language, in culture and in mindset. Once you see beyond certain national differences, you see that they are so alike in mindset. Why is it that nations such as Denmark and Sweden have had so many wars between them over the centuries that the only two nations that have had more wars is England and France? This is a fact that many people in Scandinavia are not aware of. Why is this, my beloved?

Therefore, there is a potential, a very real potential, that the Scandinavian countries can suddenly step up to a higher level of consciousness and say: "Why are we distrusting each other? Why are we not cooperating more?" This, of course, can happen in other parts of the world as well where there are nations that are very close to each other. They have simply been trapped in a spiral where they do not know why they do not trust each other, they just do not. Nobody is willing to stand back and say: "Does it actually make sense that we carry on with this distrust that might have been reasonable decades or centuries ago but is it relevant, is it even relevant today?"

Transcending problems rather than solving them

My beloved, you can see how what I am attempting to give you here is an overall vision. We have made you aware of many problems. We need you to make the calls on them so that we can step in and do our part. Of course, I do not want you to think that the main process of manifesting the Golden Age is overcoming all of these problems. Even if we overcame all of these problems tomorrow, this would not automatically manifest the Golden Age. The Golden Age is something that needs to be co-created between people in embodiment and myself. It needs to be brought forth gradually so that people feel that it has not been dropped upon them but that they have played a part in manifesting it. They have a sense of involvement and ownership, and the greater part of bringing this Golden Age is to shift the consciousness. When you shift the consciousness, the problems fade away. They are transcended.

Now, why do we need you to make the calls on these problems? Well, partly because we are having you make calls on raising the consciousness, but we also are having you make the calls that allow us to step in and bind and consume the demons and the entities and remove the fallen beings who are aggressively perpetuating the problems and have created them in the first place. You see that it is a two-pronged process. If you do not remove the dark forces, people will not be able to shift their consciousness into a positive approach. When you remove the dark forces, this shift becomes so much easier and when the shift happens, it is not that all of the problems will be solved in a linear way. It is not that the cause of the problem will be destroyed, as we have said before, but people will simply transcend the consciousness. Suddenly, the problem either fades away or people no longer focus on it because they are focused on the solution, on the possibility of manifesting a better society. This is what will truly manifest the Golden Age, but it cannot be done as long as people's attention is pulled into all of these negative spirals perpetuated by the fallen beings and the dark forces. It simply cannot be done.

Well, you could say that it can be done as it has been done over the past 2,000 years but it will be a much more slow process. Therefore, what we envision is to speed up the process so that by removing these dark forces, people will suddenly wake up and feel free from this weight that used to pull them into all of these reactionary patterns and spirals. When they no longer have this pull, they will be free to step back and say: "Why are we having this distrust? Why are we doing things this way? Why aren't we looking for better solutions? Surely, there must be better solutions out there." Suddenly, there is a raising of the awareness that yes here is a better solution and suddenly people will see that it is not a matter of forcing this upon society or forcing it upon other people. It is simply self-evident that this is the next step in the evolution of society.

The Golden Age must come gradually

You see, my beloved, there are sometimes ascended master students who get so eager to bring the Golden Age that they would like to see it manifest in an instant, in some dramatic shift. They want to see these dramatic shifts so suddenly some miraculous event, such as raising the earth into the fifth dimension or what have you, occurs and everybody now is astounded because of this seemingly miraculous event.

My vision is entirely different. My vision is a gradual process where instead of seeing this as some miraculous event, people see it as self-evident, as the obvious next step for society and therefore they implement it with that level of awareness, with that approach. Not that it is dropped upon them from heaven but that it is simply the natural self-evident step to take in order to continue the process of manifesting a better and better society where people feel good about themselves.

This is the vision I want to give you for now. I know I have painted with broad strokes, given you relatively few specifics of how this will be implemented. Do you see why? It is not a matter of defining that we need to change the economy and therefore we need to implement this, that and the next thing so that we can map out a plan. No, it is a matter of raising the consciousness so that step-by-step many different people in many different places suddenly see it as self-evident that we need to do this.

That is my vision. In fact, in some way I am perfectly happy to remain unknown to the majority of the people. I am perfectly happy to see the manifestation of the Golden Age without most people recognizing Saint Germain or thinking that all of these ideas are coming from me. I am perfectly happy to have the majority of the people feel that: "Oh, this idea just appeared at the right time and everybody could see that it was self-evident and that is why we implemented it."

This is what many people think about democracy, for example, but it did not appear out of nowhere. It was brought from the ascended realm and it was, in fact, a long process going way back into history to bring forth the current modern democracies. Many, many ideas had to be brought into the world before this could happen. Nevertheless, we are perfectly happy to have the people think that they came up with this because it gives them a sense of being involved, of being engaged. My beloved, I am not looking for people to be mindless followers of this almighty Saint Germain who is the ruler, the hierarch, of the Aquarian age. I am looking for people to feel the creative flow through them and know that they are bringing forth something from within themselves wherever they see it coming from. This is my vision for now.

Will there come a point where people will be more aware of the source? Yes, certainly. But I am in no rush to be recognized as the engineer of the Aquarian age, of the Golden Age. I am just happy to see the growth on this planet so that people can live more and more fulfilled positive lives. This is my joy. This is my reward. Why would I need recognition or worship or adulation? My joy is to see people grow. There is no greater joy for an ascended master working with a planet like earth.

16 | INVOKING GOLDEN AGE SPIRITUALITY

In the name I AM THAT I AM, Jesus Christ, I call to all ascended masters working on manifesting the Golden Age, especially Saint Germain, to radiate into the collective consciousness a new awareness of spirituality and religion in the Golden Age. Help people see that we can build a new future by working with the ascended masters and letting go of the old way of looking at life, including...

[Make personal calls.]

Part 1

1. I accept that we cannot, on a planet like earth, bring forth a new age, let alone a Golden Age, by only focusing on the positive and ignoring the not-so-positive.

O Saint Germain, you do inspire,
my vision raised forever higher,
with you I form a figure-eight,
your Golden Age I co-create.

**O Saint Germain, what love you bring,
it truly makes all matter sing,
your violet flame does all restore,
with you we are becoming more.**

2. I accept that it is necessary to make precise calls on issues because only when those in embodiment make these calls, can the ascended masters step in and deal with the issues and the dark forces behind them. If we do not do this, we simply will not manifest a better age. It cannot be done.

O Saint Germain, what Freedom Flame,
released when we recite your name,
acceleration is your gift,
our planet it will surely lift.

**O Saint Germain, what love you bring,
it truly makes all matter sing,
your violet flame does all restore,
with you we are becoming more.**

3. I accept that we can make the calls and this authorizes the masters to step in. While *we* may not have the power to over-come the dark forces, *they* do. They simply need the authority.

O Saint Germain, in love we claim,
our right to bring your violet flame,

from you Above, to us below,
it is an all-transforming flow.

**O Saint Germain, what love you bring,
it truly makes all matter sing,
your violet flame does all restore,
with you we are becoming more.**

4. I accept that if we are not willing to look at various issues, we cannot solve them and the reason is that the earth is an educational institution.

O Saint Germain, I love you so,
my aura filled with violet glow,
my chakras filled with violet fire,
I am your cosmic amplifier.

**O Saint Germain, what love you bring,
it truly makes all matter sing,
your violet flame does all restore,
with you we are becoming more.**

5. I accept that we learn by the push-pull of immersing ourselves in and identifying ourselves with the material realm and then awakening ourselves from that identification.

O Saint Germain, I am now free,
your violet flame is therapy,
transform all hang-ups in my mind,
as inner peace I surely find.

**O Saint Germain, what love you bring,
it truly makes all matter sing,**

your violet flame does all restore,
with you we are becoming more.

6. I accept that the awakening process is a twofold process where we both come to see the issues that are limiting us, that have caused us to be identified with the material realm, and we also come to see that we are much more. We are spiritual beings and there is a positive vision of a higher society and a higher state on earth.

O Saint Germain, my body pure,
your violet flame for all is cure,
consume the cause of all disease,
and therefore I am all at ease.

O Saint Germain, what love you bring,
it truly makes all matter sing,
your violet flame does all restore,
with you we are becoming more.

7. I accept that if we do not look at the issues that have limited us, we cannot free ourselves from them and consciously separate ourselves from them. It is in separating ourselves from the limitations that we expand our consciousness, that we raise our consciousness to a new level.

O Saint Germain, I'm karma-free,
the past no longer burdens me,
a brand new opportunity,
I am in Christic unity.

O Saint Germain, what love you bring,
it truly makes all matter sing,

your violet flame does all restore,
with you we are becoming more.

8. I call for the cutting free of new-age people to see that helping to radiate good vibrations will not in itself transform the earth. We need to see that we have an ego, we have internal spirits, we have ties to the fallen beings, otherwise we will not grow.

O Saint Germain, we are now one,
I am for you a violet sun,
as we transform this planet earth,
your Golden Age is given birth.

O Saint Germain, what love you bring,
it truly makes all matter sing,
your violet flame does all restore,
with you we are becoming more.

9. I accept that we do not need to focus on issues with fear because we can take a love-based approach where we simply make the calls that allow the masters to step in.

O Saint Germain, the earth is free,
from burden of duality,
in oneness we bring what is best,
your Golden Age is manifest.

O Saint Germain, what love you bring,
it truly makes all matter sing,
your violet flame does all restore,
with you we are becoming more.

Part 2

1. I accept that a hundred or two hundred years from now, people will look back at our time and consider that we were in the Dark Ages because they know so much more about the world than we know today.

> O Saint Germain, you do inspire,
> my vision raised forever higher,
> with you I form a figure-eight,
> your Golden Age I co-create.

> **O Saint Germain, what love you bring,**
> **it truly makes all matter sing,**
> **your violet flame does all restore,**
> **with you we are becoming more.**

2. I accept that even though science has discovered much about the material universe, there is still a certain level of ignorance and it will be overcome as we move into the Golden Age. This overcoming of ignorance is a gradual process.

> O Saint Germain, what Freedom Flame,
> released when we recite your name,
> acceleration is your gift,
> our planet it will surely lift.

> **O Saint Germain, what love you bring,**
> **it truly makes all matter sing,**
> **your violet flame does all restore,**
> **with you we are becoming more.**

3. I accept that we need to move out of the peculiar form of ignorance where we know a lot about the external world but as a society we know very little about the internal world of the psyche, of what consciousness is, how it works, what is the potential of consciousness.

O Saint Germain, in love we claim,
our right to bring your violet flame,
from you Above, to us below,
it is an all-transforming flow.

O Saint Germain, what love you bring,
it truly makes all matter sing,
your violet flame does all restore,
with you we are becoming more.

4. I accept that we are bringing up our children in a state of ignorance about who we are, what our real potential is. This means that most people today have been brought up without having one of their basic needs fulfilled.

O Saint Germain, I love you so,
my aura filled with violet glow,
my chakras filled with violet fire,
I am your cosmic amplifier.

O Saint Germain, what love you bring,
it truly makes all matter sing,
your violet flame does all restore,
with you we are becoming more.

5. I accept that one of the basic human needs is a sense of purpose. We need to have a sense of purpose in life or we are

likely to go into a state of depression, mental illness, substance abuse or some form of escapism.

> O Saint Germain, I am now free,
> your violet flame is therapy,
> transform all hang-ups in my mind,
> as inner peace I surely find.

> **O Saint Germain, what love you bring,**
> **it truly makes all matter sing,**
> **your violet flame does all restore,**
> **with you we are becoming more.**

6. I accept that as we move further into the Golden Age, a critical mass of people will come to accept that we are more than material beings. We have a need for a sense of purpose, and society should bring up children to have some knowledge of who they are, how the psychology works, what the potential for human consciousness is.

> O Saint Germain, my body pure,
> your violet flame for all is cure,
> consume the cause of all disease,
> and therefore I am all at ease.

> **O Saint Germain, what love you bring,**
> **it truly makes all matter sing,**
> **your violet flame does all restore,**
> **with you we are becoming more.**

7. I accept that it is possible to express many spiritual ideas in a universal way so that they are not tied to any particular religion, spiritual philosophy and not even tied to ascended masters.

O Saint Germain, I'm karma-free,
the past no longer burdens me,
a brand new opportunity,
I am in Christic unity.

O Saint Germain, what love you bring,
it truly makes all matter sing,
your violet flame does all restore,
with you we are becoming more.

8. I accept that at some point in the Golden Age, societies will recognize ascended masters. Those who recognize it and openly and consciously cooperate with the masters, will prosper and those who do not will fall behind.

O Saint Germain, we are now one,
I am for you a violet sun,
as we transform this planet earth,
your Golden Age is given birth.

O Saint Germain, what love you bring,
it truly makes all matter sing,
your violet flame does all restore,
with you we are becoming more.

9. I accept that for the foreseeable future, it is not necessary that society recognizes ascended masters, but it is necessary that people begin to recognize and accepts some of these universal ideas.

O Saint Germain, the earth is free,
from burden of duality,

in oneness we bring what is best,
your Golden Age is manifest.

O Saint Germain, what love you bring,
it truly makes all matter sing,
your violet flame does all restore,
with you we are becoming more.

Part 3

1. I accept that human consciousness is something that can
be expanded, something that can have different levels. This is
the only way to explain that there can be such a difference in
human behavior.

O Saint Germain, you do inspire,
my vision raised forever higher,
with you I form a figure-eight,
your Golden Age I co-create.

O Saint Germain, what love you bring,
it truly makes all matter sing,
your violet flame does all restore,
with you we are becoming more.

2. I accept that it is possible for a human being to spend an
entire lifetime consciously seeking to raise its level of consciousness. If all children were brought up with this awareness,
this would give the vast majority of people a new sense of purpose and direction in their lives.

O Saint Germain, what Freedom Flame,
released when we recite your name,
acceleration is your gift,
our planet it will surely lift.

**O Saint Germain, what love you bring,
it truly makes all matter sing,
your violet flame does all restore,
with you we are becoming more.**

3. I accept that when children have a sense of purpose, they become more and more fulfilled. They have a sense of being at peace with themselves, at peace with life and feeling good about themselves, being who they are, being in embodiment on earth and making a positive contribution to society.

O Saint Germain, in love we claim,
our right to bring your violet flame,
from you Above, to us below,
it is an all-transforming flow.

**O Saint Germain, what love you bring,
it truly makes all matter sing,
your violet flame does all restore,
with you we are becoming more.**

4. I accept that when people have a sense of purpose, the eco-nomical resources that are tied up in social problems are freed so that society can spend that money on building something constructive.

O Saint Germain, I love you so,
my aura filled with violet glow,

my chakras filled with violet fire,
I am your cosmic amplifier.

O Saint Germain, what love you bring,
it truly makes all matter sing,
your violet flame does all restore,
with you we are becoming more.

5. I accept that when people have a sense of purpose, there will be an increase in productivity, an increase in creativity, because those who get into various forms of mental illness and depression are often the children that came in to make a positive contribution to society. I accept that instead of going into a negative spiral, these people are making a positive contribution to society.

O Saint Germain, I am now free,
your violet flame is therapy,
transform all hang-ups in my mind,
as inner peace I surely find.

O Saint Germain, what love you bring,
it truly makes all matter sing,
your violet flame does all restore,
with you we are becoming more.

6. I accept that society will develop a purpose for how we can help other nations. Developed nations will go together and raise an underdeveloped nation to a higher level.

O Saint Germain, my body pure,
your violet flame for all is cure,

consume the cause of all disease,
and therefore I am all at ease.

O Saint Germain, what love you bring,
it truly makes all matter sing,
your violet flame does all restore,
with you we are becoming more.

7. I accept a growing awareness of the collective consciousness so that instead of dragging down the collective consciousness, people are now raising up the collective consciousness. This will lead to a shift in nations so that they decide to engage in helping others.

O Saint Germain, I'm karma-free,
the past no longer burdens me,
a brand new opportunity,
I am in Christic unity.

O Saint Germain, what love you bring,
it truly makes all matter sing,
your violet flame does all restore,
with you we are becoming more.

8. I accept that nations who do this will gain both a sense of purpose as a nation and more affluence. The moment a nation begins to spend resources on selflessly helping others, then the ascended masters can multiply that effort and the nation will have more abundance.

O Saint Germain, we are now one,
I am for you a violet sun,

as we transform this planet earth,
your Golden Age is given birth.

O Saint Germain, what love you bring,
it truly makes all matter sing,
your violet flame does all restore,
with you we are becoming more.

9. I accept that we are transcending the stranglehold of religion, especially Christianity and scientific materialism and that this will free our educational systems.

O Saint Germain, the earth is free,
from burden of duality,
in oneness we bring what is best,
your Golden Age is manifest.

O Saint Germain, what love you bring,
it truly makes all matter sing,
your violet flame does all restore,
with you we are becoming more.

Part 4

1. I accept that as we transcend the conflict between science and religion, the modern democracies can teach their children universal spiritual principles without feeling they have too much of a religious connotation.

O Saint Germain, you do inspire,
my vision raised forever higher,

with you I form a figure-eight,
your Golden Age I co-create.

O Saint Germain, what love you bring,
it truly makes all matter sing,
your violet flame does all restore,
with you we are becoming more.

2. I accept that schools teach children about their psychology but also many other things about how life works, how the universe works, how the psyche works. I accept that we have a form of education that is much more directly related to people's personal lives.

O Saint Germain, what Freedom Flame,
released when we recite your name,
acceleration is your gift,
our planet it will surely lift.

O Saint Germain, what love you bring,
it truly makes all matter sing,
your violet flame does all restore,
with you we are becoming more.

3. I accept that when we come to school, we are taught topics that are directly related to our personal lives, how we see the world, how the world works. We are taught this in a way that is not broken up in separate topics but is tied together.

O Saint Germain, in love we claim,
our right to bring your violet flame,
from you Above, to us below,
it is an all-transforming flow.

**O Saint Germain, what love you bring,
it truly makes all matter sing,
your violet flame does all restore,
with you we are becoming more.**

4. I accept that we are taught in a way that is not passive but is interactive, where we are participating. All of the separate topics become alive because instead of learning something without knowing why or learning something for the sake of learning it, we now have a motivation for learning.

O Saint Germain, I love you so,
my aura filled with violet glow,
my chakras filled with violet fire,
I am your cosmic amplifier.

**O Saint Germain, what love you bring,
it truly makes all matter sing,
your violet flame does all restore,
with you we are becoming more.**

5. I accept that people who get a university degree are not so focused on one particular topic, but have a much more holistic awareness of how life works. They have a sense of connection between what they have been learning and how society works.

O Saint Germain, I am now free,
your violet flame is therapy,
transform all hang-ups in my mind,
as inner peace I surely find.

**O Saint Germain, what love you bring,
it truly makes all matter sing,**

**your violet flame does all restore,
with you we are becoming more.**

6. I accept that we have a much more direct connection between what we are learning at school and what we are going to do after school, whether it be in a work situation or in some other field.

O Saint Germain, my body pure,
your violet flame for all is cure,
consume the cause of all disease,
and therefore I am all at ease.

**O Saint Germain, what love you bring,
it truly makes all matter sing,
your violet flame does all restore,
with you we are becoming more.**

7. I accept that children are educated not to simply find a particular job, but to be sustaining themselves with some creative endeavor; starting their own company, inventing something, going into music, art, philosophy, creativity or writing.

O Saint Germain, I'm karma-free,
the past no longer burdens me,
a brand new opportunity,
I am in Christic unity.

**O Saint Germain, what love you bring,
it truly makes all matter sing,
your violet flame does all restore,
with you we are becoming more.**

8. I accept that all people have the right to have a basic income, so there are people who from an early age can go through their educational process and educate themselves to go into some creative field. They may not be able to make money perhaps for many years, perhaps not ever, but they know from an early age that they have the economic basis for pursuing and expressing their creativity.

> O Saint Germain, we are now one,
> I am for you a violet sun,
> as we transform this planet earth,
> your Golden Age is given birth.

> **O Saint Germain, what love you bring,**
> **it truly makes all matter sing,**
> **your violet flame does all restore,**
> **with you we are becoming more.**

9. I accept that those nations who will allow this to happen, will attract some extremely advanced and creative souls to take embodiment there. These souls will bring forth new ideas, new inventions, that will have a positive impact on those nations.

> O Saint Germain, the earth is free,
> from burden of duality,
> in oneness we bring what is best,
> your Golden Age is manifest.

> **O Saint Germain, what love you bring,**
> **it truly makes all matter sing,**
> **your violet flame does all restore,**
> **with you we are becoming more.**

Part 5

1. I accept that as people become more aware of the possibility of raising consciousness, they will see that traditional religions have very little to offer and that we do not need an external religion that tells us what to believe about life.

O Saint Germain, you do inspire,
my vision raised forever higher,
with you I form a figure-eight,
your Golden Age I co-create.

O Saint Germain, what love you bring,
it truly makes all matter sing,
your violet flame does all restore,
with you we are becoming more.

2. I accept that the only way to raise our level of consciousness is to expand our intuitive faculties. When we do, we attract a mystical teaching and we get answers from inside ourselves.

O Saint Germain, what Freedom Flame,
released when we recite your name,
acceleration is your gift,
our planet it will surely lift.

O Saint Germain, what love you bring,
it truly makes all matter sing,
your violet flame does all restore,
with you we are becoming more.

3. I accept that when we get answers from inside ourselves, we do not need a traditional religion that instead of giving us answers gives us doctrines and dogmas and tells us to have blind faith or we will go to hell.

> O Saint Germain, in love we claim,
> our right to bring your violet flame,
> from you Above, to us below,
> it is an all-transforming flow.

> **O Saint Germain, what love you bring,**
> **it truly makes all matter sing,**
> **your violet flame does all restore,**
> **with you we are becoming more.**

4. I accept that there will not be one main religion that will dominate the Golden Age, because people will find a more individual way. Therefore, no monolithic religion will have a direct influence on society and the political process.

> O Saint Germain, I love you so,
> my aura filled with violet glow,
> my chakras filled with violet fire,
> I am your cosmic amplifier.

> **O Saint Germain, what love you bring,**
> **it truly makes all matter sing,**
> **your violet flame does all restore,**
> **with you we are becoming more.**

5. I accept that it is necessary for the full functioning of a democracy that there is not one religion that dominates that

society. It is not possible to have a truly free democracy if the thinking is dominated by one religion.

O Saint Germain, I am now free,
your violet flame is therapy,
transform all hang-ups in my mind,
as inner peace I surely find.

O Saint Germain, what love you bring,
it truly makes all matter sing,
your violet flame does all restore,
with you we are becoming more.

6. I accept that we will look at how the universe actually works instead of having a theory and seeking to impose that theory upon the universe, therefore forcing the results of science to conform to the theory.

O Saint Germain, my body pure,
your violet flame for all is cure,
consume the cause of all disease,
and therefore I am all at ease.

O Saint Germain, what love you bring,
it truly makes all matter sing,
your violet flame does all restore,
with you we are becoming more.

7. I accept that we will make observations and experiments and look at the results and look at what that says about how things actually work. Therefore, we can discard the theories that we cannot support through these observations.

O Saint Germain, I'm karma-free,
the past no longer burdens me,
a brand new opportunity,
I am in Christic unity.

O Saint Germain, what love you bring,
it truly makes all matter sing,
your violet flame does all restore,
with you we are becoming more.

8. I accept that we will take this approach to the human psyche, to the concept of consciousness, and investigate consciousness. We will look at how the psyche actually works, what works, what does not work.

O Saint Germain, we are now one,
I am for you a violet sun,
as we transform this planet earth,
your Golden Age is given birth.

O Saint Germain, what love you bring,
it truly makes all matter sing,
your violet flame does all restore,
with you we are becoming more.

9. I accept that we will conduct observations, conduct experiments and come up with something that is completely based on experience and experiment. We will come up with an entirely new view of the psyche that is not religious or even spiritual.

O Saint Germain, the earth is free,
from burden of duality,

in oneness we bring what is best,
your Golden Age is manifest.

O Saint Germain, what love you bring,
it truly makes all matter sing,
your violet flame does all restore,
with you we are becoming more.

Part 6

1. I accept that we will develop a natural, objective, neutral awareness of how the human psyche works, what a human being is, what our potential really is. We will de-mystify the topic and this is not a religious approach because we are not actually asked to believe this, we are asked to test it ourselves.

O Saint Germain, you do inspire,
my vision raised forever higher,
with you I form a figure-eight,
your Golden Age I co-create.

O Saint Germain, what love you bring,
it truly makes all matter sing,
your violet flame does all restore,
with you we are becoming more.

2. I accept that more people begin to demonstrate that raising consciousness works, and this will bring about a shift where raising awareness has become the new norm, the newly accepted truth.

O Saint Germain, what Freedom Flame,
released when we recite your name,
acceleration is your gift,
our planet it will surely lift.

O Saint Germain, what love you bring,
it truly makes all matter sing,
your violet flame does all restore,
with you we are becoming more.

3. I accept that we transcend all stigma related to mental illness, so that instead of waiting for a mental illness to occur, we teach children from an early age how to avoid mental illness. We help children function better and help our citizens function better and come to feel good about themselves.

O Saint Germain, in love we claim,
our right to bring your violet flame,
from you Above, to us below,
it is an all-transforming flow.

O Saint Germain, what love you bring,
it truly makes all matter sing,
your violet flame does all restore,
with you we are becoming more.

4. I accept that this is not religious, it is not spiritual, it is not mystical. It is seen as absolutely natural and absolutely self-evident and people will look back and can scarcely understand that there was a time where individuals and societies resisted what now seems so self-evident.

O Saint Germain, I love you so,
my aura filled with violet glow,
my chakras filled with violet fire,
I am your cosmic amplifier.

**O Saint Germain, what love you bring,
it truly makes all matter sing,
your violet flame does all restore,
with you we are becoming more.**

5. I accept that people will pursue questions about the spiritual aspects of life on an individual basis. I accept that ascended masters will become more known, but there will be room for other spiritual teachings.

O Saint Germain, I am now free,
your violet flame is therapy,
transform all hang-ups in my mind,
as inner peace I surely find.

**O Saint Germain, what love you bring,
it truly makes all matter sing,
your violet flame does all restore,
with you we are becoming more.**

6. I accept that there will be room for many different kind of spiritual communities. Some will not even be called spiritual communities because they will be seen as a form of community where people can come together and support each other in the raising of consciousness, in the answering of their questions about life and fulfilling that basic human need, namely that we need some understanding of who we are, how the world works and how we fit into the world.

O Saint Germain, my body pure,
your violet flame for all is cure,
consume the cause of all disease,
and therefore I am all at ease.

O Saint Germain, what love you bring,
it truly makes all matter sing,
your violet flame does all restore,
with you we are becoming more.

7. I accept that there will be a greater awareness of the need to practice some form of technique in order to raise awareness, and people will choose this individually.

O Saint Germain, I'm karma-free,
the past no longer burdens me,
a brand new opportunity,
I am in Christic unity.

O Saint Germain, what love you bring,
it truly makes all matter sing,
your violet flame does all restore,
with you we are becoming more.

8. I accept that as we move much further into the Golden Age, crime will disappear. We have a basic income that allows us to sustain ourselves materially and we have a sense of purpose and direction and we have freedom to express ourselves creatively so we do not need to steal from anyone else.

O Saint Germain, we are now one,
I am for you a violet sun,

as we transform this planet earth,
your Golden Age is given birth.

**O Saint Germain, what love you bring,
it truly makes all matter sing,
your violet flame does all restore,
with you we are becoming more.**

9. I accept that as people have a healthy knowledge about psychology, they do not need the escapism of drugs, so the drug trade will disappear and will no longer tie up resources in the justice systems of the world.

O Saint Germain, the earth is free,
from burden of duality,
in oneness we bring what is best,
your Golden Age is manifest.

**O Saint Germain, what love you bring,
it truly makes all matter sing,
your violet flame does all restore,
with you we are becoming more.**

Sealing

In the name of the Divine Mother, I call to all ascended masters for the sealing of myself and all people in my circle of influence in the creative flow of the Divine Mother, the River of Life. I call for the multiplication of my calls by all ascended masters so that we form the perfect figure-eight flow of "As Above, so below." Thus, I accept that this is fully manifest, because the mouth of the Lord, the Divine Mother that I AM, has spoken it. Amen.

17 | INVOKING GOLDEN AGE BUSINESS AND ECONOMY

In the name I AM THAT I AM, Jesus Christ, I call to all ascended masters working on manifesting the Golden Age, especially Saint Germain, to radiate into the collective consciousness a new awareness of how businesses and the economy will evolve in the Golden Age. Help people see that we can build a new future by working with the ascended masters and letting go of the old way of looking at life, including…

[Make personal calls.]

Part 1

1. I accept that the justice system will shift away from punishment because of the realization that people have free will and if they are not interested in working on their psychology, then society cannot force them to do so as long as they live within the law.

O Saint Germain, you do inspire,
my vision raised forever higher,
with you I form a figure-eight,
your Golden Age I co-create.

O Saint Germain, what love you bring,
it truly makes all matter sing,
your violet flame does all restore,
with you we are becoming more.

2. I accept that when a person breaks the law and therefore harms the whole with what is clearly anti-social behavior, then society has a right to say that you cannot now escape looking at your own psychology and doing whatever is needed to overcome the state of consciousness that caused you to commit a crime.

O Saint Germain, what Freedom Flame,
released when we recite your name,
acceleration is your gift,
our planet it will surely lift.

O Saint Germain, what love you bring,
it truly makes all matter sing,
your violet flame does all restore,
with you we are becoming more.

3. I accept that criminals will be given a choice between a traditional form of punishment and a process of psychological healing that can help them get out more quickly and therefore lead a more constructive life.

O Saint Germain, in love we claim,
our right to bring your violet flame,
from you Above, to us below,
it is an all-transforming flow.

O Saint Germain, what love you bring,
it truly makes all matter sing,
your violet flame does all restore,
with you we are becoming more.

4. I accept that when people enter this treatment process, those in charge can judge that a person is ready to re-enter society, and then the person will be let out and will be given help to re-integrate into society or to find a positive way to sustain itself.

O Saint Germain, I love you so,
my aura filled with violet glow,
my chakras filled with violet fire,
I am your cosmic amplifier.

O Saint Germain, what love you bring,
it truly makes all matter sing,
your violet flame does all restore,
with you we are becoming more.

5. I accept that enactment of the basic payment will prevent many people from going into crime, plus making it easier for them to get out of crime and go into an education.

O Saint Germain, I am now free,
your violet flame is therapy,

transform all hang-ups in my mind,
as inner peace I surely find.

**O Saint Germain, what love you bring,
it truly makes all matter sing,
your violet flame does all restore,
with you we are becoming more.**

6. I accept a shift where society sees that people who have gone into crime and have gone through the treatment process deserve a second chance. Many people will be willing to help these people get on a constructive track with their lives.

O Saint Germain, my body pure,
your violet flame for all is cure,
consume the cause of all disease,
and therefore I am all at ease.

**O Saint Germain, what love you bring,
it truly makes all matter sing,
your violet flame does all restore,
with you we are becoming more.**

7. I accept a shift in the business field where people realize that the old-fashioned capitalist model of businesses has become obsolete.

O Saint Germain, I'm karma-free,
the past no longer burdens me,
a brand new opportunity,
I am in Christic unity.

**O Saint Germain, what love you bring,
it truly makes all matter sing,
your violet flame does all restore,
with you we are becoming more.**

8. I accept that we are not material beings but we have the potential to expand our awareness, and therefore business will shift away from the current capitalistic model where it is the more aggressive businesses that survive and thrive.

O Saint Germain, we are now one,
I am for you a violet sun,
as we transform this planet earth,
your Golden Age is given birth.

**O Saint Germain, what love you bring,
it truly makes all matter sing,
your violet flame does all restore,
with you we are becoming more.**

9. I accept that businesses will no longer seek to out-compete each other, seek to destroy the competition or seek to gain a monopoly.

O Saint Germain, the earth is free,
from burden of duality,
in oneness we bring what is best,
your Golden Age is manifest.

**O Saint Germain, what love you bring,
it truly makes all matter sing,
your violet flame does all restore,
with you we are becoming more.**

Part 2

1. I accept a shift so that those businesses who have the **greatest** creativity will prosper because they are the ones who will
come up with the new ideas. They are the ones who will **invent**,
or rather be the instrument for receiving from Saint Germain,
entire new industries that the old-fashioned capitalists could
not even envision or could not take seriously.

> O Saint Germain, you do inspire,
> my vision raised forever higher,
> with you I form a figure-eight,
> your Golden Age I co-create.

> **O Saint Germain, what love you bring,**
> **it truly makes all matter sing,**
> **your violet flame does all restore,**
> **with you we are becoming more.**

2. I accept that business leaders will begin to see that the real
key to the future is creativity, and thus we need to expand and
promote creativity.

> O Saint Germain, what Freedom Flame,
> released when we recite your name,
> acceleration is your gift,
> our planet it will surely lift.

> **O Saint Germain, what love you bring,**
> **it truly makes all matter sing,**
> **your violet flame does all restore,**
> **with you we are becoming more.**

3. I accept that when people raise their awareness, they free their creative resources and thus business leaders will start promoting this in their businesses, they will start demanding that society does this on a large scale.

> O Saint Germain, in love we claim,
> our right to bring your violet flame,
> from you Above, to us below,
> it is an all-transforming flow.

> **O Saint Germain, what love you bring,**
> **it truly makes all matter sing,**
> **your violet flame does all restore,**
> **with you we are becoming more.**

4. I accept a shift away from the more aggressive forms of doing business and into a focus on creativity. Businesses will continue to innovate instead of becoming concerned about maintaining market share or defending a monopoly.

> O Saint Germain, I love you so,
> my aura filled with violet glow,
> my chakras filled with violet fire,
> I am your cosmic amplifier.

> **O Saint Germain, what love you bring,**
> **it truly makes all matter sing,**
> **your violet flame does all restore,**
> **with you we are becoming more.**

5. I accept that business leaders will become more aware of how to avoid stagnation, and they will realize that in order to attract creative people, they need to find a new ownership

model. It is not enough that one person or a small group of shareholders own the business and most of the employees work for a salary without ever getting a sense of ownership or physical ownership of the business.

> O Saint Germain, I am now free,
> your violet flame is therapy,
> transform all hang-ups in my mind,
> as inner peace I surely find.

> **O Saint Germain, what love you bring,**
> **it truly makes all matter sing,**
> **your violet flame does all restore,**
> **with you we are becoming more.**

6. I accept that people will acknowledge that the businesses that are most creative cannot allow themselves to be taken over by a financial power elite who are shareholders and do not care about the business or the people working there because they just want to make a quick profit.

> O Saint Germain, my body pure,
> your violet flame for all is cure,
> consume the cause of all disease,
> and therefore I am all at ease.

> **O Saint Germain, what love you bring,**
> **it truly makes all matter sing,**
> **your violet flame does all restore,**
> **with you we are becoming more.**

7. I accept that there will be a new type of business leaders who will see the need for an ownership model where the

people who are working in the company are the ones who own the business and are reaping the rewards of its success, instead of having some shareholders that have not contributed to the business but are simply extracting money from it.

O Saint Germain, I'm karma-free,
the past no longer burdens me,
a brand new opportunity,
I am in Christic unity.

O Saint Germain, what love you bring,
it truly makes all matter sing,
your violet flame does all restore,
with you we are becoming more.

8. I accept that many new ownership models will give the people who work in the business world a greater sense of purpose, a greater sense of personal involvement and ownership, a greater sense they are a part of something.

O Saint Germain, we are now one,
I am for you a violet sun,
as we transform this planet earth,
your Golden Age is given birth.

O Saint Germain, what love you bring,
it truly makes all matter sing,
your violet flame does all restore,
with you we are becoming more.

9. I accept that businesses in which people are allowed to be creative and allowed to make a contribution will prosper and they will begin to take over the economy in many nations.

O Saint Germain, the earth is free,
from burden of duality,
in oneness we bring what is best,
your Golden Age is manifest.

O Saint Germain, what love you bring,
it truly makes all matter sing,
your violet flame does all restore,
with you we are becoming more.

Part 3

1. I accept that there will be a breakthrough of awareness of the power elite and how the power elite has manipulated the economy and the money system.

O Saint Germain, you do inspire,
my vision raised forever higher,
with you I form a figure-eight,
your Golden Age I co-create.

O Saint Germain, what love you bring,
it truly makes all matter sing,
your violet flame does all restore,
with you we are becoming more.

2. I accept a revolutionary shift in consciousness where people realize that it is one of the primary responsibilities of a democratic government to make sure that the economy of their country and even the economy of the world cannot be

dominated and controlled by a small power elite who do not have the interests of the people at heart.

O Saint Germain, what Freedom Flame,
released when we recite your name,
acceleration is your gift,
our planet it will surely lift.

**O Saint Germain, what love you bring,
it truly makes all matter sing,
your violet flame does all restore,
with you we are becoming more.**

3. I accept that we need to rethink how the money system works, we need to get out of a debt-based economy. We cannot allow a small power elite to create money and reap the profit from lending it with interest.

O Saint Germain, in love we claim,
our right to bring your violet flame,
from you Above, to us below,
it is an all-transforming flow.

**O Saint Germain, what love you bring,
it truly makes all matter sing,
your violet flame does all restore,
with you we are becoming more.**

4. I accept that the state needs to be in control of the money system so that only the state benefits and thereby the people benefit. If the state makes money off of money, people do not have to pay so much taxes.

O Saint Germain, I love you so,
my aura filled with violet glow,
my chakras filled with violet fire,
I am your cosmic amplifier.

O Saint Germain, what love you bring,
it truly makes all matter sing,
your violet flame does all restore,
with you we are becoming more.

5. I accept that the only institution in society that has a right to make money off of money is the state. The state has an interest in creating a money system that allows for the greatest amount of creativity, movability of the money, the greatest ability to finance new businesses.

O Saint Germain, I am now free,
your violet flame is therapy,
transform all hang-ups in my mind,
as inner peace I surely find.

O Saint Germain, what love you bring,
it truly makes all matter sing,
your violet flame does all restore,
with you we are becoming more.

6. I accept that there is such an awareness of the existence of power elites, how the power elites work and how anti-democratic it is that they will be put out of commission by the democratic nations.

O Saint Germain, my body pure,
your violet flame for all is cure,

consume the cause of all disease,
and therefore I am all at ease.

**O Saint Germain, what love you bring,
it truly makes all matter sing,
your violet flame does all restore,
with you we are becoming more.**

7. I accept that if we do not reform the money system, then our debt-based economies are going to collapse. The debt has reached such proportions that no country can pay it back and it is not democratic that the population of an entire country is enslaved financially.

O Saint Germain, I'm karma-free,
the past no longer burdens me,
a brand new opportunity,
I am in Christic unity.

**O Saint Germain, what love you bring,
it truly makes all matter sing,
your violet flame does all restore,
with you we are becoming more.**

8. I accept that it is not in accordance with the ideals of democracy and freedom that for the next many decades a majority of people's resources will go to pay back the interest to a small power elite.

O Saint Germain, we are now one,
I am for you a violet sun,
as we transform this planet earth,
your Golden Age is given birth.

**O Saint Germain, what love you bring,
it truly makes all matter sing,
your violet flame does all restore,
with you we are becoming more.**

9. I accept that the people realize how the economy is being exploited by a small elite, and that we cannot allow this to happen and therefore we must create a new money system.

O Saint Germain, the earth is free,
from burden of duality,
in oneness we bring what is best,
your Golden Age is manifest.

**O Saint Germain, what love you bring,
it truly makes all matter sing,
your violet flame does all restore,
with you we are becoming more.**

Part 4

1. I accept that a democratic money system will not allow the concentration of wealth in the hands of a small percentage of the population, but instead spread it out over the entire population, whereby the economy will grow.

O Saint Germain, you do inspire,
my vision raised forever higher,
with you I form a figure-eight,
your Golden Age I co-create.

**O Saint Germain, what love you bring,
it truly makes all matter sing,
your violet flame does all restore,
with you we are becoming more.**

2. I accept that we will free up the money so that it is not tied up in these investment schemes that have only the purpose of creating greater and greater numbers on certain peoples financial accounts so that they can feel that they are richer and richer.

O Saint Germain, what Freedom Flame,
released when we recite your name,
acceleration is your gift,
our planet it will surely lift.

**O Saint Germain, what love you bring,
it truly makes all matter sing,
your violet flame does all restore,
with you we are becoming more.**

3. I accept that we cannot allow people to carry out an insatiable need to accumulate more and more money. When this is not allowed, the money will now no longer be tied up, it will become liquefied, invested into new businesses and there will be a tremendous growth in the economy.

O Saint Germain, in love we claim,
our right to bring your violet flame,
from you Above, to us below,
it is an all-transforming flow.

**O Saint Germain, what love you bring,
it truly makes all matter sing,
your violet flame does all restore,
with you we are becoming more.**

4. I accept that the United States cannot be the richest nation in the world when 2% of the people control 90% of the wealth. The United States is the richest exclusive, elitist club in the world but it is not the richest nation because it cannot even afford to give basic health care to all of its citizens.

O Saint Germain, I love you so,
my aura filled with violet glow,
my chakras filled with violet fire,
I am your cosmic amplifier.

**O Saint Germain, what love you bring,
it truly makes all matter sing,
your violet flame does all restore,
with you we are becoming more.**

5. I accept that it is the responsibility as a democratic government to prevent that 90% of the wealth is concentrated in the hands of 2% of the people. Thereby, the national economy will grow to ten times its current size and if that money was spent to benefit all of the people, then you could say that the United States is the richest nation in the world.

O Saint Germain, I am now free,
your violet flame is therapy,
transform all hang-ups in my mind,
as inner peace I surely find.

**O Saint Germain, what love you bring,
it truly makes all matter sing,
your violet flame does all restore,
with you we are becoming more.**

6. I accept that the potential for economic growth is unfathomable to most people. When some of these ideas begin to be implemented, then the economy can grow much faster than it has done in the last 50 or 100 years.

O Saint Germain, my body pure,
your violet flame for all is cure,
consume the cause of all disease,
and therefore I am all at ease.

**O Saint Germain, what love you bring,
it truly makes all matter sing,
your violet flame does all restore,
with you we are becoming more.**

7. I accept that there will be a growth in the economy that even the most advanced economist would scarcely be willing to accept because they think this would lead to inflation. But the inflationary cycle is a product of the power elite and the debt-based economy.

O Saint Germain, I'm karma-free,
the past no longer burdens me,
a brand new opportunity,
I am in Christic unity.

**O Saint Germain, what love you bring,
it truly makes all matter sing,**

your violet flame does all restore,
with you we are becoming more.

8. I accept that when we transcend this, we can create an economy that can grow much faster without producing inflation. When we have a better money system, there will be no inflationary factor built into the money system. Therefore, there is no limit to how the economy can grow without creating an inflationary spiral.

O Saint Germain, we are now one,
I am for you a violet sun,
as we transform this planet earth,
your Golden Age is given birth.

O Saint Germain, what love you bring,
it truly makes all matter sing,
your violet flame does all restore,
with you we are becoming more.

9. I accept that a free economy cannot overheat because in a free economy we do not create money artificially. We create money only to pay for goods and services. If the money is backed by something that has real value, how can there be inflation, how can the economy overheat?

O Saint Germain, the earth is free,
from burden of duality,
in oneness we bring what is best,
your Golden Age is manifest.

O Saint Germain, what love you bring,
it truly makes all matter sing,

**your violet flame does all restore,
with you we are becoming more.**

Sealing

In the name of the Divine Mother, I call to all ascended masters for the sealing of myself and all people in my circle of influence in the creative flow of the Divine Mother, the River of Life. I call for the multiplication of my calls by all ascended masters so that we form the perfect figure-eight flow of "As Above, so below." Thus, I accept that this is fully manifest, because the mouth of the Lord, the Divine Mother that I AM, has spoken it. Amen.

18 | INVOKING HIGHER EQUALITY AMONG NATIONS

In the name I AM THAT I AM, Jesus Christ, I call to all ascended masters working on manifesting the Golden Age, especially Saint Germain, to radiate into the collective consciousness a new awareness of the need for the most developed nations to help the less developed nations. Help people see that we can build a new future by working with the ascended masters and letting go of the old way of looking at life, including…

[Make personal calls.]

Part 1

1. I accept that the developed nations will no longer live with the unequal distribution of wealth in the world, and thus they will engage in a systematic effort to raise the standard of living in other nations.

O Saint Germain, you do inspire,
my vision raised forever higher,
with you I form a figure-eight,
your Golden Age I co-create.

O Saint Germain, what love you bring,
it truly makes all matter sing,
your violet flame does all restore,
with you we are becoming more.

2. I accept that new ideas will be released in the nations that need it the most and thus the rest of the world will be brought up to a material standard of living that is closer to what the most affluent nations have today.

O Saint Germain, what Freedom Flame,
released when we recite your name,
acceleration is your gift,
our planet it will surely lift.

O Saint Germain, what love you bring,
it truly makes all matter sing,
your violet flame does all restore,
with you we are becoming more.

3. I accept that there is less of a distance between the rich and the not so rich nations, meaning there will be less disease and no starvation. We will no longer accept that there are children dying of starvation.

O Saint Germain, in love we claim,
our right to bring your violet flame,

from you Above, to us below,
it is an all-transforming flow.

O Saint Germain, what love you bring,
it truly makes all matter sing,
your violet flame does all restore,
with you we are becoming more.

4. I accept that we are not on earth to fight with each other and destroy ourselves in either a war or some environmental collapse. We have a higher purpose.

O Saint Germain, I love you so,
my aura filled with violet glow,
my chakras filled with violet fire,
I am your cosmic amplifier.

O Saint Germain, what love you bring,
it truly makes all matter sing,
your violet flame docs all restore,
with you we are becoming more.

5. I accept that people begin to see that we have a higher purpose individually, and thus we have a higher purpose as a whole, as the human race. One such purpose is to give all people equal opportunity to raise their awareness and live a fulfilled life where they feel good about themselves.

O Saint Germain, I am now free,
your violet flame is therapy,
transform all hang-ups in my mind,
as inner peace I surely find.

O Saint Germain, what love you bring,
it truly makes all matter sing,
your violet flame does all restore,
with you we are becoming more.

6. I accept that it is our collective responsibility to create a planet where people have the material abundance that makes it possible for them to feel good about themselves.

O Saint Germain, my body pure,
your violet flame for all is cure,
consume the cause of all disease,
and therefore I am all at ease.

O Saint Germain, what love you bring,
it truly makes all matter sing,
your violet flame does all restore,
with you we are becoming more.

7. I accept that as people begin to see that we are not material beings, and they begin to understand the basic dynamic of the power elite, then the world will transcend the consciousness where warfare is seen as a solution to any kind of problem.

O Saint Germain, I'm karma-free,
the past no longer burdens me,
a brand new opportunity,
I am in Christic unity.

O Saint Germain, what love you bring,
it truly makes all matter sing,
your violet flame does all restore,
with you we are becoming more.

8. I accept that some nations will dare to take the step to abandon the military. There will come a point where all nations will have either no military or a very small military that has many other tasks than actually killing other human beings.

O Saint Germain, we are now one,
I am for you a violet sun,
as we transform this planet earth,
your Golden Age is given birth.

O Saint Germain, what love you bring,
it truly makes all matter sing,
your violet flame does all restore,
with you we are becoming more.

9. I accept that some nations will say that the money we are now spending on the military, we will spend on creating a force that can go into other countries and in the short term help with natural disasters or starvation but in the long term help build that country.

O Saint Germain, the earth is free,
from burden of duality,
in oneness we bring what is best,
your Golden Age is manifest.

O Saint Germain, what love you bring,
it truly makes all matter sing,
your violet flame does all restore,
with you we are becoming more.

Part 2

1. I accept that helping third world countries will be seen as a major priority for our nations, and instead of spending money on the military we are spending it on building other countries.

> O Saint Germain, you do inspire,
> my vision raised forever higher,
> with you I form a figure-eight,
> your Golden Age I co-create.

> **O Saint Germain, what love you bring,**
> **it truly makes all matter sing,**
> **your violet flame does all restore,**
> **with you we are becoming more.**

2. I accept that there is a shift where people recognize that if we are not material beings and we have the opportunity to raise our consciousness, that means we have a basic humanity within us. We have a certain worth as a human being.

> O Saint Germain, what Freedom Flame,
> released when we recite your name,
> acceleration is your gift,
> our planet it will surely lift.

> **O Saint Germain, what love you bring,**
> **it truly makes all matter sing,**
> **your violet flame does all restore,**
> **with you we are becoming more.**

3. I accept that people begin to connect to the basic humanity in others and national divisions and other kinds of divisions will begin to fade away. There will be greater cooperation, a greater sense of community.

> O Saint Germain, in love we claim,
> our right to bring your violet flame,
> from you Above, to us below,
> it is an all-transforming flow.

> **O Saint Germain, what love you bring,**
> **it truly makes all matter sing,**
> **your violet flame does all restore,**
> **with you we are becoming more.**

4. I accept that there will be nations who decide to merge because what is the point of having national boundaries? There will be the emergence of greater regions where armed conflict becomes unthinkable.

> O Saint Germain, I love you so,
> my aura filled with violet glow,
> my chakras filled with violet fire,
> I am your cosmic amplifier.

> **O Saint Germain, what love you bring,**
> **it truly makes all matter sing,**
> **your violet flame does all restore,**
> **with you we are becoming more.**

5. I accept that we will reach a state where war becomes a remote possibility; a remote occurrence. There is a shift where people in many nations stop feeling threatened.

O Saint Germain, I am now free,
your violet flame is therapy,
transform all hang-ups in my mind,
as inner peace I surely find.

O Saint Germain, what love you bring,
it truly makes all matter sing,
your violet flame does all restore,
with you we are becoming more.

6. I accept that certain fallen beings will be taken out of the four levels of matter by the ascended masters, and warfare will fade away as a realistic risk. Nations will step into an entirely different approach to life. Those who can do this, will prosper financially and in terms of the peoples' wellbeing and the increase in creativity.

O Saint Germain, my body pure,
your violet flame for all is cure,
consume the cause of all disease,
and therefore I am all at ease.

O Saint Germain, what love you bring,
it truly makes all matter sing,
your violet flame does all restore,
with you we are becoming more.

7. I accept a shift so that people will begin to move their focus away from the problems and look at the possibilities, the potential.

O Saint Germain, I'm karma-free,
the past no longer burdens me,

a brand new opportunity,
I am in Christic unity.

O Saint Germain, what love you bring,
it truly makes all matter sing,
your violet flame does all restore,
with you we are becoming more.

8. I accept that instead of thinking that the problems are real
and the potential is a fantasy, people will see that the problems
are unreal and it is the potential that has reality to it.

O Saint Germain, we are now one,
I am for you a violet sun,
as we transform this planet earth,
your Golden Age is given birth.

O Saint Germain, what love you bring,
it truly makes all matter sing,
your violet flame does all restore,
with you we are becoming more.

9. I accept that people shift into a more positive view of life,
into a more trusting view of life. They feel they live in a more
friendly universe than their grandparents did, and certainly a
more friendly world.

O Saint Germain, the earth is free,
from burden of duality,
in oneness we bring what is best,
your Golden Age is manifest.

**O Saint Germain, what love you bring,
it truly makes all matter sing,
your violet flame does all restore,
with you we are becoming more.**

Part 3

1. I accept that people realize that the material realm, the mother realm, wants to nurture them and give them everything they need materially so that they can pursue the raising of consciousness.

O Saint Germain, you do inspire,
my vision raised forever higher,
with you I form a figure-eight,
your Golden Age I co-create.

**O Saint Germain, what love you bring,
it truly makes all matter sing,
your violet flame does all restore,
with you we are becoming more.**

2. I accept that this shift will have a widespread impact on how people feel about themselves and each other. If we do not distrust the universe, why do we need to distrust our neighbors, especially when we experience the basic humanity in both ourselves and our neighbors.

O Saint Germain, what Freedom Flame,
released when we recite your name,

acceleration is your gift,
our planet it will surely lift.

**O Saint Germain, what love you bring,
it truly makes all matter sing,
your violet flame does all restore,
with you we are becoming more.**

3. I accept that neighboring nations who have had conflicts, nations who have had distrust of each other, will resolve this and they can scarcely understand how they used to look at each other with distrust. They realize that: "Why shouldn't we trust each other, after all we are so alike?"

O Saint Germain, in love we claim,
our right to bring your violet flame,
from you Above, to us below,
it is an all-transforming flow.

**O Saint Germain, what love you bring,
it truly makes all matter sing,
your violet flame does all restore,
with you we are becoming more.**

4. I accept that the Scandinavian countries are stepping up to a higher level of consciousness and say: "Why are we distrusting each other? Why are we not cooperating more?" This is happening in other parts of the world as well.

O Saint Germain, I love you so,
my aura filled with violet glow,
my chakras filled with violet fire,
I am your cosmic amplifier.

O Saint Germain, what love you bring,
it truly makes all matter sing,
your violet flame does all restore,
with you we are becoming more.

5. I accept that even if we overcame all of these problems tomorrow, this would not automatically manifest the Golden Age. The Golden Age is something that needs to be co-created between people in embodiment and Saint Germain.

O Saint Germain, I am now free,
your violet flame is therapy,
transform all hang-ups in my mind,
as inner peace I surely find.

O Saint Germain, what love you bring,
it truly makes all matter sing,
your violet flame does all restore,
with you we are becoming more.

6. I accept that when we shift the consciousness, the problems fade away. They are transcended, partly because the ascended masters will step in and bind and consume the demons and the entities and remove the fallen beings who are aggressively perpetuating the problems and have created them in the first place.

O Saint Germain, my body pure,
your violet flame for all is cure,
consume the cause of all disease,
and therefore I am all at ease.

O Saint Germain, what love you bring,
it truly makes all matter sing,
your violet flame does all restore,
with you we are becoming more.

7. I accept that if we do not remove the dark forces, people will not be able to shift their consciousness into a positive approach. When we remove the dark forces, this shift becomes so much easier and when the shift happens it is not that all of the problems will be solved in a linear way. It is not that the cause of the problem will be destroyed.

O Saint Germain, I'm karma-free,
the past no longer burdens me,
a brand new opportunity,
I am in Christic unity.

O Saint Germain, what love you bring,
it truly makes all matter sing,
your violet flame does all restore,
with you we are becoming more.

8. I accept that people will transcend the consciousness so that the problem either fades away or people no longer focus on it because they are focused on the possibility of manifesting a better society.

O Saint Germain, we are now one,
I am for you a violet sun,
as we transform this planet earth,
your Golden Age is given birth.

O Saint Germain, what love you bring,
it truly makes all matter sing,
your violet flame does all restore,
with you we are becoming more.

9. I accept that by removing the dark forces, people will wake up and feel free from the weight that used to pull them into reactionary patterns and spirals. They will step back and say: "Why are we having this distrust? Why are we doing things this way? Why aren't we looking for better solutions? Surely, there must be better solutions out there."

O Saint Germain, the earth is free,
from burden of duality,
in oneness we bring what is best,
your Golden Age is manifest.

O Saint Germain, what love you bring,
it truly makes all matter sing,
your violet flame does all restore,
with you we are becoming more.

Part 4

1. I accept that as we raise awareness, people see that there are better solutions. It is not a matter of forcing this upon society or forcing it upon other people. It is self-evident that this is the next step in the evolution of society.

O Saint Germain, you do inspire,
my vision raised forever higher,

with you I form a figure-eight,
your Golden Age I co-create.

O Saint Germain, what love you bring,
it truly makes all matter sing,
your violet flame does all restore,
with you we are becoming more.

2. I accept that people are awakened from the dream of having a Golden Age manifest as the result of some miraculous event that instantly manifests dramatic changes.

O Saint Germain, what Freedom Flame,
released when we recite your name,
acceleration is your gift,
our planet it will surely lift.

O Saint Germain, what love you bring,
it truly makes all matter sing,
your violet flame does all restore,
with you we are becoming more.

3. I accept that Saint Germain's vision is a gradual process where instead of seeing this as a miracle, people see it as self-evident, as the obvious next step for society and therefore they implement it with that level of awareness, with that approach.

O Saint Germain, in love we claim,
our right to bring your violet flame,
from you Above, to us below,
it is an all-transforming flow.

**O Saint Germain, what love you bring,
it truly makes all matter sing,
your violet flame does all restore,
with you we are becoming more.**

4. I accept that the Golden Age will not be dropped upon us from heaven because we will see it as the natural self-evident step to take in order to continue the process of manifesting a better society where people feel good about themselves.

O Saint Germain, I love you so,
my aura filled with violet glow,
my chakras filled with violet fire,
I am your cosmic amplifier.

**O Saint Germain, what love you bring,
it truly makes all matter sing,
your violet flame does all restore,
with you we are becoming more.**

5. I accept that it is not a matter of defining what we need to change and mapping out a plan. It is a matter of raising the consciousness so that step-by-step many different people in many different places suddenly see it as self-evident that we need to do this.

O Saint Germain, I am now free,
your violet flame is therapy,
transform all hang-ups in my mind,
as inner peace I surely find.

**O Saint Germain, what love you bring,
it truly makes all matter sing,**

your violet flame does all restore,
with you we are becoming more.

6. I accept that Saint Germain is perfectly happy to see the manifestation of the Golden Age without most people recognizing Saint Germain or thinking that all of these ideas are coming from him.

O Saint Germain, my body pure,
your violet flame for all is cure,
consume the cause of all disease,
and therefore I am all at ease.

O Saint Germain, what love you bring,
it truly makes all matter sing,
your violet flame does all restore,
with you we are becoming more.

7. I accept that Saint Germain is perfectly happy to have the majority of the people feel that: "Oh, this idea just appeared at the right time and everybody could see that it was self-evident and that is why we implemented it."

O Saint Germain, I'm karma-free,
the past no longer burdens me,
a brand new opportunity,
I am in Christic unity.

O Saint Germain, what love you bring,
it truly makes all matter sing,
your violet flame does all restore,
with you we are becoming more.

8. I accept that any new idea is brought from the ascended realm and it is a long process to bring forth something new, such as the modern democracies. Many, many ideas had to be brought into the world before this could happen.

O Saint Germain, we are now one,
I am for you a violet sun,
as we transform this planet earth,
your Golden Age is given birth.

O Saint Germain, what love you bring,
it truly makes all matter sing,
your violet flame does all restore,
with you we are becoming more.

9. I accept that Saint Germain is not looking for people to be mindless followers of this almighty Saint Germain who is the ruler of the Aquarian age. He is looking for people to feel the creative flow through them and know that they are bringing forth something from within themselves, wherever they see it coming from.

O Saint Germain, the earth is free,
from burden of duality,
in oneness we bring what is best,
your Golden Age is manifest.

O Saint Germain, what love you bring,
it truly makes all matter sing,
your violet flame does all restore,
with you we are becoming more.

Sealing

In the name of the Divine Mother, I call to all ascended masters for the sealing of myself and all people in my circle of influence in the creative flow of the Divine Mother, the River of Life. I call for the multiplication of my calls by all ascended masters so that we form the perfect figure-eight flow of "As Above, so below." Thus, I accept that this is fully manifest, because the mouth of the Lord, the Divine Mother that I AM, has spoken it. Amen.

19 | BUREAUCRACY AND GOVERNMENT IN THE GOLDEN AGE

So, I AM indeed, the Ascended Master Saint Germain. I come to give you a discourse in the series on how to manifest the Golden Age. This applies to all nations and is not specifically targeted at any particular nation.

Corruption and elitism

One of the important aspects of manifesting the Golden Age is, of course, to overcome corruption. Now, you may look at some of the corruption indexes that have been compiled by international organizations. It is not difficult to see, as a simple matter of fact, that the countries who have the lowest level of corruption have the highest material standard of living and, generally speaking, have a well-functioning, often growing economy. What is then the connection between the two?

Well, it is that corruption allows a small elite to gather more and more privileges to themselves, and how do they do this? In practical terms, they do it by paying off certain people in the government apparatus so that they can get the special favors that other people are not able to get. What is truly behind this is that, in any nation where an elite forms (and that means pretty much any nation) the elite does not want to share their privileges. They want to keep the population down, they want to keep competition down.

What is the effect of this? It is that it also keeps creativity down. More than that, it also means that we of the ascended masters are not allowed to multiply the efforts of people in the nation where there is too big of a disparity between rich and poor, between the privileged and the non-privileged. You see in general that countries that eradicate corruption, they have more of a multiplication factor, and therefore their economies are doing better. This is something that anybody can see by simply studying the facts.

Therefore, you will see that in the Golden Age, those countries that make the greatest effort to eradicate corruption, will indeed have a more well-functioning economy. They will have more equal opportunity for all people, and therefore they will have, generally speaking, a more happy and satisfied population.

Bureaucracy in the Golden Age

Now, what is behind corruption? Well, corruption, of course, could not exist if there was not a bureaucracy, and so we need to talk about the role of bureaucracy in the Golden Age. In order to understand this topic, you need to understand that the fallen beings exist on this planet both in embodiment and in higher realms. They are seeking to use absolutely anything in order to achieve their ends, which may be to gain power and control or it may be to simply create destruction and chaos, or to stop growth. There are different groups of fallen beings; they have different aims. Sometimes they clash with each other. In some cases they actually magnify each other, and so it is a complicated situation we face on earth.

Now, it may surprise some of you to hear me say this, given my history of talking about Communism, that if there was a higher state of collective consciousness, then a communist system with state ownership of the means of production could actually function. The economy could survive in the long run, and it could even bring forth a fairly egalitarian society where the people could be reasonably happy.

Karl Marx was not the first person in the world to think of such a society. You can go back even in known history, but certainly beyond known history, and find societies that had, basically, common ownership of the means of production and of land. These societies were well-functioning. There were such societies on Atlantis that were functioning on a much higher level than anything you see today.

What it is that distorts the communist society so that the economy cannot function? Well, it is that there emerges this power elite. It is the influence of the fallen beings who are not seeking to make the society function, but who are seeking to use it for the purposes of control, or even on a greater agenda of creating conflict in the world that could lead to destruction.

If you were to turn this around and look at what traditionally you would call a capitalist society, you would see that in unrestrained Capitalism, a power elite will form. They will take to themselves special privileges, and therefore in the outermost consequence, there will be a small elite who owns all of the means to production. You have a situation that is not very different from the situation in a communist country. What prevents a capitalist economy from functioning in the long run is again the formation of an elite and the influence of the fallen beings. What you realize next is that the fallen beings will use absolutely anything for their ends. They will use Capitalism, they will use Communism, they will use any type of society. They will use any institution in society. So now let us look at bureaucracy.

Why do you have a bureaucracy? Well, most people would say that it is in order to create a functioning state, to ensure that all people have equal rights before the law, equal opportunity, that things are functioning well, that people do not build houses that fall down upon themselves, and that they drive safely on the roads, and that there is an infrastructure that actually functions.

Yes, this is, of course, the higher meaning of a bureaucracy but this is not the way bureaucracies function at the present moment because they have been heavily influenced by the fallen beings. What do the fallen beings do? Well, many things, but one of the things they do is that they always seek to complicate everything, to make things more and more complex, more and more complicated. They set up these systems, these mechanisms, where the complexity of the system creates certain inherent problems. Then, what is the solution to these problems that the fallen beings always recommend? It is more control, more bureaucracy, more laws, more rules, more regulations.

You might say that the way bureaucracies are functioning right now, it is a typical example of the process that I described before: The fallen ones create a problem and then set themselves up as the only ones who have the solution to the problem. Their solution to the problem does not solve the problem. It just makes it more and more complicated. You see, in many nations in the world, how bureaucracies have become more and more complicated, more and more difficult to administer. There are more rules, more regulations. You can see the EU, which is practically drowning in rules and regulations.

The effect of this in the long run will be to not only shut down the people's creativity, but also dampen the economy. It will also have the effect of giving special privileges to the businesses who are already big and established because they can afford to hire the people, including lawyers, to comply with all of the government regulations whereas smaller businesses cannot afford to do this. You can, through sufficient regulation, create virtual monopolies. This, of course, shuts down that flow of creativity – the flow that we can multiply – and therefore it puts a lid on economic growth.

Naturally, as we move further and further into the Golden Age, the collective consciousness will be raised. This will have two effects. One is that the fallen beings will lose their power. Many of them will be taken either out of embodiment or removed from the emotional, mental and identity realms. You do not anymore have that downward pull or that chaotic influence of the fallen beings that seeks to use any system to create complexity and chaos, even destruction. The other thing that will happen is that people's consciousness will be raised.

Now, you may say: "What is one of the legitimate functions of bureaucracy?" Well, it is to prevent people from exploiting each other, taking advantage of each other, by creating certain rules and enforcing them. That is why, in the purest form, you have a police force. A police force was never meant to suppress the general population, but of course only correct those who violated or exploited others. When a police force becomes the source of exploitation in itself, well that is, of course, not sustainable in a Golden Age.

Shifting to a positive outlook on life

When you have that raising of the collective consciousness, it becomes a very subtle shift where people begin to realize that they do not need to steal from others, they do not need to manipulate others, they do not need to exploit others because there are plenty of business opportunities, or work opportunities. You can earn a living, and a good living, in a perfectly legitimate way that does not exploit other people.

My beloved, you have this shift into a positive outlook on life, and that means people are no longer seeking to exploit each other, they are no longer seeking to avoid work. Everybody is focused on expressing their creativity or their industriousness in the best possible way so they can make money in a legitimate way. This means that everybody is contributing to the growth of the economy, which means we have even more to multiply, and then the economy grows even further. When this positive shift happens, and people are not so focused on exploiting each other, the need for a bureaucracy gradually decreases to the point where you end up having a bureaucracy that is far, far smaller than what you have today in most countries.

This means that the bureaucracy becomes less complex. It also means that the people in a bureaucracy start shifting their mindset. They are not so focused on preventing a negative as on promoting a positive. Instead of thinking they have to correct the people and rein them in and control them, they are focused on how they can actually promote growth. This also means that there will come a point where the laws of the nations – at least for the forerunners of the Golden Age – will shift.

Instead of being focused on preventing this exploitation and making things illegal (and making it more difficult to cheat others, or cheat the state), you create new kinds of laws that are actually meant to ensure that people have the best possible opportunity to express their creativity in the ways that benefit the whole. Suddenly, the law becomes less complex. There are less hindrances put in the way. Certainly, there are laws that do not favor big businesses, but allow all businesses a legitimate opportunity. Suddenly, you have this very positive shift where, again, everybody is focused on growth rather than being focused on preventing some kind of calamity or disorder or the overthrow of the status quo, the overthrow of society, or this or that.

There is no need for violent revolutions in the Golden Age because societies are in the process of progressive growth, progressive expansion, progressive evolution. Suddenly, those who are in charge of societies begin to realize that they can relax, they can take it easy, because the danger of these violent revolutions that was there is dissipated because there is no longer the tension among the people. People are focused on what they all want in the end: They want a good life for themselves.

No need for violent revolutions

There will come later stages in the Golden Age where the majority of the population in many nations will have moved to the point where they are seeking to selflessly serve the whole or serve other people. But in the beginning stages of the Golden Age, people will be focused on creating a good life for themselves. When they do this in the way I have described, creating a good life for yourself actually helps to create a better life for the whole, therefore a better life for other people. Suddenly, there is no need for these kind of repressive, controlling societies that you see today. It is not that people will go to violent revolutions to overthrow such repressive societies, they will simply gradually fade away because there will be no need for them. People will not accept them. They will simply stand up and make it known that they want to live in a different society, and there is no question that the leaders will eventually have to comply.

Those who do not comply, will simply disappear. They will go out of embodiment, they will lose their power, whatever you have. If the majority of the people in a nation decide that they want a different society, then the leaders who will not go along with this will disappear. There is no question about it. There is no reason, or no need, for a violent revolution to overthrow such leaders. It is simply a matter of a critical number of the people deciding: "We will not accept this anymore in our nation. We want to live in a different kind of nation, and this is the kind of nation we want to live in."

How governments will change

My beloved, this will bring so many shifts around the world, and suddenly you will see that the governments will begin to change. I have talked about the need to experiment with direct democracy where the people begin to vote on various issues. Of course, it is not practical that the people vote on all issues. There will still be a need for a governmental apparatus with representatives, with bureaucrats that can carry out the will of the people.

These will shift to the point where what you see now in so many countries is an awareness or a consciousness that there is a certain distance between the politicians and the bureaucrats and the people. This often breeds this certain sense of superiority among the politicians and the bureaucrats, even among business leaders or the media, or institutions of society, such as educational institutions. These people feel superior to the general population. They feel it is their role to govern society and tell the people what they should want for their own good. In the Golden Age, this will simply fade away.

Again, there will be a change of the guard where the people who cannot move on with these changes as the consciousness is raised, will simply disappear from their positions. They will withdraw, they will retire, they will find some other thing to do. This will give rise to an entirely new generation of those politicians and bureaucrats who will catch on to the need to serve the whole, to serve the people. Suddenly, you will no longer have this sense of distance between the government and the population, and therefore the people in the government will not feel superior to the population. The people themselves will not feel afraid, they will not feel distanced, they will not feel suspicious of their governments.

My beloved, as the fallen beings are removed from the planet, as the consciousness is raised, all of the conspiracy theories will fade away because whatever conspiracies have some reality to them will fade away. The people will be raised where they no longer believe in some of these fantasies that are put out there. You see, my beloved, the shift will be a shift in a positive direction.

The gap between people and politicians

Now, if you look back in history, you may look at some of these dynamics that have been happening in many nations between the population and the government, and you may ask yourself: "Why has there been this animosity, this conflict, this suspicion? Why has this existed for so long?" It is truly very difficult to understand from a logical, rational standpoint. Many people who research conditions in society have actually looked at this and asked themselves: "What could explain this? Why hasn't, even in the democratic nations, there been a shift so that the people feel closer to the politicians and vice versa so there isn't a gap, there isn't the room for suspicion."

From a rational, scientific viewpoint, you cannot explain this. There is no rational explanation. The explanation is, of course, what we have given you: The existence of fallen beings and their influence, and the level of the collective consciousness. Once this becomes clear to some of the people who are very knowledgeable about society and how society functions, it will create another shift where the more advanced people in societies will not necessarily come to recognize the existence of ascended masters or fallen beings, but they will come to recognize that there has always been a power elite that has not been a force for good. You cannot really build a constructive society without recognizing this and without taking the necessary steps to prevent such an elite from controlling a society and therefore holding back growth.

It will also be acknowledged, from a purely universal perspective, that there must be a collective consciousness. There will even come a time when there will be more clear scientific proof of this than you have today—where you actually have enough scientific proof to convince anyone who is in a neutral state of mind. There will come a point where this gains widespread acceptance, and where the leaders of society begin to recognize that it is necessary to look at, and to raise, the collective consciousness in order to improve society.

It is not a matter of going out and seeking to force the people, or control the people, or create more laws and regulations. It is actually a matter of helping the people resolve the wounds and the divisions in their own psyches, in their own psychologies, so that they become more whole human beings and therefore are able to live more constructive lives. There will also, of course, be an awareness that why this has not happened before is because the power elite did not want it to happen because to them, the more unwhole, the more divided, the more psychologically crippled that the population was, the easier it was to control them.

Substance abuse pacifies people

You will see countries today where there is a high level of substance abuse, drugs and alcohol. You will see that this clearly pacifies people and therefore makes them easier to control. You will see that in certain societies that you have seen from the past (and the Soviet Union is one example of this) the level of alcoholism was so high that it was a major factor in upholding the system. People were simply so pacified that they could not come into any kind of coherent state where they could change status quo.

You might actually ask yourself, if you are willing, why it is primarily men who become subject to alcoholism? I know it is not exclusively men, but it is, in many societies, clearly a larger percentage of the men who are alcoholics than women. If you look at, as an example, the Soviet Union, you will see that this ties in to what Portia talked about where men are more susceptible to declaring their allegiance to an idea, to an ideal, to a system. They declare this allegiance, and therefore they feel that it is necessary to make personal sacrifices because the whole, the system, the idea, is more important than the individual, more important than their material lives. Of course, once they have, so to speak, sold their soul to the system, they realize that this comes with a price. They may have some comfortable position in the system, but they have no room for creativity, and therefore they can never feel fulfilled. They can never actually feel good about themselves, and so what do they do in order to avoid being confronted with the fact that they feel bad about themselves every working day? Well, they drink so that they forget, so that they change their state of mind chemically, which they are not able to do in their minds on their own because they have no spiritual path.

This is why you see this form of escapism in societies where it is actually the men who have the power to change status quo, but they somehow have this fixed point in their psychologies where they have sworn allegiance to something, feeling they have to be patriotic or loyal to the system. Or they are simply afraid of rocking the boat, and so they dare not speak out, they dare not bring change. That is why the status quo becomes their god, and that is why they feel bad about themselves because what they are experiencing is a missed opportunity.

You can look at Soviet society and you can see that, although there was a certain progression, it was a much slower progression than there was in other nations and that there could have been. The reason is — *pay attention to this* — that even in the Soviet system, there could have been much more growth, and if there had been that growth, then perhaps even the Soviet Union would have survived longer. Because there was not the willingness to change with the times, then there came that point where the only realistic outcome was a collapse of the system.

The reason why there was not this growth was that there were too many people that were not willing to bring that change. It is not here a matter of questioning the system itself. It is a matter of coming to this point where you say: "We have been doing things a certain way now for a very long time. Why are we doing it the same way? Why aren't we trying to find a different way that will produce better results?" You will see that if more people had been willing to ask this question, there would have been change in many levels. This is not a matter of overthrowing the system, it is simply a matter of realizing that any society must change or die.

This is what history proves. If there is any validity to the concept of a historical necessity, well it is certainly that any society that becomes a closed system will be overturned by history. History will run away from it and the Soviet Union is one of the many proofs of this. You see here that there were many men in the Soviet Union who were in a position where they could have brought some improvement somewhere, and if many men had brought small improvements, it would have had an impact on the entire system.

When you are in a position where you have the opportunity to bring improvement, and you do not take it, you subconsciously sense this. You subconsciously feel that missed opportunity. That is why you saw so many men in the Soviet Union who were dissatisfied with their lives, dissatisfied with themselves. They felt that life really was not worth living because they could not stand living with that sense that there was something they had missed, some opportunity they had missed. Some blamed the system. Others did not even know who to blame and so they just wanted to get away from it all and the only escape they could see was a clear bottle with a clear liquid.

All people want to improve their lives

My beloved, what will happen in the Golden Age is, of course, that substance abuse will simply fade away because, as people are given an opportunity to improve their lives and see that when they make an effort, it makes a difference in their personal lives (it even makes a difference in society), then there is no need to escape. Of course, when more and more people are made aware of the possibility to heal their psychological wounds – even heal the wounds they come into embodiment with – well then, the other reason for escapism will disappear. They are not trying to run away from themselves, they are not trying to run away from their outer situation, and suddenly you have people who start feeling better and better about themselves.

Truly, can there be any nation on earth where the people do not want a better material life and where they do not want a better inner life where they feel better about themselves? I am not aware of such a nation. When you look at this logically, can there really be any government on earth who will not want its own people to have a better and better material life and who will not want its own people to feel better and better about themselves? Well, there can be, if a government is controlled by the fallen beings or the fallen mindset, but as we move into the Golden Age, this will also fade away.

Suddenly, you will have the emergence of governments who might even look at their past and say: "Why were we trapped in these patterns for so long? Why were we trapped in these power plays, this completely unnecessary conflict with other nations or even with our own people? Why weren't we just simply focused on improving material life and improving how people feel about themselves and about their society? Why were we trapped in this for so long?" Well, actually, they might say: "It doesn't even matter *why* we were trapped in it for so long because now we see it and now we are not trapped in it, and we are going to shift our focus into manifesting a better society."

Unfathomable growth

My beloved, when the collective consciousness is raised to the point where this is what people focus on, when more and more of the fallen beings are removed from the planet, then there will be a period of growth such as has never been seen before in recorded history, and that has very rarely been seen in previous civilizations. You already see the technological possibilities, and I can assure you, my beloved, that once there is that shift where people focus on the positive, I will pour out so many new ideas and so much new technology that the planet will shift into this almost unfathomable growth, unfathomable for the people of today who have never known such growth.

There will come a point where nobody really needs to look back at history and say who was to blame and what was the problem. They actually have a certain understanding of the forces of history, and they are aware that they cannot allow this to repeat itself. Given that the fallen beings are not on the planet, it is not really a risk that it will repeat itself, and therefore there will come a point where societies will actually shift. They will not ignore history, but they will not seek to analyze and place blame. They will look forward and focus on the task of creating a better society, a golden age society.

That, my beloved, is my – I hope you find – *positive* vision for today. I thank you for being here, for being the anchors in the physical octave whereby I could use your chakras to radiate this into the collective consciousness. I truly begin the shift both in this nation and in many other nations who are ready for it so that we can approach that point of no return where we move into the phase of physically manifesting my Golden Age.

You have – all of you who are the students of the ascended masters, all of you who are serious spiritual students, seeking to transcend your consciousness – you have all been a part of bringing us closer to this point. I, of course, look to you to continue your efforts so that you will bring the planet over that critical turning point where, we might say, that the manifestation of the Golden Age has become irreversible.

I would actually say that the manifestation of the Golden Age has already become irreversible, but nevertheless, the fallen beings might be able to delay it. I trust that with your willingness to make the calls and raise your consciousness, we shall instead surprise them by accelerating the growth and moving to that point of no return far faster than the fallen beings can even predict. Therefore, they simply will not have time to adjust to the changes. They will be among those people who stand back wondering what happened.

20 | INVOKING GOLDEN AGE BUREAUCRACY AND GOVERNMENT

In the name I AM THAT I AM, Jesus Christ, I call to all ascended masters working on manifesting the Golden Age, especially Saint Germain, to radiate into the collective consciousness a new awareness of how bureaucracy and government will evolve in the Golden Age. Help people see that we can build a new future by working with the ascended masters and letting go of the old way of looking at life, including…

[Make personal calls.]

Part 1

1. I call for people to be cut free to see that corruption allows a small elite to gather more and more privileges to themselves by paying off certain people in the

government apparatus, so that they can get the special favors that other people are not able to get.

> O Saint Germain, you do inspire,
> my vision raised forever higher,
> with you I form a figure-eight,
> your Golden Age I co-create.

> **O Saint Germain, what love you bring,**
> **it truly makes all matter sing,**
> **your violet flame does all restore,**
> **with you we are becoming more.**

2. I call for people to be cut free to see that in any nation where an elite forms, members of the elite do not want to share their privileges. They want to keep the population down, they want to keep competition down.

> O Saint Germain, what Freedom Flame,
> released when we recite your name,
> acceleration is your gift,
> our planet it will surely lift.

> **O Saint Germain, what love you bring,**
> **it truly makes all matter sing,**
> **your violet flame does all restore,**
> **with you we are becoming more.**

3. I call for people to be cut free to see that this also keeps creativity down. The ascended masters are not allowed to multiply the efforts of people in the nation where there is too big of a disparity between rich and poor, between the privileged and the non-privileged.

O Saint Germain, in love we claim,
our right to bring your violet flame,
from you Above, to us below,
it is an all-transforming flow.

O Saint Germain, what love you bring,
it truly makes all matter sing,
your violet flame does all restore,
with you we are becoming more.

4. I call for people to be cut free to see that countries that eradicate corruption have more of a multiplication factor, and therefore their economies are doing better.

O Saint Germain, I love you so,
my aura filled with violet glow,
my chakras filled with violet fire,
I am your cosmic amplifier.

O Saint Germain, what love you bring,
it truly makes all matter sing,
your violet flame does all restore,
with you we are becoming more.

5. I call for people to be cut free to see that in the Golden Age, those countries that make the greatest effort to eradicate corruption, will have a more well-functioning economy. They will have more equal opportunity for all people, and therefore they will have a more happy and satisfied population.

O Saint Germain, I am now free,
your violet flame is therapy,

transform all hang-ups in my mind,
as inner peace I surely find.

**O Saint Germain, what love you bring,
it truly makes all matter sing,
your violet flame does all restore,
with you we are becoming more.**

6. I call for people to be cut free to see that the fallen beings exist on this planet both in embodiment and in higher realms. They are seeking to use absolutely anything in order to achieve their ends, which may be to gain power and control or it may be to simply create destruction and chaos, or to stop growth.

O Saint Germain, my body pure,
your violet flame for all is cure,
consume the cause of all disease,
and therefore I am all at ease.

**O Saint Germain, what love you bring,
it truly makes all matter sing,
your violet flame does all restore,
with you we are becoming more.**

7. I call for people to be cut free to see that the fallen beings will use capitalism, they will use communism, they will use any type of society. They will use any institution in society.

O Saint Germain, I'm karma-free,
the past no longer burdens me,
a brand new opportunity,
I am in Christic unity.

**O Saint Germain, what love you bring,
it truly makes all matter sing,
your violet flame does all restore,
with you we are becoming more.**

8. I call for people to be cut free to see that the way bureaucracies function is heavily influenced by the fallen beings. They seek to complicate everything, to make things more and more complex.

O Saint Germain, we are now one,
I am for you a violet sun,
as we transform this planet earth,
your Golden Age is given birth.

**O Saint Germain, what love you bring,
it truly makes all matter sing,
your violet flame does all restore,
with you we are becoming more.**

9. I call for people to be cut free to see that the fallen beings set up these systems, these mechanisms, where the complexity of the system creates certain inherent problems. Then, the solution that the fallen beings always recommend is more control, more bureaucracy, more laws, more rules, more regulations.

O Saint Germain, the earth is free,
from burden of duality,
in oneness we bring what is best,
your Golden Age is manifest.

**O Saint Germain, what love you bring,
it truly makes all matter sing,**

**your violet flame does all restore,
with you we are becoming more.**

Part 2

1. I call for people to be cut free to see that the fallen beings create a problem and then set themselves up as the only ones who have the solution to the problem. Their solution to the problem does not solve the problem. It just makes it more and more complicated.

> O Saint Germain, you do inspire,
> my vision raised forever higher,
> with you I form a figure-eight,
> your Golden Age I co-create.

> **O Saint Germain, what love you bring,
> it truly makes all matter sing,
> your violet flame does all restore,
> with you we are becoming more.**

2. I call for people to be cut free to see that when bureaucracies become more complicated and more difficult to administer, this shuts down the people's creativity and dampens the economy.

> O Saint Germain, what Freedom Flame,
> released when we recite your name,
> acceleration is your gift,
> our planet it will surely lift.

**O Saint Germain, what love you bring,
it truly makes all matter sing,
your violet flame does all restore,
with you we are becoming more.**

3. I call for people to be cut free to see that a complicated bureaucracy gives special privileges to the businesses who are already big and established, because they can afford to hire the people to comply with all of the government regulations whereas smaller businesses cannot afford to do this.

O Saint Germain, in love we claim,
our right to bring your violet flame,
from you Above, to us below,
it is an all-transforming flow.

**O Saint Germain, what love you bring,
it truly makes all matter sing,
your violet flame does all restore,
with you we are becoming more.**

4. I call for people to be cut free to see that the fallen beings can, through sufficient regulation, create virtual monopolies. This shuts down the flow of creativity – the flow that the masters can multiply – and therefore it puts a lid on economic growth.

O Saint Germain, I love you so,
my aura filled with violet glow,
my chakras filled with violet fire,
I am your cosmic amplifier.

**O Saint Germain, what love you bring,
it truly makes all matter sing,
your violet flame does all restore,
with you we are becoming more.**

5. I call for the fallen beings to be taken out of embodiment or removed from the emotional, mental and identity realms. I call for the consuming of the downward pull and the chaotic influence of the fallen beings that seeks to use any system to create complexity and chaos, even destruction.

O Saint Germain, I am now free,
your violet flame is therapy,
transform all hang-ups in my mind,
as inner peace I surely find.

**O Saint Germain, what love you bring,
it truly makes all matter sing,
your violet flame does all restore,
with you we are becoming more.**

6. I call for people to be cut free to see that a legitimate function of bureaucracy is to prevent people from exploiting each other by creating certain rules and enforcing them. A police force was never meant to suppress the general population, but only to correct those who violated or exploited others.

O Saint Germain, my body pure,
your violet flame for all is cure,
consume the cause of all disease,
and therefore I am all at ease.

O Saint Germain, what love you bring,
it truly makes all matter sing,
your violet flame does all restore,
with you we are becoming more.

7. I call for people to be cut free to realize that they do not need to steal from others, manipulate others or exploit others because there are plenty of business or work opportunities. We can earn a good living in a perfectly legitimate way that does not exploit other people.

O Saint Germain, I'm karma-free,
the past no longer burdens me,
a brand new opportunity,
I am in Christic unity.

O Saint Germain, what love you bring,
it truly makes all matter sing,
your violet flame does all restore,
with you we are becoming more.

8. I call for people to be cut free to shift into a positive outlook on life, so they are no longer seeking to exploit each other, they are no longer seeking to avoid work. Everybody is focused on expressing their creativity or their industriousness in the best possible way so they can make money in a legitimate way.

O Saint Germain, we are now one,
I am for you a violet sun,
as we transform this planet earth,
your Golden Age is given birth.

O Saint Germain, what love you bring,
it truly makes all matter sing,
your violet flame does all restore,
with you we are becoming more.

9. I call for people to be cut free to see that when they are not so focused on exploiting each other, the need for a bureaucracy gradually decreases to the point where we end up having a bureaucracy that is far smaller than what we have today.

O Saint Germain, the earth is free,
from burden of duality,
in oneness we bring what is best,
your Golden Age is manifest.

O Saint Germain, what love you bring,
it truly makes all matter sing,
your violet flame does all restore,
with you we are becoming more.

Part 3

1. I call for people in the bureaucracy to be cut free to shift their mindset so they are not focused on preventing a negative but on promoting a positive. Instead of thinking they have to correct the people and control them, they are focused on how they can promote growth.

O Saint Germain, you do inspire,
my vision raised forever higher,

with you I form a figure-eight,
your Golden Age I co-create.

**O Saint Germain, what love you bring,
it truly makes all matter sing,
your violet flame does all restore,
with you we are becoming more.**

2. I call for people to be cut free to see that the laws of the nations must shift so that instead of being focused on preventing exploitation and making things illegal, we create new kinds of laws that are meant to ensure that people have the best possible opportunity to express their creativity in ways that benefit the whole.

O Saint Germain, what Freedom Flame,
released when we recite your name,
acceleration is your gift,
our planet it will surely lift.

**O Saint Germain, what love you bring,
it truly makes all matter sing,
your violet flame does all restore,
with you we are becoming more.**

3. I call for people to be cut free to see that the law must become less complex so there are less hindrances for creativity and so that laws do not favor big businesses, but allow all businesses a legitimate opportunity.

O Saint Germain, in love we claim,
our right to bring your violet flame,

from you Above, to us below,
it is an all-transforming flow.

O Saint Germain, what love you bring,
it truly makes all matter sing,
your violet flame does all restore,
with you we are becoming more.

4. I call for people to be cut free to make the positive shift
where they are focused on growth rather than being focused
on preventing a calamity or the overthrow of the status quo.

O Saint Germain, I love you so,
my aura filled with violet glow,
my chakras filled with violet fire,
I am your cosmic amplifier.

O Saint Germain, what love you bring,
it truly makes all matter sing,
your violet flame does all restore,
with you we are becoming more.

5. I call for people to be cut free to see that there is no need
for violent revolutions in the Golden Age because societies are
in the process of progressive growth, progressive expansion,
progressive evolution.

O Saint Germain, I am now free,
your violet flame is therapy,
transform all hang-ups in my mind,
as inner peace I surely find.

**O Saint Germain, what love you bring,
it truly makes all matter sing,
your violet flame does all restore,
with you we are becoming more.**

6. I call for the cutting free of those who are in charge of societies so they can relax, they can take it easy, because the danger of violent revolutions is dissipated as there is no longer the tension among the people. People are focused on producing a good life for themselves.

O Saint Germain, my body pure,
your violet flame for all is cure,
consume the cause of all disease,
and therefore I am all at ease.

**O Saint Germain, what love you bring,
it truly makes all matter sing,
your violet flame does all restore,
with you we are becoming more.**

7. I call for people to be cut free to see that creating a good life for ourselves helps to create a better life for the whole, therefore a better life for other people.

O Saint Germain, I'm karma-free,
the past no longer burdens me,
a brand new opportunity,
I am in Christic unity.

**O Saint Germain, what love you bring,
it truly makes all matter sing,**

**your violet flame does all restore,
with you we are becoming more.**

8. I call for people to be cut free to see that there is no need for the repressive, controlling societies that we see today. It is not that people will go to violent revolutions to overthrow such repressive societies, they will simply fade away because there will be no need for them.

O Saint Germain, we are now one,
I am for you a violet sun,
as we transform this planet earth,
your Golden Age is given birth.

**O Saint Germain, what love you bring,
it truly makes all matter sing,
your violet flame does all restore,
with you we are becoming more.**

9. I call for people to be cut free to stand up and make it known that they want to live in a different society. I call for the leaders to be cut free to see that they must comply or they will disappear.

O Saint Germain, the earth is free,
from burden of duality,
in oneness we bring what is best,
your Golden Age is manifest.

**O Saint Germain, what love you bring,
it truly makes all matter sing,
your violet flame does all restore,
with you we are becoming more.**

Part 4

1. I call for people to be cut free to see that when the majority of the people in a nation decide that they want a different society, then the leaders who will not go along with this will disappear.

> O Saint Germain, you do inspire,
> my vision raised forever higher,
> with you I form a figure-eight,
> your Golden Age I co-create.
>
> **O Saint Germain, what love you bring,**
> **it truly makes all matter sing,**
> **your violet flame does all restore,**
> **with you we are becoming more.**

2. I call for people to be cut free to see that there is no need for a violent revolution to overthrow such leaders. It is a matter of a critical number of the people deciding: "We will not accept this anymore in our nation. We want to live in a different kind of nation, and this is the kind of nation we want to live in."

> O Saint Germain, what Freedom Flame,
> released when we recite your name,
> acceleration is your gift,
> our planet it will surely lift.
>
> **O Saint Germain, what love you bring,**
> **it truly makes all matter sing,**
> **your violet flame does all restore,**
> **with you we are becoming more.**

3. I call for politicians, bureaucrats and business leaders to be cut free from any sense of being superior to the general population. Cut them free from the illusion that it is their role to govern society and tell the people what they should want—for their own good.

> O Saint Germain, in love we claim,
> our right to bring your violet flame,
> from you Above, to us below,
> it is an all-transforming flow.

> **O Saint Germain, what love you bring,**
> **it truly makes all matter sing,**
> **your violet flame does all restore,**
> **with you we are becoming more.**

4. I call for the cutting free of the new generation of politicians and bureaucrats who will catch on to the need to serve the whole, to serve the people.

> O Saint Germain, I love you so,
> my aura filled with violet glow,
> my chakras filled with violet fire,
> I am your cosmic amplifier.

> **O Saint Germain, what love you bring,**
> **it truly makes all matter sing,**
> **your violet flame does all restore,**
> **with you we are becoming more.**

5. I call for the cutting free of those who can see the need to overcome the distance between the government and the

population, so the people in the government will not feel superior to the population.

> O Saint Germain, I am now free,
> your violet flame is therapy,
> transform all hang-ups in my mind,
> as inner peace I surely find.

> **O Saint Germain, what love you bring,**
> **it truly makes all matter sing,**
> **your violet flame does all restore,**
> **with you we are becoming more.**

6. I call for people to be cut free so they will not feel afraid,
they will not feel distanced, they will not feel suspicious of
their governments.

> O Saint Germain, my body pure,
> your violet flame for all is cure,
> consume the cause of all disease,
> and therefore I am all at ease.

> **O Saint Germain, what love you bring,**
> **it truly makes all matter sing,**
> **your violet flame does all restore,**
> **with you we are becoming more.**

7. I call for people to be cut free to see that the reason for the
distance between the leaders and the people is that there has
always been a power elite that has not been a force for good.

> O Saint Germain, I'm karma-free,
> the past no longer burdens me,

a brand new opportunity,
I am in Christic unity.

O Saint Germain, what love you bring,
it truly makes all matter sing,
your violet flame does all restore,
with you we are becoming more.

8. I call for people to be cut free to see that we cannot build a constructive society without recognizing this and without taking the necessary steps to prevent such an elite from controlling society and therefore holding back growth.

O Saint Germain, we are now one,
I am for you a violet sun,
as we transform this planet earth,
your Golden Age is given birth.

O Saint Germain, what love you bring,
it truly makes all matter sing,
your violet flame does all restore,
with you we are becoming more.

9. I call for people to be cut free to see that there must be a collective consciousness. Therefore, it is necessary to raise the collective consciousness in order to improve society. Society needs to help people resolve the wounds and the divisions in their own psyches so that they become more whole human beings and are able to live more constructive lives.

O Saint Germain, the earth is free,
from burden of duality,

in oneness we bring what is best,
your Golden Age is manifest.

**O Saint Germain, what love you bring,
it truly makes all matter sing,
your violet flame does all restore,
with you we are becoming more.**

Part 5

1. I call for people to be cut free to see that this has not happened because the power elite does not want it to happen. To the elite, the more unwhole, divided and psychologically crippled the population is, the easier it is to control people.

O Saint Germain, you do inspire,
my vision raised forever higher,
with you I form a figure-eight,
your Golden Age I co-create.

**O Saint Germain, what love you bring,
it truly makes all matter sing,
your violet flame does all restore,
with you we are becoming more.**

2. I call for people to be cut free to see that substance abuse pacifies people and makes them easier to control, making alcoholism a major factor in upholding the Soviet system.

O Saint Germain, what Freedom Flame,
released when we recite your name,

acceleration is your gift,
our planet it will surely lift.

**O Saint Germain, what love you bring,
it truly makes all matter sing,
your violet flame does all restore,
with you we are becoming more.**

3. I call for people to be cut free to see that men are more susceptible to declaring their allegiance to an idea and a system. Once they have sold their soul to the system, the need for creativity can never feel fulfilled so they numb themselves in order to forget.

O Saint Germain, in love we claim,
our right to bring your violet flame,
from you Above, to us below,
it is an all-transforming flow.

**O Saint Germain, what love you bring,
it truly makes all matter sing,
your violet flame does all restore,
with you we are becoming more.**

4. I call for people to be cut free to see that people only change their state of mind chemically when they have no spiritual path. This is why escapism is common in societies where it is the men who have the power to change status quo, but they have this fixed point in their psychologies where they have sworn allegiance to the system.

O Saint Germain, I love you so,
my aura filled with violet glow,

my chakras filled with violet fire,
I am your cosmic amplifier.

**O Saint Germain, what love you bring,
it truly makes all matter sing,
your violet flame does all restore,
with you we are becoming more.**

5. I call for people to be cut free to see that it is not necessarily a matter of questioning the system itself. It is a matter of coming to this point where we say: "We have been doing things a certain way now for a very long time. Why are we doing it the same way? Why aren't we trying to find a different way that will produce better results?"

O Saint Germain, I am now free,
your violet flame is therapy,
transform all hang-ups in my mind,
as inner peace I surely find.

**O Saint Germain, what love you bring,
it truly makes all matter sing,
your violet flame does all restore,
with you we are becoming more.**

6. I call for people to be cut free to see that any society must change or die. Any society that becomes a closed system will be overturned by history.

O Saint Germain, my body pure,
your violet flame for all is cure,
consume the cause of all disease,
and therefore I am all at ease.

**O Saint Germain, what love you bring,
it truly makes all matter sing,
your violet flame does all restore,
with you we are becoming more.**

7. I call for people to be cut free to see that in the Golden Age substance abuse will fade away because people will be given an opportunity to improve their lives and there is no need to escape. When we know how to heal our psychological wounds, the need for escapism will disappear.

O Saint Germain, I'm karma-free,
the past no longer burdens me,
a brand new opportunity,
I am in Christic unity.

**O Saint Germain, what love you bring,
it truly makes all matter sing,
your violet flame does all restore,
with you we are becoming more.**

8. I call for people to be cut free to see that in any nation the inhabitants want a better material life and a better inner life where they feel better about themselves. Any government on earth will want its own people to have a better material life and will not want its own people to feel better about themselves. Only a government controlled by the fallen beings will not want growth.

O Saint Germain, we are now one,
I am for you a violet sun,
as we transform this planet earth,
your Golden Age is given birth.

**O Saint Germain, what love you bring,
it truly makes all matter sing,
your violet flame does all restore,
with you we are becoming more.**

9. I call for the emergence of governments who will look at their past and say: "Why were we trapped in these patterns for so long? Why were we trapped in these power plays, this completely unnecessary conflict with other nations or even with our own people? Why weren't we focused on improving material life and improving how people feel about themselves and about their society? Why were we trapped in this for so long?"

O Saint Germain, the earth is free,
from burden of duality,
in oneness we bring what is best,
your Golden Age is manifest.

**O Saint Germain, what love you bring,
it truly makes all matter sing,
your violet flame does all restore,
with you we are becoming more.**

Part 6

1. I call for the emergence of governments who will say: "It doesn't even matter *why* we were trapped in it for so long because now we see it and now we are not trapped in it, and we are going to shift our focus into manifesting a better society."

O Saint Germain, you do inspire,
my vision raised forever higher,
with you I form a figure-eight,
your Golden Age I co-create.

**O Saint Germain, what love you bring,
it truly makes all matter sing,
your violet flame does all restore,
with you we are becoming more.**

2. I accept that when the collective consciousness is raised to
the point where this is what people focus on, and when more
and more of the fallen beings are removed from the planet,
then there will be a period of growth such as has never been
seen in recorded history.

O Saint Germain, what Freedom Flame,
released when we recite your name,
acceleration is your gift,
our planet it will surely lift.

**O Saint Germain, what love you bring,
it truly makes all matter sing,
your violet flame does all restore,
with you we are becoming more.**

3. I accept that once there is that shift where people focus on
the positive, Saint Germain will pour out so many new ideas
and so much new technology that the planet will shift into this
almost unfathomable growth, unfathomable for the people of
today who have never known such growth.

> O Saint Germain, in love we claim,
> our right to bring your violet flame,
> from you Above, to us below,
> it is an all-transforming flow.

> **O Saint Germain, what love you bring,**
> **it truly makes all matter sing,**
> **your violet flame does all restore,**
> **with you we are becoming more.**

4. I accept that there will come a point where nobody needs to look back at history and say who was to blame and what was the problem. We have a certain understanding of the forces of history, and we are aware that we cannot allow this to repeat itself.

> O Saint Germain, I love you so,
> my aura filled with violet glow,
> my chakras filled with violet fire,
> I am your cosmic amplifier.

> **O Saint Germain, what love you bring,**
> **it truly makes all matter sing,**
> **your violet flame does all restore,**
> **with you we are becoming more.**

5. I accept that societies will shift so they will not ignore history, but they will not seek to analyze and place blame. They will look forward and focus on the task of creating a better society, a golden age society.

> O Saint Germain, I am now free,
> your violet flame is therapy,

transform all hang-ups in my mind,
as inner peace I surely find.

O Saint Germain, what love you bring,
it truly makes all matter sing,
your violet flame does all restore,
with you we are becoming more.

6. I accept that there is a shift in my own nation and in many other nations who are ready for it so that we can reach that point of no return where we move into the phase of physically manifesting Saint Germain's Golden Age.

O Saint Germain, my body pure,
your violet flame for all is cure,
consume the cause of all disease,
and therefore I am all at ease.

O Saint Germain, what love you bring,
it truly makes all matter sing,
your violet flame does all restore,
with you we are becoming more.

7. I accept that the manifestation of the Golden Age has already become irreversible and that the fallen beings will not be able to delay it.

O Saint Germain, I'm karma-free,
the past no longer burdens me,
a brand new opportunity,
I am in Christic unity.

O Saint Germain, what love you bring,
it truly makes all matter sing,
your violet flame does all restore,
with you we are becoming more.

8. I accept that we are accelerating the growth and moving to that point of no return far faster than the fallen beings can even predict.

O Saint Germain, we are now one,
I am for you a violet sun,
as we transform this planet earth,
your Golden Age is given birth.

O Saint Germain, what love you bring,
it truly makes all matter sing,
your violet flame does all restore,
with you we are becoming more.

9. I accept that Saint Germain's Golden Age is a physical reality on earth right NOW!

O Saint Germain, the earth is free,
from burden of duality,
in oneness we bring what is best,
your Golden Age is manifest.

O Saint Germain, what love you bring,
it truly makes all matter sing,
your violet flame does all restore,
with you we are becoming more.

Sealing

In the name of the Divine Mother, I call to all ascended masters for the sealing of myself and all people in my circle of influence in the creative flow of the Divine Mother, the River of Life. I call for the multiplication of my calls by all ascended masters so that we form the perfect figure-eight flow of "As Above, so below." Thus, I accept that this is fully manifest, because the mouth of the Lord, the Divine Mother that I AM, has spoken it. Amen.

21 | TRANSCENDING FEAR-BASED SOCIETIES

I AM the Ascended Master Saint Germain. I am joyful over being given the opportunity to deliver this dictation with such a large audience where your chakras can become, metaphorically speaking, the loudspeakers that will radiate my vibration, my Presence, my ideas into the collective consciousness and therefore cause them to go further than they would otherwise go. Therefore, we speed up the time to where my release begins to have an impact in the physical level.

The wild horse of the Christ consciousness

Now, Jesus has given you his magnificent discourse on the Christ consciousness and some of the rarely understood aspects of the Christ consciousness [*Healing Your Spiritual Traumas*]. I would like to build upon this by giving you a certain image that the Christ consciousness is like a wild horse. It is untamed, it is untamable, it is constantly moving very, very fast. As it is running across the plains, it is whirling up dust. Most people on earth are at such a low level of consciousness that they cannot see the horse, but they can see the dust. What happens is that the Christ consciousness always represents change. When it comes thundering into town, it comes to signal that there is a need to bring change in a society.

Once in a while there is a human being who hears the thundering of the horse, who runs out, attempts to grab a hold of its mane and either swing himself on top of it, which very few manage to do, or at least run alongside the horse for a time, until people usually fall flat on their faces and then walk out of the cloud of dust, covered in that dust. The people who are able to do this are those who have some kind of attunement to the need for change. Some of them may get a glimpse of the horse, some of them may touch it, some of them may be able to run alongside of it. The thing is that once they come out of the cloud of dust, then the people can see that these leaders are covered in dust and they cannot tell the difference between the horse and the dust. They see the glimmering of the dust and they think this means that the person, the leader, has something they do not have, has some element of Christ consciousness. That is why they begin to follow that leader, and many times they follow a leader without questioning him or her once they have made that decision to submit themselves to that leader.

This explains many of the situations that you have seen in history where some people have caught the need for change. They have gone into the cloud of dust, come out of it covered in dust, and therefore had some kind of charisma that the people responded to. Once the people had submitted, they did not question the leader. In many cases, unfortunately, once the leader has gained a following and attained the position, he does not question himself, or she does not question herself.

That is why you saw, as Jesus explained, that many leaders can have a growth period and then stagnate and go into decline. Many empires can have a growth period, stagnate and go into decline. What you need to recognize here is that what brings change is always some element of the Christ consciousness, some alignment with the Christ consciousness.

The question is: "Can the people align themselves with the need to raise all life, or will they seek to raise only themselves, their group, their company, their nation, their empire?" If they cannot overcome the focus on themselves and seek to serve the whole, that is when they become subject to the second law of thermodynamics and go into a decline that can lead to their destruction.

Moving out of a fear-based society

Based on this, I would like to give you some discourse on one of the more subtle changes that needs to happen before I can truly release the matrices for my Golden Age. That change is that we need to have a certain critical mass of the most mature, advanced, open-minded people grasp the need to move from a fear-based to a non-fear-based society. Take note: I am not saying from a fear-based to a love-based because many people would not be able to grasp this. They have a human concept of love.

In the beginning, they need to consider that for a very, very long time all societies on earth have been fear-based. They need to begin to consider how this fear-based outlook on life, this fear-based approach to life, has affected societies in many very subtle ways. Then, they need to begin to consider that the alternative to a fear-based society is one that is not based on fear, but that is based on perhaps trust or another positive quality that they can grasp. The real issue is that they need to grasp the move from fear-based to non-fear-based societies.

Now, Jesus gave you the understanding that there are sometimes those who are even in the fallen consciousness, or perhaps even fallen beings, who can for a brief period be in alignment with the mind of Christ and the need to bring change. This can actually have a positive effect in the sense that even though it may precipitate a violent event, it still gives the people an opportunity to consider their fear-based mindset and transcend it. I wish to speak to you about one of the elements that needs to be examined critically as you consider this move from fear-based to non-fear-based societies.

When governments distrust their own people

Now, given that we are in Russia, let us look at the Soviet Union and how you had a more primitive version of what many people today call the surveillance society. The communist government of the Soviet Union felt threatened, often by its own people, and they did whatever they could, given the technology, to always survey the people and to set up a very elaborate, complex system for making sure that they knew whenever someone did something that could be a threat to the state.

This, of course, is easy to understand when you look at how the Bolshevik revolution happened. It happened through violence, through manipulation, through lying, through cheating. People who are in this state of consciousness, they know they have risen to power by doing to others these things. It enabled them to get to power, but the price they pay is that they will forever, or at least indefinitely, live with the fear that others will do to them as they have done to others. In other words, that others will use the same means to overthrow them that they used to overthrow the previous power elite. This becomes the motivation for why they had this surveillance society.

If we now go forward to the more modern times after the collapse of the Soviet Union, and look at one of the major developments that has taken place, it is, naturally, the Internet and digital technology. If the Soviet leaders would have had access to this kind of technology, they obviously could have created an even tighter mesh of surveillance around their citizens. They did not have it and now it was developed, especially during the 1990's.

Governments in the West were, of course, aware of this. They were starting to make some use of it, but they knew their people would be very critical about increased surveillance. They faced a certain dilemma where you cannot easily claim that you are a free democratic nation and at the same time institute tighter and tighter surveillance of your own citizens. The fallen beings, who always seek to take over societies, of course, loved this kind of technology.

It should be said here that, naturally, the Internet and digital technology were released by me because it also increased the amount of information available to people. You will see that one of the reasons the Soviet leaders could not use computer technology is that they were actually afraid to release computers to their scientists. They faced the dilemma that they knew that if they gave their scientists computers, they could not control what kind of information they could access and how they could communicate with people in the West. It is, of course, the same in western governments that they cannot fully control the Internet and the amount of information that people have access to.

A new perspective on 9/11

The fallen beings, of course, were not happy with this, but as they always do, they seek to plot a way that they can make use of new technology to further their ends of control. They very cleverly engineered the situation where certain people traveled to the United States, started taking flying lessons, and then captured four airplanes and flew them into a couple of buildings in the United States on September 11, 2001.

Now, my beloved, here is where things will get very, very strange for many people, including many ascended master students. The western nations at the time were in certain ways in a period of stagnation because there were certain issues they had not been willing to face. The September 11 event was clearly engineered by the fallen beings, and they had a very clear purpose for doing this, mainly to provide the perfect excuse for democratic governments to increase surveillance of their own citizens in the name of combating terrorism.

However, given the stalemate in western nations at the time, we can actually say that this event did bring the kind of change that is necessary in order to bring society forward and force a society to face certain issues. In a brief moment and from a certain viewpoint, this was in alignment with the mind of Christ and the need to bring change. Naturally, it was not supported by the ascended masters or the mind of Christ in any way, but it was, as Jesus said, one of those examples where the Law of Free Will mandates we must step back and allow things to unfold. When the second law of thermodynamics or the fallen beings precipitate one of these shocking events, then this does serve to awaken the people and force them to look at certain issues. You saw, of course, how most people in the United States and many other nations responded in a fear-based way to this – some would say "new" – threat of terrorism—but had there not been that threat for a very long time? What was really new about this was that this event was so shocking that it was difficult to ignore, and therefore governments responded according to their level of consciousness. One of the effects of this is, of course, that all western democratic nations have started using all kinds of surveillance technology from cameras on the street, to monitoring the Internet in order to, as they see it, prevent further terrorist attacks. This is, of course, to a large degree an excuse for doing something that the fallen beings have wanted them to do for a long time, namely increase control.

Naturally, the democratic governments are not consciously doing this in order to increase control, but it is the outcome of what they are doing. There are free democratic societies that now have such a level of surveillance of their own citizens that if this had happened in the Soviet Union, these free democratic governments would have been appalled at how this totalitarian regime of the Soviet Union could monitor their own citizens. Now they are doing the exact same thing, only with much more sophisticated technology. One of the ironies of history, one might say. This is, of course, not to say that the modern post-Soviet Russian government is not doing the same thing. Naturally, it is.

What you see here is that this is one of those examples of how we sometimes need to use a certain type of technology that we know can and will be misused, but still that technology will bring society forward. What have you also seen as a result of the Internet? Well, you have seen several times where an individual has downloaded information from classified secret government networks and made it public. Once it is made public, there is no way to stop the distribution of it. You see how the very technology that the governments are using for the surveillance of the people can also be used against the government to hold them accountable.

A society where nothing is hidden

It was a calculated risk that I took by releasing this technology at the time and it has had an overall positive effect. Now, what will happen as we move closer to the Golden Age? What will happen as societies begin to move out of the fear-based mindset? Well, here is where we come to one of these subtleties precipitated by the fallen beings. What is the essence of the fear-based mindset? It is the sense of lack. There is a sense of lack about the resources available in the material realm.

Therefore, there is a sense of competition about those resources and there are groups, even nations, who want to grab for themselves as much as possible. This is a fear-based reaction. The other element of this fear-based mindset is that because there is lack, if you have something, there is probably someone who wants to take it from you. Therefore, you need to protect yourself, and one of the ways you protect yourself is to hide what you have, to keep something hidden. What you see is that for centuries, even thousands of years, many societies have been based on this sense of lack and this sense that it is perfectly natural, unavoidable, and legitimate that people, even institutions and governments, can have secrets, that they can keep something hidden from public view.

You see, my beloved, how this very consciousness has infused many, many societies. The Soviet Union, of course, was one example of how the leaders found it absolutely necessary to make sure that the people did not know what they were doing. At the same time, they wanted to know what the people were doing. You will see also in western societies – even in those who call themselves free democracies – that the governments believe that it is necessary and legitimate that they keep certain things secret from their own people. Many corporations believe that they have a right to keep their production secrets and even keep secret from their own employees the decisions made by the leaders of those companies—even though they could have a great impact on the lives of the employees.

Abusing the right to privacy

This has filtered down to where the fallen beings have been very, very smart at using this consciousness to manipulate the situation so that most of the population in free democratic nations actually believe that it is necessary and legitimate that there are secrets kept at all levels of their society, including in their personal lives. One of the basic human rights instituted in many constitutions is the right to privacy. Well, my beloved, the challenge that I threw at human beings with the release of digital technology was the necessity to question: "Do you actually have a right to privacy?" You may say: "Well, I certainly don't want anybody to put a camera in my bathroom and stream it live to the Internet." But that is not what I am talking about.

What I am talking about is: "Do you actually need to live in a society where people can keep secrets from each other?" Now, you may think that the rest of the world wants to look at that live streaming of what you do in your bathroom, but most people would not care. What you are doing is upholding the right to privacy in order to protect certain elements of your private life that really do not need protection. The price that societies pay is that this focus on the right to privacy and the right to keep something secret is the absolute perfect cover for the fallen beings and their manipulation of society, even their manipulation of governments. As we move closer and closer to the Golden Age, we need people to start questioning this entire consciousness.

Is it actually legitimate and necessary to have a society that claims to be free, my beloved, but at the same time allows people to keep secrets and do things that affect other people, but the people who are affected do not know about it? Is that truly a free society? What you recognize here is that the average good-hearted, honest citizen really has no secrets that he or she needs to keep from the government or the public. Naturally, you have a right to privacy in your own home. That is not the same as being able to keep secrets.

You see that there are so many aspects of society where the fallen beings have abused the right to privacy in order to cover up how they are manipulating the people. This, of course, cannot be sustained in the Golden Age. Because people have not been willing to question this consciousness, well, I decided to release the digital technology and the fallen beings precipitated the 9/11 event. There were two ways society could have responded to that event. They could have responded as they did, or in a higher way where they said (as some people did say but very few acted upon): "We cannot allow these terrorists to get us to compromise basic democratic rights." Many of the governments in the West said this after 9/11 but they still followed right along and built the surveillance society that all western nations have today.

Because they did this, well you are now in the School of Hard Knocks, my beloved. There is only one outcome of this, and that is that the new surveillance and digital technology is used to the extent where nobody can hide anything. You already know, my beloved, that when you go on the Internet, the moment you log on to any website, you are being monitored by the NSA, the CIA, Google, and Facebook. You decide which one is the worst of those.

Is hiding something a right?

You know that the moment you step into virtual reality, well, you have no privacy. You will see how this will be extended as society becomes more and more digitized. There will come a point where it will simply be recognized that we cannot put the cat back into the bag, we cannot turn time back, we cannot get rid of this technology. We have actually moved into the information age and we have established information societies. We need to take the only logical consequence, namely that we do not allow anyone to hide anything that affects other people.

If you are in your own home doing things that only affect yourself and your family, naturally you have your privacy. When you are doing something that affects other people, you do not have a right to privacy. You do not have a right to keep this secret because the people who are affected have a right to know what you are doing and how it affects them, what your motives are. This, of course, is not a threat for the average citizen. Are you cheating anybody? Are you manipulating anybody? Nay! But who *are* manipulating others? Well, the power elite, the fallen beings, the hidden elite that is seeking to control society. They are the ones who have something to hide, and they are trying to use your right to privacy to legitimize that they can continue to hide something.

In the Golden Age, there will come this shift where the logical consequence of the information society is, of course, that you have to give up secrecy. This will then change the equation in many, many subtle ways because, suddenly, individuals, companies, and nations, governments, armed forces, spy agencies will realize they cannot do anything for which they cannot be held accountable.

The desire to escape accountability

Do you recognize, my beloved, that the very modus operandi of the fallen beings, and of the power elites you have seen throughout history, is that they want to be able to do whatever they want without being held accountable? Well, this can only happen in a society where there is secrecy. In a society where there is full information, you will always be held accountable for your actions and that, my beloved, is one aspect of the Christ Consciousness. Naturally, to the Christ consciousness, nothing is hidden.

Now we have talked about that fact that even some of our more mature students still see a distance between themselves and the ascended masters and you have various things that you often want to hide from us. We have also attempted to help you understand that only when you give up this desire to hide something from us, can you step up to greater oneness with us. Naturally, in oneness there can be nothing hidden. How can you be one with me if you want to hide something from me? It cannot be done. What will actually happen is that within the not-so-distant future, I foresee a shift in the collective consciousness where I can release a new type of information technology that I have mentioned before so that society will be able to read what we have traditionally called the Akashic Records.

Now, they will not get the ability to do it in as sophisticated of a way as we can do it in our retreats. They will be able to do it to the point where they can go back in the relatively near past and they can read the actions, or display them on a screen, exactly what happened at a given place. It is somewhat similar to what you can do now with a surveillance camera. It is just that here you do not need a camera because the recording takes place in the records of Akasha. When you can access this, you can go back, for example, to the scene of a crime and you can replay what happened and see what people did what.

This, of course, will in the beginning meet a lot of opposition and resistance. It is clear that in the beginning it will be used specifically to solve crimes but the real effect of it will be to prevent crime. Because if you know that you cannot get away with committing a crime, well, then most people would not commit the crime, would they? It is only because they think they can get away with it that they break the law.

In the longer run, this can also be used, of course, to expose all kinds of hidden manipulations in society. It truly will turn the tables on the fallen beings and those who are serving them in physical embodiment. They will not be able to hide anything and so this can lead to a shift in the attitude.

Now, there is a famous American author, called John Steinbeck, who wrote a series of stories about a small village on the Californian coast, a small fishing village. There is a merchant in one of the stories who has spent his entire life seeking to cheat and con people out of their money. He has been the embodiment of dishonesty, but one day he has a revelation and suddenly realizes that the ultimate con, the ultimate way to cheat, is complete honesty. If everybody is honest, then you cannot cheat somebody else, but nobody else can cheat you so you do not need to live in this constant fear of being cheated.

We can go even further and recognize that when a society becomes based on trust and honesty, and people are not seeking to cheat each other, then there will be an increase in the multiplication from the ascended realm. The economy of that society will rise to an entirely different level that the people can scarcely imagine today. You have already seen this in some nations where they have created greater transparency, greater honesty in the business world because everybody has realized that there is value in co-operation. If nobody is seeking to cheat anybody, everybody prospers from it.

As this shift begins to filter down to all levels of society, people will recognize that they have to let go of this consciousness of lack because there is no need to be dishonest in a society where there is abundance. It is often more trouble to cheat or steal from others than to make the money yourself. That is not the way many people perceive it in the present society, but in a society with greater affluence, that is the way it will be. You will, in fact, see that those nations who have raised the material standard of living have overcome a certain type of crimes because it was actually easier and safer for people to get a job than to steal—and they felt better about themselves.

Leaving the authoritarian mindset

This is a very subtle, and it will be a gradual, shift, but it is a very important shift that has many different ramifications. One of them that I wish to comment on here is that as it becomes clear that you cannot exercise power without accountability, a society will move out of what we could call the authoritarian mindset. What do you see today in so many societies? There are people who in various ways have set themselves up where they feel they are in a position of authority and many times the population in a certain country agrees with this assessment.

You have, of course, the extreme example of this as a dictator that has all power and therefore is seen by those of his people who are still alive as the ultimate authority. You have in all societies, even those who call themselves free democratic nations, people in a position of authority. It can be those who are elected representatives and have some position in the government, such as a minister. In many cases, these people are not elected by the people, they are the bureaucrats who hold powerful positions in the bureaucracy, they are those in the police force, in the secret police, those who are in charge of the surveillance society. It can be those in the army and military. It can be those in businesses, especially large businesses.

You will see that most of the people who reach a position of authority cannot exercise that authority in a way that is not fear-based. Most of them go into feeling they have to do something to maintain their position of authority. Therefore, they start to manipulate the people or the system in various ways. They go into this mode of feeling that they have a right to keep this secret from the people because they will not admit that what they are doing is not what the people want. They think it is actually what the people want, if only the people knew what they wanted. Since the people do not know what they want, it is the person in authority who is knowing what the people *should* want and therefore has a right to manipulate the situation and keep it secret from the people.

You have seen in many societies – including, of course, the Soviet one, but also in many western societies – where the people have been afraid of those in authority positions. Of course, as you move away from a fear-based society, this fear of authority figures will completely and utterly fade away. This will mean that many of those who are in authority positions now, simply cannot stay in those positions. They will either go out of embodiment or they will, quite frankly, be deposed by the people. Many of them will choose to retire, and this will give room for an entirely new kind of leaders who are what you popularly call servant leaders. They have that element of Christ consciousness where they are focused on serving the whole and this, again, will bring an important shift. Suddenly, the people will no longer sense any fear toward their leaders. If you do not have fear of your leaders, why do you need to distrust your leaders, especially when you begin to realize that these leaders are trying to serve you in an honest and straight-forward manner and they are willing to take accountability for what they do? They are willing to be transparent.

Transparent leadership

There will come a time, my beloved, where it will be seen that the most advanced, the most prosperous, form of leadership is transparent leadership. It will be seen as an absolute necessity and it *is* a necessity because neither a society nor a company can step away from the fear-based mindset without instituting complete transparency in its leadership. This will get rid of all kinds of dishonesty, it will get rid of corruption, and suddenly, again, society can shift. You will, for example, see that many societies will free up many, many people to start producing something that actually increases the economy.

Look at the Soviet Union again and see how many people were employed by the government to keep an eye on the rest of the population. This meant that these people were not free to do constructive work, and that is a considerable factor in why the economy failed. Now you see that in western nations more and more people work in a bureaucracy, and more and more people are employed specifically to conduct surveillance of the rest of the population, or at least those who are considered the extremist elements. This again ties up resources and creativity. It cannot lead to a growth in the economy because when people are working on something that does not raise society, we of the ascended masters cannot multiply their efforts. Only when people do something that raises the whole, can we give that multiplication, and only then will the economy grow.

My beloved, these are some very important things to keep in your minds as ascended master students. It is important for you to make the calls to reinforce this impulse that I have released into the collective consciousness so that you truly pave the way for – you open the way for – a more widespread acceptance of this. You can make the calls that those who are in positions to bring about these changes are cut free so they can grasp these ideas and take the necessary actions.

Truly, my beloved, who would not want to live in a society that is not based on fear? Who wants to live in a fear-based society if they think there is an alternative? When enough people start grasping these ideas, they will realize that there *is* an alternative. It is an obvious alternative. It has been there all along, but humanity has not been at the point where they could institute it, but now this is changing and more and more people are ready to move towards a society that is not based on fear.

Do you need a military?

Of course, another outcome is: "If you are not in fear, do you need a military?" As I have said before, obviously there will come a point in the Golden Age where no nation has a military. There will be a transition period where some nations still maintain a military because they recognize that there are other nations that are not quite out of the fear-based mindset and so they need to maintain a deterrent. They do not do this from a fear-based mindset.

This can then lead to an evolution where some of the smaller nations will simply say: "But why are we forced by Donald Trump to spend two percent of our gross national product on a military that we realistically speaking don't need? And why should we go along with this? So let us, instead of going along, go our own way and take the lead, and take what is the historically necessary step of daring to abandon our military and trust that this will truly bring us to a higher level where it becomes obvious that we don't need it."

My beloved, you will also see that many forms of aggression will fade away. You cannot go in and seek to manipulate the election of other countries, for example, whether done by computers or in other ways if this can be exposed. Then, you will be held accountable for it. You cannot spy on businesses if you could be held accountable for it. All of these things that you today think are inevitable (and think you can never have a world without this form of aggression and cheating and spying and manipulation), they can simply fade away and the people will begin to trust that they can actually live in and manifest a society that is not based on fear. Just imagine what a tremendous shift that would be.

Dare to imagine and then allow yourselves to feel how you would feel if you lived in that society. Some of you may say: "Well that's easy for those who have grown up in certain nations where they didn't have to fear their government, but it is not so easy if you have grown up in certain nations where you had, and perhaps still have, a legitimate fear of your government." I am still asking you, as the students of the ascended masters, to go into that state of non-fear. Allow yourself to feel what you would feel if you lived in a society that was not based on fear, and then choose to maintain that feeling. My beloved, if you who are ascended master students cannot achieve and maintain that feeling, how can you be the forerunners for a shift into the golden age consciousness?

We look to you to be willing to make that change regardless of where you live, and maintain that feeling that you are not fearing your own society. Your approach to life is not based on fear, and so allow yourself to feel good about yourselves and about your situation. How can you feel good about yourself, if you are fearing the very society in which you live every day? Thus, my beloved, once again, I thank you for being the electrodes of this release.

22 | INVOKING THE TRANSCENDENCE OF FEAR-BASED SOCIETIES

In the name I AM THAT I AM, Jesus Christ, I call to all ascended masters working on manifesting the Golden Age, especially Saint Germain, to radiate into the collective consciousness a new awareness of how to free ourselves from the fear put upon humanity by the fallen beings. Help people see that we can build a new future by working with the ascended masters and letting go of the old way of looking at life, including…

[Make personal calls.]

Part 1

1. I call for people to be cut free to see that the Christ consciousness is like a wild horse that represents change. The horse is whirling up dust, and most people

are at such a low level of consciousness that they cannot see the horse, but they can see the dust.

> O Saint Germain, you do inspire,
> my vision raised forever higher,
> with you I form a figure-eight,
> your Golden Age I co-create.

> **O Saint Germain, what love you bring,**
> **it truly makes all matter sing,**
> **your violet flame does all restore,**
> **with you we are becoming more.**

2. I call for people to be cut free to see that a few people can run alongside the horse and come out covered in dust. The people can see that these leaders are covered in dust and they cannot tell the difference between the horse and the dust.

> O Saint Germain, what Freedom Flame,
> released when we recite your name,
> acceleration is your gift,
> our planet it will surely lift.

> **O Saint Germain, what love you bring,**
> **it truly makes all matter sing,**
> **your violet flame does all restore,**
> **with you we are becoming more.**

3. I call for people to be cut free to see that the glimmering of the dust does not mean that the leader has something they do not have, has some element of Christ consciousness. They should not follow that leader without questioning him or her.

O Saint Germain, in love we claim,
our right to bring your violet flame,
from you Above, to us below,
it is an all-transforming flow.

O Saint Germain, what love you bring,
it truly makes all matter sing,
your violet flame does all restore,
with you we are becoming more.

4. I call for people to be cut free to see that there are many situations where leaders have caught the need for change and have had some kind of charisma that the people responded to.

O Saint Germain, I love you so,
my aura filled with violet glow,
my chakras filled with violet fire,
I am your cosmic amplifier.

O Saint Germain, what love you bring,
it truly makes all matter sing,
your violet flame does all restore,
with you we are becoming more.

5. I call for people to be cut free to see that once the they have submitted, they do not question the leader, and once the leader has gained a following and attained the position, he does not question himself.

O Saint Germain, I am now free,
your violet flame is therapy,
transform all hang-ups in my mind,
as inner peace I surely find.

**O Saint Germain, what love you bring,
it truly makes all matter sing,
your violet flame does all restore,
with you we are becoming more.**

6. I call for people to be cut free to see that this is why many leaders can have a growth period and then stagnate and go into decline. Many empires can have a growth period, stagnate and go into decline.

O Saint Germain, my body pure,
your violet flame for all is cure,
consume the cause of all disease,
and therefore I am all at ease.

**O Saint Germain, what love you bring,
it truly makes all matter sing,
your violet flame does all restore,
with you we are becoming more.**

7. I call for people to be cut free to see that what brings change is always some element of the Christ consciousness, some alignment with the Christ consciousness. The question is: "Can the people align themselves with the need to raise all life, or will they seek to raise only themselves, their group, their company, their nation, their empire?"

O Saint Germain, I'm karma-free,
the past no longer burdens me,
a brand new opportunity,
I am in Christic unity.

**O Saint Germain, what love you bring,
it truly makes all matter sing,
your violet flame does all restore,
with you we are becoming more.**

8. I call for people to be cut free to see that if we cannot over-come the focus on ourselves and seek to serve the whole, that is when we become subject to the second law of thermody-namics and go into a decline that can lead to our destruction.

O Saint Germain, we are now one,
I am for you a violet sun,
as we transform this planet earth,
your Golden Age is given birth.

**O Saint Germain, what love you bring,
it truly makes all matter sing,
your violet flame does all restore,
with you we are becoming more.**

9. I accept that before Saint Germain can release the matrices for the Golden Age, we need to have a critical mass of the most mature, advanced, open-minded people grasp the need to move from a fear-based to a non-fear-based society.

O Saint Germain, the earth is free,
from burden of duality,
in oneness we bring what is best,
your Golden Age is manifest.

**O Saint Germain, what love you bring,
it truly makes all matter sing,**

**your violet flame does all restore,
with you we are becoming more.**

Part 2

1. I call for people to be cut free to see that for a very long time all societies on earth have been fear-based. This fear-based outlook on life has affected societies in many subtle ways.

O Saint Germain, you do inspire,
my vision raised forever higher,
with you I form a figure-eight,
your Golden Age I co-create.

**O Saint Germain, what love you bring,
it truly makes all matter sing,
your violet flame does all restore,
with you we are becoming more.**

2. I call for people to be cut free to see that the alternative to a fear-based society is one that is not based on fear, but that is based on trust or another positive quality that people can grasp.

O Saint Germain, what Freedom Flame,
released when we recite your name,
acceleration is your gift,
our planet it will surely lift.

**O Saint Germain, what love you bring,
it truly makes all matter sing,**

**your violet flame does all restore,
with you we are becoming more.**

3. I call for people to be cut free to see that there are sometimes those who are in the fallen consciousness, or perhaps are fallen beings, who can for a brief period be in alignment with the mind of Christ and the need to bring change.

O Saint Germain, in love we claim,
our right to bring your violet flame,
from you Above, to us below,
it is an all-transforming flow.

**O Saint Germain, what love you bring,
it truly makes all matter sing,
your violet flame does all restore,
with you we are becoming more.**

4. I call for people to be cut free to see that this can have a positive effect in the sense that even though it may precipitate a violent event, it still gives the people an opportunity to consider their fear-based mindset and transcend it.

O Saint Germain, I love you so,
my aura filled with violet glow,
my chakras filled with violet fire,
I am your cosmic amplifier.

**O Saint Germain, what love you bring,
it truly makes all matter sing,
your violet flame does all restore,
with you we are becoming more.**

5. I call for people to be cut free to see that when the second law of thermodynamics or the fallen beings precipitate one of these shocking events, this does serve to awaken the people and force them to look at certain issues.

O Saint Germain, I am now free,
your violet flame is therapy,
transform all hang-ups in my mind,
as inner peace I surely find.

O Saint Germain, what love you bring,
it truly makes all matter sing,
your violet flame does all restore,
with you we are becoming more.

6. I call for people to be cut free to see that all western democratic nations responded to the 9/11 event by using more surveillance technology. This is to a large degree an excuse for doing something that the fallen beings have wanted them to do for a long time, namely increase control.

O Saint Germain, my body pure,
your violet flame for all is cure,
consume the cause of all disease,
and therefore I am all at ease.

O Saint Germain, what love you bring,
it truly makes all matter sing,
your violet flame does all restore,
with you we are becoming more.

7. I call for people to be cut free to see that the democratic governments are not consciously doing this in order to increase

control, but it is the outcome of what they are doing. There are free democratic societies that now have such a level of surveillance that if this had happened in the Soviet Union, these nations would have been appalled.

O Saint Germain, I'm karma-free,
the past no longer burdens me,
a brand new opportunity,
I am in Christic unity.

O Saint Germain, what love you bring,
it truly makes all matter sing,
your violet flame does all restore,
with you we are becoming more.

8. I call for people to be cut free to see that the ascended masters sometimes need to release a certain type of technology that they know can and will be misused, but still that technology will bring society forward. The positive potential of the Internet is that the very technology that the governments are using for the surveillance of the people can also be used against the governments to hold them accountable.

O Saint Germain, we are now one,
I am for you a violet sun,
as we transform this planet earth,
your Golden Age is given birth.

O Saint Germain, what love you bring,
it truly makes all matter sing,
your violet flame does all restore,
with you we are becoming more.

9. I accept that as we move closer to the Golden Age, societies begin to move out of the fear-based mindset. The essence of the fear-based mindset is the sense of lack. There is a sense of lack about the resources available in the material realm.

> O Saint Germain, the earth is free,
> from burden of duality,
> in oneness we bring what is best,
> your Golden Age is manifest.

> **O Saint Germain, what love you bring,**
> **it truly makes all matter sing,**
> **your violet flame does all restore,**
> **with you we are becoming more.**

Part 3

1. I call for people to be cut free to see that another element of the fear-based mindset is that because there is lack, if you have something, there is probably someone who wants to take it from you. Therefore, you need to protect yourself, and one of the ways you protect yourself is to hide what you have, to keep something hidden.

> O Saint Germain, you do inspire,
> my vision raised forever higher,
> with you I form a figure-eight,
> your Golden Age I co-create.

> **O Saint Germain, what love you bring,**
> **it truly makes all matter sing,**

**your violet flame does all restore,
with you we are becoming more.**

2. I call for people to be cut free to see that for thousands of years many societies have been based on this sense of lack and this sense that it is perfectly natural, unavoidable, and legitimate that people, even institutions and governments, can have secrets, that they can keep something hidden from public view.

O Saint Germain, what Freedom Flame,
released when we recite your name,
acceleration is your gift,
our planet it will surely lift.

**O Saint Germain, what love you bring,
it truly makes all matter sing,
your violet flame does all restore,
with you we are becoming more.**

3. I call for people to be cut free to see that even those who call themselves free democracies believe that it is necessary and legitimate that the government keeps certain things secret from their own people. Many corporations believe that they have a right to keep secrets.

O Saint Germain, in love we claim,
our right to bring your violet flame,
from you Above, to us below,
it is an all-transforming flow.

**O Saint Germain, what love you bring,
it truly makes all matter sing,**

your violet flame does all restore,
with you we are becoming more.

4. I call for people to be cut free to see that this has filtered down to where the fallen beings have been using this consciousness to manipulate the situation so that most of the population in free democratic nations believe that it is necessary and legitimate that there are secrets kept at all levels of their society, including in their personal lives.

O Saint Germain, I love you so,
my aura filled with violet glow,
my chakras filled with violet fire,
I am your cosmic amplifier.

O Saint Germain, what love you bring,
it truly makes all matter sing,
your violet flame does all restore,
with you we are becoming more.

5. I call for people to be cut free to see that although one of the basic human rights is the right to privacy, with the release of digital technology, do we actually have a right to privacy?

O Saint Germain, I am now free,
your violet flame is therapy,
transform all hang-ups in my mind,
as inner peace I surely find.

O Saint Germain, what love you bring,
it truly makes all matter sing,
your violet flame does all restore,
with you we are becoming more.

6. I call for people to be cut free to see that we do not actually need to live in a society where people can keep secrets from each other. We are upholding the right to privacy in order to protect certain elements of our private lives that really do not need protection.

> O Saint Germain, my body pure,
> your violet flame for all is cure,
> consume the cause of all disease,
> and therefore I am all at ease.

> **O Saint Germain, what love you bring,**
> **it truly makes all matter sing,**
> **your violet flame does all restore,**
> **with you we are becoming more.**

7. I call for people to be cut free to see that the price societies pay is that this focus on the right to privacy and the right to keep something secret is the perfect cover for the fallen beings and their manipulation of society, even their manipulation of governments.

> O Saint Germain, I'm karma-free,
> the past no longer burdens me,
> a brand new opportunity,
> I am in Christic unity.

> **O Saint Germain, what love you bring,**
> **it truly makes all matter sing,**
> **your violet flame does all restore,**
> **with you we are becoming more.**

8. I call for people to be cut free to see that as we move closer to the Golden Age, we need to start questioning this entire consciousness. Is it legitimate and necessary to have a society that claims to be free, but at the same time allows people to keep secrets and do things that affect other people, but the people who are affected do not know about it? Is that truly a free society?

> O Saint Germain, we are now one,
> I am for you a violet sun,
> as we transform this planet earth,
> your Golden Age is given birth.

> **O Saint Germain, what love you bring,**
> **it truly makes all matter sing,**
> **your violet flame does all restore,**
> **with you we are becoming more.**

9. I call for people to be cut free to see that the average good-hearted, honest citizen really has no secrets that he or she needs to keep from the government or the public. We have a right to privacy in our own homes, but that is not the same as being able to keep secrets.

> O Saint Germain, the earth is free,
> from burden of duality,
> in oneness we bring what is best,
> your Golden Age is manifest.

> **O Saint Germain, what love you bring,**
> **it truly makes all matter sing,**
> **your violet flame does all restore,**
> **with you we are becoming more.**

Part 4

1. I call for people to be cut free to see that in many aspects of society the fallen beings have abused the right to privacy in order to cover up how they are manipulating the people. This cannot be sustained in the Golden Age.

O Saint Germain, you do inspire,
my vision raised forever higher,
with you I form a figure-eight,
your Golden Age I co-create.

O Saint Germain, what love you bring,
it truly makes all matter sing,
your violet flame does all restore,
with you we are becoming more.

2. I call for people to be cut free to see that societies could have responded to the 9/11 event by saying: "We cannot allow these terrorists to get us to compromise basic democratic rights." Many of the governments in the West said this after 9/11 but they still built the surveillance society that all western nations have today.

O Saint Germain, what Freedom Flame,
released when we recite your name,
acceleration is your gift,
our planet it will surely lift.

O Saint Germain, what love you bring,
it truly makes all matter sing,

your violet flame does all restore,
with you we are becoming more.

3. I call for people to be cut free to see that we are now in the School of Hard Knocks. The only outcome is that surveillance and digital technology is used to the extent where nobody can hide anything because theres is no privacy on the Internet.

O Saint Germain, in love we claim,
our right to bring your violet flame,
from you Above, to us below,
it is an all-transforming flow.

O Saint Germain, what love you bring,
it truly makes all matter sing,
your violet flame does all restore,
with you we are becoming more.

4. I call for people to be cut free to see that this will be extended as society becomes more digitized. There will come a point where it will be recognized that we cannot put the cat back into the bag, we cannot turn time back, we cannot get rid of this technology.

O Saint Germain, I love you so,
my aura filled with violet glow,
my chakras filled with violet fire,
I am your cosmic amplifier.

O Saint Germain, what love you bring,
it truly makes all matter sing,
your violet flame does all restore,
with you we are becoming more.

5. I call for people to be cut free to see that we have moved into the information age and we have established information societies. We need to take the only logical consequence, namely that we don't allow anyone to hide anything that affects other people.

> O Saint Germain, I am now free,
> your violet flame is therapy,
> transform all hang-ups in my mind,
> as inner peace I surely find.

> **O Saint Germain, what love you bring,**
> **it truly makes all matter sing,**
> **your violet flame does all restore,**
> **with you we are becoming more.**

6. I call for people to be cut free to see that when we are in our own homes doing things that only affect ourselves and our family, we have our privacy. When we are doing something that affects other people, we do not have a right to privacy. We do not have a right to keep this secret because the people who are affected have a right to know what we are doing and how it affects them.

> O Saint Germain, my body pure,
> your violet flame for all is cure,
> consume the cause of all disease,
> and therefore I am all at ease.

> **O Saint Germain, what love you bring,**
> **it truly makes all matter sing,**
> **your violet flame does all restore,**
> **with you we are becoming more.**

7. I call for people to be cut free to see that this is not a threat for the average citizen. It is a threat to the power elite, the fallen beings, the hidden elite that is seeking to control society. They are the ones who have something to hide, and they are trying to use our right to privacy to legitimize that they can continue to hide something.

> O Saint Germain, I'm karma-free,
> the past no longer burdens me,
> a brand new opportunity,
> I am in Christic unity.

> **O Saint Germain, what love you bring,**
> **it truly makes all matter sing,**
> **your violet flame does all restore,**
> **with you we are becoming more.**

8. I call for people to be cut free to see that in the Golden Age, there will come a shift where the logical consequence of the information society is that we have to give up secrecy. This will change the equation in subtle ways because individuals, companies, governments, armed forces, spy agencies will realize they cannot do anything for which they cannot be held accountable.

> O Saint Germain, we are now one,
> I am for you a violet sun,
> as we transform this planet earth,
> your Golden Age is given birth.

> **O Saint Germain, what love you bring,**
> **it truly makes all matter sing,**

**your violet flame does all restore,
with you we are becoming more.**

9. I call for people to be cut free to see that the modus operandi of the fallen beings, and of the power elites we have seen throughout history, is that they want to be able to do whatever they want without being held accountable. This can only happen in a society where there is secrecy.

O Saint Germain, the earth is free,
from burden of duality,
in oneness we bring what is best,
your Golden Age is manifest.

**O Saint Germain, what love you bring,
it truly makes all matter sing,
your violet flame does all restore,
with you we are becoming more.**

Part 5

1. I call for people to be cut free to see that in a society where there is full information, we will always be held accountable for our actions and that is one aspect of the Christ Consciousness. To the Christ consciousness, nothing is hidden.

O Saint Germain, you do inspire,
my vision raised forever higher,
with you I form a figure-eight,
your Golden Age I co-create.

O Saint Germain, what love you bring,
it truly makes all matter sing,
your violet flame does all restore,
with you we are becoming more.

2. I accept that there will be a shift in the collective consciousness so Saint Germain can release a new type of information technology so that society will be able to read the Akashic Records.

O Saint Germain, what Freedom Flame,
released when we recite your name,
acceleration is your gift,
our planet it will surely lift.

O Saint Germain, what love you bring,
it truly makes all matter sing,
your violet flame does all restore,
with you we are becoming more.

3. I accept that societies will get the ability to go back in the relatively near past and read what happened at a given place. It is similar to a surveillance camera, but we do not need a camera because the recording takes place in the records of Akasha. We can go back to the scene of a crime and replay what happened.

O Saint Germain, in love we claim,
our right to bring your violet flame,
from you Above, to us below,
it is an all-transforming flow.

O Saint Germain, what love you bring,
it truly makes all matter sing,

your violet flame does all restore,
with you we are becoming more.

4. I accept that in the beginning it will be used specifically to solve crimes but the real effect will be to prevent crime. If people know that they cannot get away with committing a crime, then most people would not do so.

O Saint Germain, I love you so,
my aura filled with violet glow,
my chakras filled with violet fire,
I am your cosmic amplifier.

O Saint Germain, what love you bring,
it truly makes all matter sing,
your violet flame does all restore,
with you we are becoming more.

5. I accept that this will also be used to expose all kinds of hidden manipulations in society. It will turn the tables on the fallen beings and those who are serving them in physical embodiment. They will not be able to hide anything and this can lead to a shift in attitude.

O Saint Germain, I am now free,
your violet flame is therapy,
transform all hang-ups in my mind,
as inner peace I surely find.

O Saint Germain, what love you bring,
it truly makes all matter sing,
your violet flame does all restore,
with you we are becoming more.

6. I call for people to be cut free to recognize that when a society becomes based on trust and honesty, and people are not seeking to cheat each other, then there will be an increase in the multiplication from the ascended realm. The economy of that society will rise to an entirely different level that we can scarcely imagine today.

> O Saint Germain, my body pure,
> your violet flame for all is cure,
> consume the cause of all disease,
> and therefore I am all at ease.

> **O Saint Germain, what love you bring,**
> **it truly makes all matter sing,**
> **your violet flame does all restore,**
> **with you we are becoming more.**

7. I call for people to be cut free to see that there is greater prosperity in nations that have created greater transparency and honesty in the business world. When everybody realizes that there is value in co-operation and nobody is seeking to cheat anybody, everybody prospers from it.

> O Saint Germain, I'm karma-free,
> the past no longer burdens me,
> a brand new opportunity,
> I am in Christic unity.

> **O Saint Germain, what love you bring,**
> **it truly makes all matter sing,**
> **your violet flame does all restore,**
> **with you we are becoming more.**

8. I call for people to be cut free to see that we need to let go of the consciousness of lack because there is no need to be dishonest in a society where there is abundance. It is often more trouble to cheat or steal from others than to make the money yourself.

O Saint Germain, we are now one,
I am for you a violet sun,
as we transform this planet earth,
your Golden Age is given birth.

O Saint Germain, what love you bring,
it truly makes all matter sing,
your violet flame does all restore,
with you we are becoming more.

9. I call for people to be cut free to see that those nations who have raised the material standard of living have overcome a certain type of crimes because it is easier and safer for people to get a job than to steal—and they feel better about themselves.

O Saint Germain, the earth is free,
from burden of duality,
in oneness we bring what is best,
your Golden Age is manifest.

O Saint Germain, what love you bring,
it truly makes all matter sing,
your violet flame does all restore,
with you we are becoming more.

Part 6

1. I call for people to be cut free to see that when it becomes clear that people cannot exercise power without accountability, a society will move out of the authoritarian mindset. In many societies some people have set themselves up in a position of authority and many times the population agrees with this.

> O Saint Germain, you do inspire,
> my vision raised forever higher,
> with you I form a figure-eight,
> your Golden Age I co-create.

> **O Saint Germain, what love you bring,**
> **it truly makes all matter sing,**
> **your violet flame does all restore,**
> **with you we are becoming more.**

2. I call for people to be cut free to see that even in democratic nations, we have people in a position of authority. It can be elected representatives but some people are not elected by the people, they are people in the bureaucracy, the police force, the secret police, the military and in large businesses.

> O Saint Germain, what Freedom Flame,
> released when we recite your name,
> acceleration is your gift,
> our planet it will surely lift.

> **O Saint Germain, what love you bring,**
> **it truly makes all matter sing,**

your violet flame does all restore,
with you we are becoming more.

3. I call for people to be cut free to see that most of the people who reach a position of authority exercise that authority in a way that is fear-based. Most of them feel they have to do something to maintain their position of authority.

O Saint Germain, in love we claim,
our right to bring your violet flame,
from you Above, to us below,
it is an all-transforming flow.

O Saint Germain, what love you bring,
it truly makes all matter sing,
your violet flame does all restore,
with you we are becoming more.

4. I call for people to be cut free to see that such people start to manipulate the population or the system in various ways. They feel they have a right to keep this secret from the people because they will not admit that what they are doing is not what the people want.

O Saint Germain, I love you so,
my aura filled with violet glow,
my chakras filled with violet fire,
I am your cosmic amplifier.

O Saint Germain, what love you bring,
it truly makes all matter sing,
your violet flame does all restore,
with you we are becoming more.

5. I call for people to be cut free to see that as we move away from a fear-based society, the fear of authority figures will fade away.

> O Saint Germain, I am now free,
> your violet flame is therapy,
> transform all hang-ups in my mind,
> as inner peace I surely find.

> **O Saint Germain, what love you bring,**
> **it truly makes all matter sing,**
> **your violet flame does all restore,**
> **with you we are becoming more.**

6. I call for people to be cut free to see that many of those who are in authority positions now cannot stay in those positions. They will either go out of embodiment or be deposed by the people. Many of them will choose to retire, and this will give room for a new kind of leaders. These are servant leaders who are focused on serving the whole.

> O Saint Germain, my body pure,
> your violet flame for all is cure,
> consume the cause of all disease,
> and therefore I am all at ease.

> **O Saint Germain, what love you bring,**
> **it truly makes all matter sing,**
> **your violet flame does all restore,**
> **with you we are becoming more.**

7. I call for people to be cut free to see that when we do not have fear of our leaders, we have no need to distrust our

leaders, especially when these leaders are trying to serve us in an honest and straightforward manner and are willing to take accountability for what they do.

> O Saint Germain, I'm karma-free,
> the past no longer burdens me,
> a brand new opportunity,
> I am in Christic unity.

> **O Saint Germain, what love you bring,**
> **it truly makes all matter sing,**
> **your violet flame does all restore,**
> **with you we are becoming more.**

8. I call for people to be cut free to see that the most advanced form of leadership is transparent leadership. It is an absolute necessity because neither a society nor a company can step away from the fear-based mindset without instituting complete transparency in its leadership.

> O Saint Germain, we are now one,
> I am for you a violet sun,
> as we transform this planet earth,
> your Golden Age is given birth.

> **O Saint Germain, what love you bring,**
> **it truly makes all matter sing,**
> **your violet flame does all restore,**
> **with you we are becoming more.**

9. I call for people to be cut free to see that transparency will remove dishonesty and corruption, and many societies will

then free up people to start producing something that increases the economy.

> O Saint Germain, the earth is free,
> from burden of duality,
> in oneness we bring what is best,
> your Golden Age is manifest.

> **O Saint Germain, what love you bring,**
> **it truly makes all matter sing,**
> **your violet flame does all restore,**
> **with you we are becoming more.**

Part 7

1. I call for people to be cut free to see that when more and more people work in a bureaucracy, and more and more people are employed to conduct surveillance of the rest of the population, this ties up resources and creativity.

> O Saint Germain, you do inspire,
> my vision raised forever higher,
> with you I form a figure-eight,
> your Golden Age I co-create.

> **O Saint Germain, what love you bring,**
> **it truly makes all matter sing,**
> **your violet flame does all restore,**
> **with you we are becoming more.**

2. I call for people to be cut free to see that this cannot lead to a growth in the economy because when people are working on something that does not raise society, the ascended masters cannot multiply their efforts. Only when people do something that raises the whole, can the masters give that multiplication, and only then will the economy grow.

> O Saint Germain, what Freedom Flame,
> released when we recite your name,
> acceleration is your gift,
> our planet it will surely lift.
>
> **O Saint Germain, what love you bring,**
> **it truly makes all matter sing,**
> **your violet flame does all restore,**
> **with you we are becoming more.**

3. I call for the cutting free of those who are in positions to bring about these changes so they can grasp these ideas and take the necessary actions and move us away from a fear-based society.

> O Saint Germain, in love we claim,
> our right to bring your violet flame,
> from you Above, to us below,
> it is an all-transforming flow.
>
> **O Saint Germain, what love you bring,**
> **it truly makes all matter sing,**
> **your violet flame does all restore,**
> **with you we are becoming more.**

4. I call for people to be cut free to see that there *is* an alternative to a fear-based society. It is an obvious alternative. It has been there all along, but humanity has not been at the point where they could institute it, but now more people are ready to move towards a society that is not based on fear.

O Saint Germain, I love you so,
my aura filled with violet glow,
my chakras filled with violet fire,
I am your cosmic amplifier.

O Saint Germain, what love you bring,
it truly makes all matter sing,
your violet flame does all restore,
with you we are becoming more.

5. I call for people to be cut free to see that if we are not in fear, we do not need a military. There will come a point in the Golden Age where no nation has a military. There will be a transition period where some nations still maintain a military as a deterrent, but they do not do this from a fear-based mindset.

O Saint Germain, I am now free,
your violet flame is therapy,
transform all hang-ups in my mind,
as inner peace I surely find.

O Saint Germain, what love you bring,
it truly makes all matter sing,
your violet flame does all restore,
with you we are becoming more.

6. I call for people to be cut free to see that some smaller nations can take what is the historically necessary step of daring to abandon the military and trust that this will bring them to a higher level where it becomes obvious that they don't need it.

> O Saint Germain, my body pure,
> your violet flame for all is cure,
> consume the cause of all disease,
> and therefore I am all at ease.

> **O Saint Germain, what love you bring,**
> **it truly makes all matter sing,**
> **your violet flame does all restore,**
> **with you we are becoming more.**

7. I call for people to be cut free to see that in a transparent society many things that we today think are inevitable, such as aggression, cheating, spying and manipulation, will fade away and people will begin to trust that they can actually live in and manifest a society that is not based on fear.

> O Saint Germain, I'm karma-free,
> the past no longer burdens me,
> a brand new opportunity,
> I am in Christic unity.

> **O Saint Germain, what love you bring,**
> **it truly makes all matter sing,**
> **your violet flame does all restore,**
> **with you we are becoming more.**

8. I call for people to be cut free to feel what they would feel if they lived in a society that was not based on fear. Let them be cut free to maintain the feeling that they are not fearing their own society.

> O Saint Germain, we are now one,
> I am for you a violet sun,
> as we transform this planet earth,
> your Golden Age is given birth.

> **O Saint Germain, what love you bring,**
> **it truly makes all matter sing,**
> **your violet flame does all restore,**
> **with you we are becoming more.**

9. I call for people to be cut free to approach life without fear, so they can allow themselves to feel good about themselves and about their situation, no longer fearing the society in which they live every day.

> O Saint Germain, the earth is free,
> from burden of duality,
> in oneness we bring what is best,
> your Golden Age is manifest.

> **O Saint Germain, what love you bring,**
> **it truly makes all matter sing,**
> **your violet flame does all restore,**
> **with you we are becoming more.**

Sealing

In the name of the Divine Mother, I call to all ascended masters for the sealing of myself and all people in my circle of influence in the creative flow of the Divine Mother, the River of Life. I call for the multiplication of my calls by all ascended masters so that we form the perfect figure-eight flow of "As Above, so below." Thus, I accept that this is fully manifest, because the mouth of the Lord, the Divine Mother that I AM, has spoken it. Amen.

23 | THE FREE ENERGY TECHNOLOGY OF THE GOLDEN AGE

NOTE: This is an excerpt of a dictation by Elohim Cyclopea, given as part of an exposé on dictatorships. The entire dictation is printed in the book *Ending the Era of Dictatorships*. The excerpt is included here because of the vision of the Golden Age.

If you look at the ideologies and the theories, whether they are religious, political or philosophical, they are in most cases based on what we have called the rational mind, the linear mind, the intellectual mind. This is the mind that is a comparative mind. It always wants to compare anything new to something known. On top of that, you have the mind that is not rational in a neutral way, but imposes that value judgment where what is known is true or good; and that which differs from what is known and accepted is therefore false, bad or evil.

By using a combination of intuitive insights, intuitive flashes, and the scientific observations of how the world seems to work, you have a powerful process for raising society beyond all of these illusions that have been created. It is not necessary that people know about fallen beings because there are enough people already who have sensed that there are illusions in the world. There are people who are beginning to realize that, even though they have so far been focused on how the Catholic church during the Middle Ages created all of these erroneous and superstitious doctrines, they are beginning to realize that religion is not the only source of such superstition. Philosophies and ideologies can also be erroneous and out of touch with how the world actually works.

There are many people, and there is this tension in the collective consciousness that has been building, where the calls of a relative small number of ascended masters students can trigger a shift so that people become aware that it is necessary to step up and become more conscious of how we use this process of combining scientific observation with intuitive insights, in order to figure out how the world actually works, not only the material world, but also how the world is actually constructed.

Scientific observations have already been made that demonstrate that there must be a realm beyond the material world, that there must be energy in this realm, and that this energy can enter the material world. Right there, you see the need to have a combination of neutral scientific observation (what they call "objective" scientific observation) combined with these intuitive insights in order to bring forth the technology that will free humanity from this lower form of energy that can so easily be monopolized by corporations, or even a state, and therefore used as a weapon to restrict the people.

A vision of free energy technology

My beloved, let me give you a vision of what will happen in a matter of decades, perhaps only a few decades, when there is a breakthrough in what they call free energy but which I would prefer to call non-material energy. Imagine that you have a society where energy is completely free, there is no cost associated with obtaining energy. Every house has a little box that is hooked up to the electrical system, and that box produces electricity. There is a cost associated with producing the box, but it can be produced in such a way that it will last a long time. Once you have bought that box, there is no ongoing cost of producing the energy. It simply just appears. It comes out of the box, it is an out-of-the-box experience as a result of out-of-box thinking.

Imagine what that will do. Do you remember, some of you, your parents telling you to turn off the light when you leave your room? Well, that will not be necessary in the future. You can leave the light on night and day. You can keep the temperature in your house constant summer and winter because there is no cost of heating or air conditioning. More than that, do you need to live in an area where they have run electrical lines to your house? No, you do not, so you can move anywhere you want.

You can, for that matter, build a house that floats on the water and you still have electricity in that house. You can build a boat that has an electrical generator that runs an electrical motor that powers the propeller, and you can sail around the world at no cost. You can have Internet connection wherever you are because that will also be the new technology. You can sit in your boat out on the ocean somewhere while you are doing your work on the Internet and making a living that way.

Now, imagine how you have cars that also have a small box that produces electricity that drives an electric engine. Therefore, you can go anywhere you want. There is no cost associated with transportation. This would mean that you could, for example, live out in the countryside and still work in the city because there would not be any cost of going back and forth. Even more than that, people would have a whole new view of their possibilities. Travel would become much less expensive.

Of course, when you have free energy, you will also, very shortly afterwards, have the release of technology whereby the free energy can actually be used to create devices that can suspend gravity. Therefore, you do not need a car that drives on the road. You can have a car where you push a button, and the free energy drives a device that makes the car float into the air, and it can now travel through the air.

Imagine that the main transportation vehicle that people have does not have to drive on the surface of the earth. You do not need roads, you do not have congestion because vehicles can travel at multiple levels. If it is too congested at the level of 10 to 15 meters above the surface, you just go up to 20 to 25 meters and there is much less traffic there.

Imagine also that you have vehicles that are, of course, driverless as what they are experimenting now with cars. Because these vehicles can move up and down, not just back and forth, it is much easier to avoid collisions. You can get in your car, enter on a screen your destination, and then you can sit back and do whatever you want to do while you are being transported there. You can take a nap, you can work on your Internet even though computers will also be much more sophisticated.

Therefore, vast new opportunities open up. Look at the city of Seoul where you have these high-rise buildings where people work in offices. They live in other high-rise buildings that, for some reason that no one really understands, are located many kilometers from the high rises where people work. This means that people have to travel back and forth with the congestion either in trains or subways or in cars, and so much time is spent on going back and forth from home to work. Imagine that this has been replaced by first of all better transportation that makes it easier to travel to your workplace. In the longer run, societies will be much more spread out. There will not be the large cities you have today where it is necessary to build up, because people can live either further from their work because of easier transportation, or their workplaces can be decentralized so that people can actually live closer to their workplace. These are just some examples of what will happen, not what can happen, but what *will* happen as humanity begins to rise above the vision of the fallen beings.

24 | INVOKING FREE ENERGY TECHNOLOGY

In the name I AM THAT I AM, Jesus Christ, I call to all ascended masters working on manifesting the Golden Age, especially Cyclopea, to radiate into the collective consciousness a new awareness of the reality of free energy technology. Help people see that we can build a new future by working with the ascended masters and letting go of the old way of looking at life, including...

[Make personal calls.]

Part 1

1. I call for people to be cut free to see that ideologies and theories, whether they are religious, political or philosophical, are in most cases based on the rational mind, the linear mind, the intellectual mind.

> Cyclopea so dear, the truth you reveal,
> the truth that duality's ailments will heal,
> your Emerald Light is like a great balm,
> our emotional bodies are perfectly calm.
>
> **Cyclopea so dear, in Emerald Sphere,**
> **in raising perception we shall persevere,**
> **as deep in our hearts your truth we revere,**
> **to immaculate vision the earth does adhere.**

2. I call for people to be cut free to see that this mind is a comparative mind. It always wants to compare anything new to something known.

> Cyclopea so dear, with you we unwind,
> all negative spirals clouding the mind,
> we know pure awareness is truly our core,
> the key to becoming the wide-open door.
>
> **Cyclopea so dear, in Emerald Sphere,**
> **in raising perception we shall persevere,**
> **as deep in our hearts your truth we revere,**
> **to immaculate vision the earth does adhere.**

3. I call for people to be cut free to see that the linear mind is not rational in a neutral way, but imposes a value judgment where what is known is true or good, and that which differs from what is known is therefore false or evil.

> Cyclopea so dear, clear our inner sight,
> empowered, we pierce the soul's fearful night,
> we now see our life through your single eye,
> beyond all disease we're ready to fly.

**Cyclopea so dear, in Emerald Sphere,
in raising perception we shall persevere,
as deep in our hearts your truth we revere,
to immaculate vision the earth does adhere.**

4. I call for people to be cut free to see that this creates a self-reinforcing illusion that blocks people from accepting the energy technology of the Golden Age. They cannot even imagine it as a realistic possibility.

Cyclopea so dear, life can only reflect,
the images that the mind does project,
the key to our healing is clearing the mind,
from the images the ego is hiding behind.

**Cyclopea so dear, in Emerald Sphere,
in raising perception we shall persevere,
as deep in our hearts your truth we revere,
to immaculate vision the earth does adhere.**

5. I call for people to be cut free to see that by using a combination of intuitive insights and scientific observations of how the world seems to work, we can raise society beyond the illusions that have been created.

Cyclopea so dear, we want to aim high,
to your healing flame we ever draw nigh,
through veils of duality we now take flight,
bathed in your penetrating Emerald Light.

**Cyclopea so dear, in Emerald Sphere,
in raising perception we shall persevere,**

as deep in our hearts your truth we revere,
to immaculate vision the earth does adhere.

6. I call for people to be cut free to see that religion is not the only source of superstition. Philosophies and ideologies can also be erroneous and out of touch with how the world actually works.

Cyclopea so dear, your Emerald Flame,
exposes every subtle, dualistic power game,
including the game of wanting to say,
that truth is defined in only one way.

Cyclopea so dear, in Emerald Sphere,
in raising perception we shall persevere,
as deep in our hearts your truth we revere,
to immaculate vision the earth does adhere.

7. I call for people to be cut free to become more conscious of the process of combining scientific observation with intuitive insights in order to figure out how the world actually works, not only the material world, but also how the entire world is constructed.

Cyclopea so dear, we're feeling the flow,
as your Living Truth upon us you bestow,
from all dual vision we are now set free,
planet earth in immaculate matrix will be.

Cyclopea so dear, in Emerald Sphere,
in raising perception we shall persevere,
as deep in our hearts your truth we revere,
to immaculate vision the earth does adhere.

8. I call for people to be cut free to see that scientific observations have already demonstrated that there must be a realm beyond the material world, that there must be energy in this realm, and that this energy can enter the material world.

> Cyclopea so dear, the truth is now clear,
> we see higher purpose for which we are here
> we know truth transcends all systems below,
> immersed in your light, we continue to grow.

> **Cyclopea so dear, in Emerald Sphere,**
> **in raising perception we shall persevere,**
> **as deep in our hearts your truth we revere,**
> **to immaculate vision the earth does adhere.**

9. I call for people to be cut free to see that a combination of neutral scientific observation combined with intuitive insights can bring forth the technology that will free humanity from this lower form of energy that can so easily be monopolized by corporations, or even a state, and therefore used as a weapon to restrict the people.

> Cyclopea so dear, we're feeling your joy,
> as creative vision we now do employ,
> in lifting earth out of serpentine cage,
> to manifest Saint Germain's Golden Age.

> **Cyclopea so dear, in Emerald Sphere,**
> **in raising perception we shall persevere,**
> **as deep in our hearts your truth we revere,**
> **to immaculate vision the earth does adhere.**

Part 2

1. I accept as a physical manifestation a breakthrough in the understanding of free energy or non-material energy.

> Cyclopea so dear, the truth you reveal,
> the truth that duality's ailments will heal,
> your Emerald Light is like a great balm,
> our emotional bodies are perfectly calm.

> **Cyclopea so dear, in Emerald Sphere,**
> **in raising perception we shall persevere,**
> **as deep in our hearts your truth we revere,**
> **to immaculate vision the earth does adhere.**

2. I accept as a physical manifestation a society where energy is completely free, there is no cost associated with obtaining energy.

> Cyclopea so dear, with you we unwind,
> all negative spirals clouding the mind,
> we know pure awareness is truly our core,
> the key to becoming the wide-open door.

> **Cyclopea so dear, in Emerald Sphere,**
> **in raising perception we shall persevere,**
> **as deep in our hearts your truth we revere,**
> **to immaculate vision the earth does adhere.**

3. I accept as a physical manifestation that every house has a little box that is hooked up to the electrical system of the house, and that box produces electricity.

Cyclopea so dear, clear our inner sight,
empowered, we pierce the soul's fearful night,
we now see our life through your single eye,
beyond all disease we're ready to fly.

Cyclopea so dear, in Emerald Sphere,
in raising perception we shall persevere,
as deep in our hearts your truth we revere,
to immaculate vision the earth does adhere.

4. I accept as a physical manifestation that there *is* a cost associated with producing the box, but it can be produced in such a way that it will last a long time.

Cyclopea so dear, life can only reflect,
the images that the mind does project,
the key to our healing is clearing the mind,
from the images the ego is hiding behind.

Cyclopea so dear, in Emerald Sphere,
in raising perception we shall persevere,
as deep in our hearts your truth we revere,
to immaculate vision the earth does adhere.

5. I accept as a physical manifestation that once we have bought that box, there is no ongoing cost of producing the energy.

Cyclopea so dear, we want to aim high,
to your healing flame we ever draw nigh,
through veils of duality we now take flight,
bathed in your penetrating Emerald Light.

**Cyclopea so dear, in Emerald Sphere,
in raising perception we shall persevere,
as deep in our hearts your truth we revere,
to immaculate vision the earth does adhere.**

6. I accept as a physical manifestation that the energy just appears. It comes out of the box, it is an out-of-the-box experience as a result of out-of-box thinking.

Cyclopea so dear, your Emerald Flame,
exposes every subtle, dualistic power game,
including the game of wanting to say,
that truth is defined in only one way.

**Cyclopea so dear, in Emerald Sphere,
in raising perception we shall persevere,
as deep in our hearts your truth we revere,
to immaculate vision the earth does adhere.**

7. I accept as a physical manifestation that we can leave the light on night and day.

Cyclopea so dear, we're feeling the flow,
as your Living Truth upon us you bestow,
from all dual vision we are now set free,
planet earth in immaculate matrix will be.

**Cyclopea so dear, in Emerald Sphere,
in raising perception we shall persevere,
as deep in our hearts your truth we revere,
to immaculate vision the earth does adhere.**

8. I accept as a physical manifestation that we can keep the temperature in our houses constant summer and winter because there is no cost of heating or air conditioning.

Cyclopea so dear, the truth is now clear,
we see higher purpose for which we are here
we know truth transcends all systems below,
immersed in your light, we continue to grow.

**Cyclopea so dear, in Emerald Sphere,
in raising perception we shall persevere,
as deep in our hearts your truth we revere,
to immaculate vision the earth does adhere.**

9. I accept as a physical manifestation that we do not need to live in an area where they have run electrical lines to our houses. We can move anywhere we want.

Cyclopea so dear, we're feeling your joy,
as creative vision we now do employ,
in lifting earth out of serpentine cage,
to manifest Saint Germain's Golden Age.

**Cyclopea so dear, in Emerald Sphere,
in raising perception we shall persevere,
as deep in our hearts your truth we revere,
to immaculate vision the earth does adhere.**

Part 3

1. I accept as a physical manifestation that we can build houses that float on the water and we still have electricity in those houses.

> Cyclopea so dear, the truth you reveal,
> the truth that duality's ailments will heal,
> your Emerald Light is like a great balm,
> our emotional bodies are perfectly calm.
>
> **Cyclopea so dear, in Emerald Sphere,**
> **in raising perception we shall persevere,**
> **as deep in our hearts your truth we revere,**
> **to immaculate vision the earth does adhere.**

2. I accept as a physical manifestation that we can build a boat that has an electrical generator that runs an electrical motor that powers the propeller, and we can sail around the world at no cost.

> Cyclopea so dear, with you we unwind,
> all negative spirals clouding the mind,
> we know pure awareness is truly our core,
> the key to becoming the wide-open door.
>
> **Cyclopea so dear, in Emerald Sphere,**
> **in raising perception we shall persevere,**
> **as deep in our hearts your truth we revere,**
> **to immaculate vision the earth does adhere.**

3. I accept as a physical manifestation that we can have Internet connection wherever we are.

> Cyclopea so dear, clear our inner sight,
> empowered, we pierce the soul's fearful night,
> we now see our life through your single eye,
> beyond all disease we're ready to fly.

> **Cyclopea so dear, in Emerald Sphere,**
> **in raising perception we shall persevere,**
> **as deep in our hearts your truth we revere,**
> **to immaculate vision the earth does adhere.**

4. I accept as a physical manifestation that we can sit on a boat out on the ocean while we are doing our work on the Internet and making a living that way.

> Cyclopea so dear, life can only reflect,
> the images that the mind does project,
> the key to our healing is clearing the mind,
> from the images the ego is hiding behind.

> **Cyclopea so dear, in Emerald Sphere,**
> **in raising perception we shall persevere,**
> **as deep in our hearts your truth we revere,**
> **to immaculate vision the earth does adhere.**

5. I accept as a physical manifestation that cars have a small box that produces electricity that drives an electric engine.

> Cyclopea so dear, we want to aim high,
> to your healing flame we ever draw nigh,

through veils of duality we now take flight,
bathed in your penetrating Emerald Light.

**Cyclopea so dear, in Emerald Sphere,
in raising perception we shall persevere,
as deep in our hearts your truth we revere,
to immaculate vision the earth does adhere.**

6. I accept as a physical manifestation that we can go anywhere we want. There is no cost associated with transportation.

Cyclopea so dear, your Emerald Flame,
exposes every subtle, dualistic power game,
including the game of wanting to say,
that truth is defined in only one way.

**Cyclopea so dear, in Emerald Sphere,
in raising perception we shall persevere,
as deep in our hearts your truth we revere,
to immaculate vision the earth does adhere.**

7. I accept as a physical manifestation that we could live out in the countryside and still work in the city because there would not be any cost of going back and forth.

Cyclopea so dear, we're feeling the flow,
as your Living Truth upon us you bestow,
from all dual vision we are now set free,
planet earth in immaculate matrix will be.

**Cyclopea so dear, in Emerald Sphere,
in raising perception we shall persevere,**

as deep in our hearts your truth we revere,
to immaculate vision the earth does adhere.

8. I accept as a physical manifestation that people have a new view of their possibilities because travel is much less expensive.

Cyclopea so dear, the truth is now clear,
we see higher purpose for which we are here
we know truth transcends all systems below,
immersed in your light, we continue to grow.

**Cyclopea so dear, in Emerald Sphere,
in raising perception we shall persevere,
as deep in our hearts your truth we revere,
to immaculate vision the earth does adhere.**

9. I accept as a physical manifestation the technology whereby the free energy is used to create devices that can suspend gravity.

Cyclopea so dear, we're feeling your joy,
as creative vision we now do employ,
in lifting earth out of serpentine cage,
to manifest Saint Germain's Golden Age.

**Cyclopea so dear, in Emerald Sphere,
in raising perception we shall persevere,
as deep in our hearts your truth we revere,
to immaculate vision the earth does adhere.**

Part 4

1. I accept as a physical manifestation that we do not need a car that drives on the road. We have a car where we push a button, and the free energy drives a device that makes the car float into the air, and it can now travel through the air.

> Cyclopea so dear, the truth you reveal,
> the truth that duality's ailments will heal,
> your Emerald Light is like a great balm,
> our emotional bodies are perfectly calm.

> **Cyclopea so dear, in Emerald Sphere,**
> **in raising perception we shall persevere,**
> **as deep in our hearts your truth we revere,**
> **to immaculate vision the earth does adhere.**

2. I accept as a physical manifestation that the main transportation vehicle that people have does not have to drive on the surface of the earth.

> Cyclopea so dear, with you we unwind,
> all negative spirals clouding the mind,
> we know pure awareness is truly our core,
> the key to becoming the wide-open door.

> **Cyclopea so dear, in Emerald Sphere,**
> **in raising perception we shall persevere,**
> **as deep in our hearts your truth we revere,**
> **to immaculate vision the earth does adhere.**

3. I accept as a physical manifestation that we do not need roads, we do not have congestion because vehicles can travel at multiple levels. If it is too congested at a certain level, we just go up to where there is less traffic.

> Cyclopea so dear, clear our inner sight,
> empowered, we pierce the soul's fearful night,
> we now see our life through your single eye,
> beyond all disease we're ready to fly.
>
> **Cyclopea so dear, in Emerald Sphere,**
> **in raising perception we shall persevere,**
> **as deep in our hearts your truth we revere,**
> **to immaculate vision the earth does adhere.**

4. I accept as a physical manifestation vehicles that are driver-less.

> Cyclopea so dear, life can only reflect,
> the images that the mind does project,
> the key to our healing is clearing the mind,
> from the images the ego is hiding behind.
>
> **Cyclopea so dear, in Emerald Sphere,**
> **in raising perception we shall persevere,**
> **as deep in our hearts your truth we revere,**
> **to immaculate vision the earth does adhere.**

5. I accept as a physical manifestation that because these vehicles can move up and down, it is much easier to avoid collisions.

> Cyclopea so dear, we want to aim high,
> to your healing flame we ever draw nigh,

through veils of duality we now take flight,
bathed in your penetrating Emerald Light.

**Cyclopea so dear, in Emerald Sphere,
in raising perception we shall persevere,
as deep in our hearts your truth we revere,
to immaculate vision the earth does adhere.**

6. I accept as a physical manifestation that we can get in a car, enter on a screen our destination, and then we can sit back and do whatever we want while we are being transported there.

Cyclopea so dear, your Emerald Flame,
exposes every subtle, dualistic power game,
including the game of wanting to say,
that truth is defined in only one way.

**Cyclopea so dear, in Emerald Sphere,
in raising perception we shall persevere,
as deep in our hearts your truth we revere,
to immaculate vision the earth does adhere.**

7. I accept as a physical manifestation that better transportation makes it easier to travel to the workplace.

Cyclopea so dear, we're feeling the flow,
as your Living Truth upon us you bestow,
from all dual vision we are now set free,
planet earth in immaculate matrix will be.

**Cyclopea so dear, in Emerald Sphere,
in raising perception we shall persevere,**

**as deep in our hearts your truth we revere,
to immaculate vision the earth does adhere.**

8. I accept as a physical manifestation that societies are more spread out, so there will not be the large cities where it is necessary to build up. People can live either further from their work because of easier transportation, or their workplaces can be decentralized so that people can actually live closer to their workplace.

Cyclopea so dear, the truth is now clear,
we see higher purpose for which we are here
we know truth transcends all systems below,
immersed in your light, we continue to grow.

**Cyclopea so dear, in Emerald Sphere,
in raising perception we shall persevere,
as deep in our hearts your truth we revere,
to immaculate vision the earth does adhere.**

9. I accept that numerous other opportunities will open up as humanity begins to rise above the vision of the fallen beings and the linear mind. When we free ourselves from thinking that what is manifest now sets limits for what can be manifest in the near future, the Golden Age will be a manifest reality.

Cyclopea so dear, we're feeling your joy,
as creative vision we now do employ,
in lifting earth out of serpentine cage,
to manifest Saint Germain's Golden Age.

**Cyclopea so dear, in Emerald Sphere,
in raising perception we shall persevere,**

**as deep in our hearts your truth we revere,
to immaculate vision the earth does adhere.**

Sealing

In the name of the Divine Mother, I call to all ascended masters for the sealing of myself and all people in my circle of influence in the creative flow of the Divine Mother, the River of Life. I call for the multiplication of my calls by all ascended masters so that we form the perfect figure-eight flow of "As Above, so below." Thus, I accept that this is fully manifest, because the mouth of the Lord, the Divine Mother that I AM, has spoken it. Amen.